T0386543

Praise for
The Secret Wealth Advantage

It's the secret hiding in plain sight. Enterprises founder – and families lose their homes – because owners are deprived of the knowledge that would have saved them from the cyclical pitfalls in the capitalist economy. The experts did not (and still do not) see these crises coming, but no-one need fall victim to the next crash. Akhil Patel documents the inside story with a blow-by-blow account of the trends that make the difference between wealth and the fatal wounds endured by those who remain wilfully blind.

—Fred Harrison, economist and author, *Boom Bust*

With an impressive grasp of financial and economic history, the author paints a colorful picture of the interplay of economic forces and investor emotion that drives market cycles and the principal periods of boom and bust that many of us have experienced. But more than that, he sets out practical ideas on how to navigate them. All investors should read this book.

—Dr Daniel Crosby, author, *The Behavioral Investor*

After allocating over $80 million of equity during stages of sheer panic as well as unbridled mania, I can tell you, the investment world is chaotic. Every day, week, month, year we are bombarded with new explanations as to why market cycles behave the way they do, and none seem to stand the test of time... until now. With this book, you'll not only intellectually understand markets and why they move, you'll be able to take full advantage of it. Every investor needs this book.

—Hunter Thompson, founder, RaisingCapital.com and Asym Capital

The Secret Wealth Advantage fills a big missing piece of a financial puzzle that has been bugging me for over 30 years: I only wish I had read this at the start of my financial career. It has now usurped *Reminiscences of a Stock Operator* as my number one investment book recommendation. I never thought that would be possible. Akhil's work is worth 1000 times the cover price, although I could be undervaluing it enormously.

—Paul Rodriguez, director, ThinkTrading.com
and host of the *State of the Markets* podcast

I've been following Akhil's work for many years, and it's completely transformed the way I think about investing. It's astonishing that these ideas aren't more widely known, but this is to your advantage: now Akhil has brought them together into such a lucid and compelling book, it's never been easier to become a more successful and confident investor.

—Rob Dix, author, *The Price of Money*

Akhil Patel's *The Secret Wealth Advantage* actually contains secrets! I was blown away by some of the correlations Patel found between the signal and the noise. *The Secret Wealth Advantage* is like having a translator to today's volatile economic environment and helps you turn uncertainty into clarity, especially when it comes to long-term planning. If you don't read this book, don't blame me.

—Lewis Schiff, author, *Business Brilliant*

The Secret Wealth Advantage is a beautifully written book, using stories to illustrate each stage of the wealth cycle, providing markers to track it in real-time and real-life actions to take advantage of the cycle. It provides clear explanations of how and why the cycle takes place and why no one sees it. If you want to save yourself a lot of money in the market from trial and error, and years of study, then this book is a must-read for all investors, young and old. Great work, Akhil!

—Jason Pizzino, private investor and cryptocurrency educator

Extremely well written; clearly thought through; and very convincing. I will certainly use the 18-year cycle in future.

—Tony Plummer, author, *Forecasting Financial Markets*
and *The Law of Vibration*

Entrepreneurs are the rockstars of the business world, disrupting industries and creating wealth. But sometimes, even the most successful entrepreneurs can't seem to catch a break. Economic cycles wreak havoc on even the most promising businesses. The problem is that many entrepreneurs are too focused on the bottom line to notice the warning signs. They don't have time to become experts in investing. That's why I endorse Akhil Patel's book *The Secret Wealth Advantage*. It's the first macroeconomic model that made sense to me and it helps entrepreneurs stay ahead of the curve. Ignore this at your peril.

—Perry Marshall, author, *80/20 Sales & Marketing*

"You don't know what you don't know" circulated through my mind as I read Akhil's book, *The Secret Wealth Advantage*. Page after page, concept after concept, much of what I thought I knew about economics and finance was challenged and enhanced. There is so much we don't know about the financial system, boom and bust cycles, credit and – money! What propels the complexity and causes crises? What makes it tick and click along? Akhil explains it all with depth and simplicity. *The Secret Wealth Advantage* is a timely and important book that will help anyone – novice or pro – gain fundamental insights that change the way we should think about, and create wealth.

—AdaPia d'Errico, principal and VP of strategy, Alpha Investing and co-founder of Womxn of Wealth

This is a brilliant book – absorbing, enlightening, unputdownable. By bringing the role of land in the economy back into view, it makes dazzlingly clear what drives the cycle and when it will turn. This is a must-read for anyone who invests in property or stocks.

—Caroline Ward, property finance broker

THE
SECRET
WEALTH
ADVANTAGE

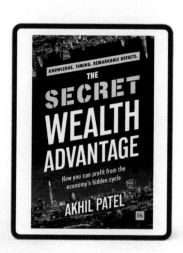

THE
SECRET
WEALTH
ADVANTAGE

How you can profit from the economy's hidden cycle

AKHIL PATEL

Harriman
House

HARRIMAN HOUSE LTD
3 Viceroy Court
Bedford Road
Petersfield
Hampshire
GU32 3LJ
GREAT BRITAIN
Tel: +44 (0)1730 233870

Email: enquiries@harriman-house.com
Website: harriman.house

First published in 2023.
Copyright © Akhil Patel

Paperback ISBN: 978-0-85719-857-0
eBook ISBN: 978-0-85719-858-7

British Library Cataloguing in Publication Data
A CIP catalogue record for this book can be obtained from the British Library.

Please visit
www.thesecretwealthadvantage.com
to access supplementary information,
charts and resources on many of the
chapters in this book.

CONTENTS

INTRODUCTION

"WHY DID NO ONE SEE
IT COMING?"

When the crisis came, the serious limitations of existing economic and financial models immediately became apparent... Macro models failed to predict the crisis and seemed incapable of explaining what was happening to the economy.

Jean-Claude Trichet, President of the European Central Bank, 18 November 2010

The question

IN 2008, THE best of times became the worst of times. The age of the seemingly endless expansion morphed into the age of the rolling, catastrophic crisis.[1] Throughout the year, waves of banking and business failures rocked the global economy, each one causing ever more destruction. In September, the failure of Lehman Brothers, the venerable Wall Street investment house, brought financial markets to the brink of collapse. The stock market, already down 40%, was still falling hard. Property prices had crashed, in some places by 50%. International trade stalled and business credit froze. The price of oil fell 75%, signalling that a deep economic depression was coming. It was, said Ben Bernanke, head of the world's largest central bank, the "worst financial crisis in global history".

This was the turbulent backdrop to a visit, by Her Majesty Queen Elizabeth II, to the London School of Economics. Invited to open a building, she had let it be known in advance that she was greatly concerned by events and wanted to find out what was going on. If a clear explanation of the chaos was to be found anywhere, it would be at the LSE, the world's oldest economics institute, whose founding creed was *rerum cognoscere causas*: understanding the causes of things.

Once the formalities had been completed, the Queen was briefed by Luis Garicano, professor of economics and strategy. He had prepared a short presentation and explained how bad things had become. "It's terrible!" the Queen exclaimed, once he had finished.

Then she asked, "If it was so big, why did no one see it coming?"

The answer

Professor Garicano awoke the next morning to find out that his encounter with the Queen had made news headlines around the world. This was *the* Queen after all. It was her first public utterance about the crisis. And she had asked the question that everyone wanted to know the answer to.

The story garnered so much attention that the British Academy, the UK's leading humanities and social sciences institution, convened a roundtable of experts to discuss her question. It summoned the wisest people in the country: leading academics, captains of industry, experienced bankers, parliamentarians and top government officials, among them 11 full professors, seven senior civil servants and seven knights of the realm. In June 2009, the Academy provided Her Majesty with a formal answer.

To summarise their response, they said that some people knew that a crisis might have been coming but no one knew when it would happen, what it would be like and how bad it would get. Everyone seemed to be doing their job, including those who were managing risks. What reason was there to question them, because at the time it all seemed to be going rather well? The world was prospering like never before as large developing countries, such as India and China, had become part of the global economy. Everyone had jobs and could spend their money on goods and services that were becoming more and more affordable. Businesses were expanding and governments were flush with tax revenues to invest in things people wanted, such as hospitals and schools.

They also believed that they could deal with the fallout if problems arose. They freely admitted that this had been a case of very wishful thinking because no one could see the bigger picture.

So they did not know it was going to be so big and they didn't see it coming because such things cannot really be foreseen, and no one had any incentive to do anything about it anyway. But they committed to learn lessons from this episode and hoped to do better next time.

The crisis, their letter concluded, "had many causes, [but] was principally a failure of the collective imagination of many bright people."

The 'failure of the collective imagination'

When you think about it, is this not a shocking statement?

In what other scientific discipline could an expert get away with attributing the most important phenomenon that he or she could study to a *failure of the collective imagination*? A phenomenon that destroyed trillions of dollars of household wealth, that resulted in millions of people losing their homes and their jobs, that saw the retirement dreams of pensioners evaporate into thin air; a phenomenon that affected everyone on the planet.

We will never know what the famously inscrutable monarch thought about the answer she received: given how many economic booms and busts she witnessed over the course of her long reign, it is likely she found it spectacularly unsatisfactory.

This was not an abstract issue for academics to debate endlessly. It had real-world, immediate consequences which, in addition to the economic devastation, could be seen in the widespread rioting, occupation of public spaces and mass protests in major cities over the next few years. Such anger was testament to the depth of the pain experienced by millions by whom the crisis was unforeseen, for which they were unprepared and from which they were unable to escape. The fury also expressed itself at the ballot box.

The 95-year-old, working-class father of one voter despaired at the collapsing stock market and, around the time of the Queen's visit to the LSE, sold his entire stock portfolio after hearing a financial professional on television declare how much worse things would get. The father had spent a lifetime working hard, paying his taxes, living frugally and investing what little money he could spare. But just as experts had failed to anticipate the crisis, they also failed to forecast the subsequent recovery. The poor man sold close to the bottom of the market and, in a stroke, lost most of his life savings. His son's rage at the father's misfortune turned to a deep and abiding hatred of the system, and he pledged to wreck it from within. As he later said, "Everything since then has come from there. All of it." And a lot did come thereafter. For in 2015 he, Steve Bannon, became the adviser to a rowdy real estate mogul and reality TV star by the name of Donald Trump who was running for the office of US President.[2]

The crisis affected me personally also. In 2009, my family's business almost went under. Small business owners like my father and uncle are at the sharp end of the capitalist system. Their companies are innovative, lean and resilient. They are the reason why our economies are so dynamic because they are constantly adapting to survive. They also employ the majority of people in any country, and many of them have relationships with their staff that large companies cannot replicate. They rely on banks to extend loans for working capital and renewing plant and equipment. This is why banks exist – to advance credit for production. But in a boom, banks overdo their lending, not to support more production but to finance speculation, mainly in property. This is where they earn highest fees and loan interest. In a crisis, banks retrench to save their balance sheets and it is small businesses, the backbone of the economy, that suffer because they are denied the credit on which their continued survival depends.

The results are catastrophic for economies and often terminal for the affected businesses. So it was with us. The bank used a feeble pretext to call in loans from an otherwise perfectly healthy pharmaceutical business, a company that, given its sector, could thrive in a recession. This callous action was almost fatal. While the business survived, it precipitated a series of problems that continue to reverberate today, over a decade later.

I sympathise with Bannon. Seeing the life's work of your parents almost go up in smoke is a deeply upsetting experience. As with Bannon, everything since has come from the crisis. In my case, however, it did not cause a mad urge to bring things down; rather, a determination to build something better out of it. I vowed to leave no stone unturned until I properly understood what had happened, and why; whether the crisis would happen again, and when; and what we would do, next time, to stay safe so that neither my family, nor families like ours, would suffer such problems again.

The search for the true cause

My initial quest proved challenging. People had much to say about why the crisis had happened: it was due to the culture of American (or Western) capitalism, or its corrupt bankers; or to the political influence of the financial industry, and the weakness of politicians in standing up to it; people were addicted to borrowing, and many policies promoted widespread (mortgaged) homeownership; further afield, some argued it was the Chinese people who, in saving too much, had pushed global interest rates too low. Many explanations were proffered but all seemed, to my mind, partial and focused on symptoms, not causes; and none gave me confidence that I would be ready for the next crisis.

I persisted despite these early setbacks, because I had a hunch that the answer I was looking for was out there. Approximately 18 years before, in the early 1990s, many countries had experienced banking crises, a slump in the property market and a deep recession. As it happens, our family business had gone through significant difficulties at that time also. My memory of those years, when I was a young teenager, was of an unsettling period. The secure world of my childhood turned out to be a mirage: it was capricious and uncertain.

The adults were worried. Spending had to be cut back. People around us were losing their jobs, their businesses and even their homes. Reflecting back on that experience in 2008, it seemed to me that the two episodes shared many similarities; but I wondered why no expert was making the connection, and whether this 18-year span was important.

Also in the early 1990s, I had received another clue, though I did not at the time understand its significance. At school every morning we attended assembly, where we gathered for a period of prayer, to get updates on school business, and listen to a passage of scripture, literature or philosophy. I would not always pay close attention; but one morning, I was transfixed when I heard an extract from a book written by a 19th-century American economist. The author described the settling of the frontier and explained the process by which the value of land increased as settlements became towns, and towns became cities. In my search for answers now, I returned to this author, Henry George. I found he had been asking the same questions in the 1870s that the Queen and I were asking now:

- Why do we keep going through periodic booms and crises?

- What drives them?

- Why does no one predict them?

- What can we do about them to stay safe?

His work, *Progress and Poverty*, I discovered, was a masterpiece, clear in its explanations and profound in its implications. He articulated universal laws of economics and marshalled them with precision to explain how economies kept moving from growth to boom to bust. I had not seen anything like it elsewhere.

I could not quite understand how someone who had all the answers was not referred to by everyone studying the crisis. George had published his work in 1879: perhaps his insights had not stood the test of time?

The economy's hidden order

Decades later, George's ideas were applied to the modern economy by a small number of brilliant researchers. Their findings were remarkable. They demonstrated that predicting such crises, and the booms that precede them, is not only possible but, once you understand how things work, actually rather straightforward, even in our highly complex and interconnected world. These crises had a very specific cause and one that was to be found in the property or, more precisely, the land market. The proof: these authors had seen the events of 2008 coming, years in advance.

Those who had written to the Queen were wrong. It was not a problem of a failure of imagination. The crisis was part of a regular pattern that has persisted for hundreds of years and is hardwired into our economies. The 18-year time period I had wondered about earlier *was* important – because this is the measure of a full economic cycle. Understand where you are within it and you know what is likely to be coming next.

These authors had identified and articulated the rhythm of our economic universe. Where most only saw complexity, they had revealed the economy's hidden order. Having now seen it, I knew I would never look at things in the same way again. I was now confident that what seemed to be a chaotic world could be mastered. In the years since, I continued my research: I was not satisfied with just explaining events. I wanted to predict them and give people ideas about what to do when they happened. I began to write a newsletter to make my forecasts public so that people could see for themselves. I continued to mine a wide range of works for investment ideas, finding practical ways to apply the knowledge of the cycle to real-life financial decisions, not just what to do but when to do it. My goal, in short, was to build an investment guide to the future.

This book is that guide and is the fulfilment of the promise I made to myself all those years ago.

Everyone is affected by the cycle, whether they are an employee embarking on or developing a career, an entrepreneur growing a business, an investor building a portfolio, or a retiree living off a lifetime of savings. Ignore the lessons in the pages that follow and you will forever be doomed to suffer from the cycle's periodic crises. If you learn them well, you will bend the cycle to your advantage. You will benefit from the boom that will take place in the coming years. When the next crisis hits, you will be well-prepared to weather it. Because there *will* be a next time.

Years after the Queen's visit to the LSE, I interviewed Professor Garicano, who had gone on to become a Member of the European Parliament. In his view, incentives were key to the crisis in 2008 arriving as it did, and none of them had changed. I asked him if any of the lessons had been learned, as had been hoped for by those at the British Academy.

His response was unequivocal: "No, they had not."

HOW THIS BOOK
IS STRUCTURED

THIS BOOK TAKES you on a journey in time – past, present and future – through the course of an 18-year economic cycle. In what follows the terms '18-year', 'economic', 'property' and 'real estate' cycle are used interchangeably.

We begin as the new cycle commences, during its hesitant early days when the economy is moribund and people fearful; we travel through periods of expansion and, along the way, endure shocks and even minor recessions; we journey then through the economic booms and bouts of wild speculation and mania that precede the cycle's climax; and then finally we get to the catastrophic crises and depressions that bring the cycle to a close, some 18 years later.

Each cycle has four great Acts:

Act I: Recovery. Out of the ashes of the prior cycle a new one is born. The economy recovers and, over the next six to seven years, expands again as confidence returns.

Act II: Mid-cycle. A minor recession takes place. Fear returns, but the slowdown is comparatively short and does not involve a crisis.

Act III: Boom. This leads to a much broader boom over the next six to seven years: there is higher growth, abundant credit, surging stock and property markets and, finally, two years of outright excess before the cycle reaches its highest point, 14 years after it began.

Act IV: Crisis. The cycle ends with a terrific crash and depression. The economy must be rescued from its deep malaise; the ruins are cleared over a period of four years. Thus an 18-year cycle ends, and a new one begins.

These four Acts inform the structure of this book.

You are about to follow a full 18-year cycle as it plays out over the course of the four Acts. Each Act contains one or more stages of the cycle, with a chapter devoted to each one. These chapters describe what happens at that stage of the cycle, illustrated using a particular historical episode and supported by analysis enabling you to track the unfolding cycle in your own era, whenever you happen to be reading this.

But the book does more than simply take you through the sequential stages. Explanatory chapters within each Act give context to the overall cycle: what causes it; why it is hidden from view and why it endures; what determines how big the booms and busts get; and why and how, over the course of the cycle, both professional advisers (inadvertently) and fraudsters (deliberately) can lead your investment decision-making astray.

Taken together, these sequential and explanatory chapters give you a complete understanding of the economy's hidden order. Understand this and you will have a clear picture of what happens, and why; where we are in the cycle and what will happen next.

The final component of the book's structure is its practical guidance. Be it investing and taking risks, or selling and taking measures to stay safe, you will learn how to respond to the cycle and when to take action. This guidance, provided at the end of each chapter, is effectively a book within a book: *The Handbook of Wealth Secrets*. This embodies the book's core purpose: to help you make better financial decisions at the right times and to give you an investment edge that even seasoned professionals can only dream of.

This is your Secret Wealth Advantage.

———— - - ■ - · ————

In preparation for our journey, we begin with a brief overview of a full 18-year cycle.

The Prologue takes you on a whistle-stop tour of perhaps the most famous cycle of them all: the one that, beginning around 1911, lasted through a world war, a pandemic and the Roaring Twenties, culminating in the Wall Street Crash of 1929, a crisis that heralded the Great Depression. The Prologue will also tell you how the 18-year cycle came to be discovered and will give you a roadmap to guide you through the cycle.

AN AGE-OLD TALE OF BOOM AND BUST

... all those who wish to examine the truth of events that happened in the past – and which, given human nature, will happen again in the future – will find my work to be valuable: it was composed to be a possession for all time...

Thucydides, *History of the Peloponnesian War*

IT WOULD BECOME the most celebrated age in economic history: the Roaring Twenties. The age of light, when the world was electrified. The age of travel, when the low-cost automobile whisked families far and wide and the airplane traversed the Atlantic. The age of equality, when women achieved voting rights and worked in offices. The age of culture, when people danced the Charleston and listened to jazz in speakeasies and on the wireless radio. The age of the soaring skyscraper. The age of broad prosperity and extravagant living.

But the first half of that age was, to put it mildly, a disaster.

Act I: Recovery

The Start

The new cycle emerged, as it always does, out of crisis: the Panic of 1907. Such episodes had become a regular feature of the American economy, repeating every two decades or so, without fail, since the country's founding some 120 years prior. But this crisis went well beyond the US. In 1907, a wave of bank failures occurred in Germany, Japan, Italy, Chile and Egypt.[1]

The US had no central bank to backstop the system. Amid the prospect of widespread banking failures, the great John Pierpont Morgan, the world's leading industrialist, was beseeched to organise a bailout by getting the banking fraternity to supply funds to those finance houses experiencing runs. This he did, even if at one point he had to lock several bankers in a room until they reached an agreement. He also impressed upon his friends the need to release uplifting news to the press and encourage religious leaders to make optimistic sermons to quell the panic.[2] He extracted a heavy price from the US government for his generous intervention: its approval to build a monopoly out of the American steel industry.

Meanwhile, many were only too happy to proffer explanations for the crisis: it was the government's fault, or crooked bankers, or unrestrained spending by women.[3] No one bothered to look into the real reason: the downturn in the property market and slump in land sales.

The crisis did not last as long as some in recent memory, such as the Depression of 1893. Confidence and business credit were soon restored. 1909 was the low point in the real estate market. The stock market anticipated the recovery: 1908 was a very good year for it and it appreciated 47%.[4]

The US government introduced a commission to look at the problems that had caused the panic, which had occurred when banks stopped lending to one another. This freeze in the banking system had happened in prior crises too – in 1819, 1837, 1857, 1873 and 1893. New regulations were therefore needed – in the form of a national central bank to provide liquidity in times of stress (the government could not rely on the ageing Morgan forever). So, in 1913, the United States Federal Reserve was created. It was hoped that it would permanently eliminate the damaging booms and busts that had periodically racked the economy.

Beyond the banking sector, the broader economy was looking to the future. There was an exciting new development: a novel, mass-produced technology that would utterly transform society.

In 1908 Henry Ford introduced the Model T to the world. It was the first affordable automobile, built, he proudly proclaimed, "for the multitude... large enough for the family, but small enough for the individual to run and care for... It will be so low in price that no man making a good salary will be unable to own one." His company had designed production processes so the car could be built quickly. In less than ten years, Ford himself watched the fifteen millionth Model T roll off the line at the factory in Michigan.

The Expansion

There was an upturn in the economy after 1911, some four years after the panic. A sign of increased activity was that new construction began again, albeit in limited fashion, and it picked up strongly in 1913 and 1914.[5] No one knew it at the time, but it would be at least 14 years before the next major downturn in the construction industry.

This era saw the apogee of the great European empires. Despite the dense trade connections between them, years of increasing tension and geopolitical manoeuvring (including a race to secure oil supplies), particularly between the German and British empires, resulted in world war in August 1914. Stock markets around the world were closed to avoid panic selling and remained closed for months.

The Peak

Non-combatant industrial powers, particularly the US (though it later joined the war in 1917) and Japan, turned to supplying the belligerents with arms and food. As a result, their economies boomed, and the price of farmland soared. The US financial system also benefited as Britain and France sold their gold holdings in return for supplies.

Act II: Mid-cycle

The Recession

The 'war to end all wars' officially ceased in November 1918. It had been a catastrophe: 20 million people were dead. Further tragedy was to follow. The trenches through which the war was fought incubated a deadly flu virus that soldiers brought home. There was a global pandemic. For the generation shattered by war, the first consequence of the peace was the death of millions more.

Commodity prices collapsed after the end of the war, when hoarded supplies were dumped back onto the market and the demand for war materials disappeared. The world slipped into a deep recession in 1919–20, roughly seven to eight years after the Start of the cycle.

There was devastation all around. An entire generation of working-age men had been wiped out in all the major economies of the world. Germany paid a high price for losing the war: loss of overseas territories and crippling reparations to the victors.

The world could not recover from this, surely?

Act III: Boom

The Land Boom

In fact, it could, as this was only the midpoint of the cycle. The move out of the recession was surprisingly swift, particularly in relation to the deep disruption of the post-war period. Interest rates and taxes were cut.[6] With lower taxes and cheaper credit, and a banking system that had held up during the recession (and so could continue to lend), the economy recovered in just 60 days.[7] The Roaring Twenties were underway.

There was work aplenty. Five million returning servicemen needed to be housed, and this ignited a construction boom supported by the building out of a highway system for the automobiles that many people now owned. Highways opened up a series of smaller towns close to the edges of cities – the first suburbs. With the agricultural sector in a slump and commodity prices low, people moved from rural areas to cities in search of jobs. Similar changes were afoot in Europe, especially France. Germany suffered hyperinflation caused by printing money to purchase foreign currency to cover the reparation payments demanded by the victorious allies. But once this was addressed, Germany, too, boomed. Japan also saw rapid growth in industrial cities such as Tokyo, Osaka and Nagasaki.

The rollout of new technologies – electricity, telephone, radio and automobile – created new industries and service sectors. Electric lighting in homes opened up a range of new cultural activities, such as playing board games after dinner. Roads took tourists to the backwaters of the country, where resorts welcomed them; they could stop off at any number of roadside motels along the way. Oil refineries sprung up, as did petrol stations along highways and roads. Production was revolutionised by 'scientific' management techniques (pioneered by Henry Ford), and productivity and jobs increased. Unemployment dropped from 11.0% in 1922 to just 3.5% by the end of the decade. The American economy roared – growing over 5% a year.[8] The radio transformed culture. For the first time, there was national participation in common leisure activities. People listened to the same music, danced the same styles and wore the same clothes, aided by the rise of national chain stores and advertising. Women were newly enfranchised; devices such as washing machines and contraceptives meant they were freed from traditional domestic roles. For the first time, they worked in offices. The androgynous styles of the era, such as the flapper dress (known as the *garçonne* in France) and short hair, reflected this emancipation. Novel construction techniques in America gave rise to a new building form: the skyscraper. Because of more intensive use of a site, land prices rose sharply wherever tall buildings could be built. This was not just in America; as the 1920s progressed, the French and German economies grew strongly, and their cities were adorned with elegant art deco buildings.

So profound were the changes in the 1920s that one could credibly feel that this was a new era, markedly different to the old pre-war world. "We appear to be entering an era of prosperity which is gradually reaching into every part of the nation," declared President Coolidge in his inaugural address of 1925, reflecting the mood of the times.

Nowhere were the good times more visible than in the land booms in and around major cities. Automobiles and trains gave access to new lands. This created not just new towns but the fantasy of a completely new life: living in permanent sunshine in Florida, or country living in the idyllic Metro-land towns of the counties closest to London (Buckinghamshire, Hertfordshire and Middlesex), while only being a short train ride away from the big city. So it was with all the great building programmes of the 1920s across the major economies of the world.

Government investment in infrastructure fuelled the boom – roads, railways, irrigation and drainage (in Florida), telegraph and telephone lines, and electricity. Low interest rates and tax incentives caused the Land Boom to kick off in earnest in 1924.[9] Rapidly escalating land prices drew builders in to develop projects based on prospective, rather than actual, demand. Everyone rushed to the new areas to be part of the action, so that few workers could be found in the places they had left.

The American banking system expanded significantly to provide credit for such companies – and to households wanting to take out a mortgage to acquire a piece of real estate. This expansion was facilitated by a number of technologies, such as the telephone, Dictaphone and calculating machine, that made operations more efficient. Mortgage lending increased almost three-fold over the course of the decade. Private debt increased by $40 billion in the 1920s, an amount equal to almost half of American GDP; it did so rapidly in France and Germany as well in the years up to 1928.[10]

In the good times, people turned towards stock market speculation with gusto. There were plenty of stories of people of humble origin making fortunes. Household ownership of stocks increased tenfold over the course of the decade.[11] This included many women who were able to divert some of their wealth into stock market speculation; many earned an income in their own right, and even traditional housewives extended their management of the household budget to the family's stock portfolio. In some cases, 40% of the stock of certain companies was owned by women. But interest in the stock market was broad: an English journalist visiting an American friend found that the ticker tape, which reported up-to-date stock prices, had been installed downstairs so that the domestic staff could follow market movements.

The Mania

In 1925, the Federal Reserve cut interest rates again to assist with the reintroduction of the gold standard in the United Kingdom. Lower interest rates after a few years of expansion ignited a speculative Mania. Between 1926 and 1929 US stocks went up more than 200%. The vehicle drawing in investors' capital was the investment trust. Through them, investors could own the shares of several companies at once and, even better, only needed to put 10% down and borrow the rest. The trusts themselves could borrow money to acquire the shares of the underlying companies, thus leveraging investor capital twice. In the 1920s bull market, this gave people inordinate profits, at least on paper. Needless to say, this turned into a bonanza of share buying of many kinds, from penny stocks to large railways.[12] The hottest items on the exchanges were electricity utilities. By 1929, they accounted for a fifth of the entire market. They also were able to leverage up with ease: in fact, by the end of the decade bankers would chase them to lend money, ignoring any applicable regulations.

But the surest sign of the Mania was found in the land market.[13] The volume of building greatly exceeded what was needed. Spending on construction rose sharply, and the industry now accounted for 20% of the American economy. Much of the building was purely speculative, including apartments in city centres and, after 1926, offices. In Manhattan, 30 million square feet of office space, almost double the existing volume, was created – which was far more than any sober analysis of demand would have proposed. Favourable tax treatment and availability of credit meant that projects were nonetheless financed. The carefree approach to lending bankers showed to utilities applied to real estate companies too; and even if some were cautious, other non-bank lenders took their place, some operating outside the normal rules that applied to commercial banks (such as savings and loans associations or real estate bond brokers). Many real estate developers made sure of the supply of credit – by chartering their own banks.

The Summit

"We in America today are nearer to the final triumph over poverty than ever before in the history of any land," said Herbert Hoover in accepting the Republican Party nomination for the election of 1928, an election he would go on to win. The good times, it seemed, were here to stay.

1926 had been the peak year for building, at least in housing, 14 years after the Start. But so strong were the boom conditions that the building of commercial and retail space went on. Those who were watching carefully, however, might have viewed a few events with some unease.

In January 1926, a ship capsized in Miami harbour, and its lumber cargo was lost, delaying building by weeks. Later that year, a hurricane in the summer storm season brought a wave of water 30 miles inland. This shocked the country and caused some investment to slow down. The Land Booms in Florida and Japan stalled in 1927, as did those in France and Germany.[14] The market for housing land entered a dull phase in contrast to the frenzy of the boom years; the period of rapid advances was over, even though banks were lending and the "property-owning community [was] still permeated with the rosy dreams that fill the air on the great upswing in land values."[15] By contrast, commercial property was unaffected and grew strongly.

For most people the good times seemed to roll on. The years of 1927 and 1928 were very good for the stock market. There seemed to be no end to the boom, but there were signs that things had gone too far. There had been overbuilding on a grand scale, and in the final years of the decade there were thousands of buildings standing vacant for want of buyers and tenants.

The Federal Reserve now faced a dilemma: to raise rates and stall the boom or to let it continue unabated. In 1928 it was forced to act. The following year, the collapse of the large Hatry business empire, and tighter market conditions, caused interest rates to be raised in London. As a result, British investors started to liquidate some of their positions in the American market. The flow of investment money slowed down. Some investors were concerned: future growth might not be quite as strong as previously thought; perhaps the level of borrowing was much higher. The market started to ignore good news and pay closer attention to bad.[16]

August 1929 saw the announcement that the world's tallest skyscraper was to be built on Fifth Avenue and named the Empire State Building. This was the latest in a series that now dominated the Manhattan skyline. The building boom had similarly transformed other cities around the country, such as San Diego, Chicago and Minneapolis.

Act IV: Crisis

The Crash

By then the stage was set for disaster. On 24 October, the Dow Jones Industrial Average fell 9% in a day. Four days later, it dropped 17%. Banks tried to organise support for the market. It did not work.

But that was the stock market. In the broader economy it seemed that difficulties had been addressed. The US government asked businesses not to cut wages so as to keep demand high and to bring forward construction plans. Some large companies announced dividend increases. The Federal Reserve reduced its short-term interest (discount) rate to 4.5% and made funds available, should they be needed. Banks stepped in to help consumer finance companies. For a time, the stock market responded, recovering half of the losses. A professor at Yale, Irving Fisher, declared that, "stock prices [had] reached a permanent high plateau... I expect to see the stock market a good deal higher than it is today."

Figure 1: The Dow Jones Industrial Average, 1925-1933

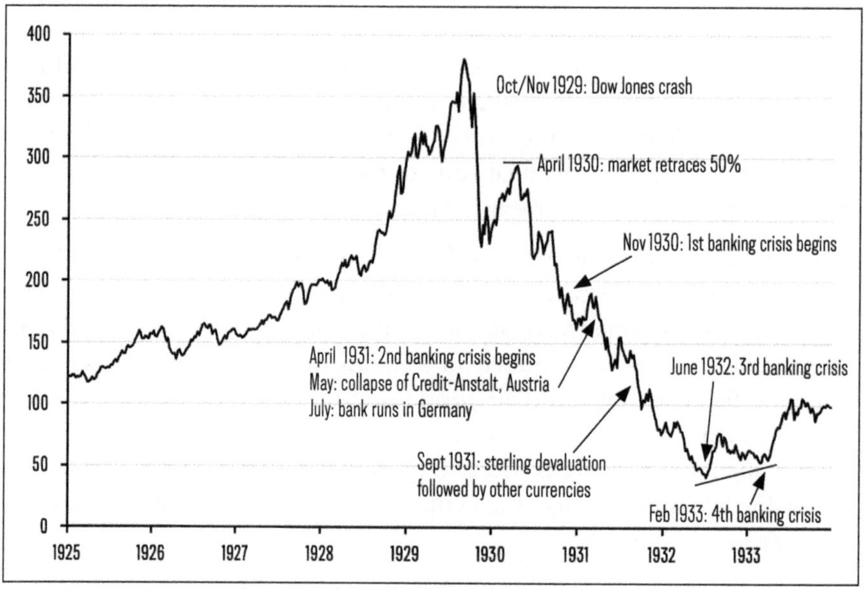

Source: Optuma (with author's own annotation).

At first, it seemed that the problems had been contained. Banks, however, were overstretched. Agricultural prices had never recovered in the 1920s and so farmers, many of whom had borrowed during the war-boom, were heavily indebted and struggled to repay loans. Many farm loan defaults had taken place during the 1920s, but the booming urban property scene had offset these losses. Now urban property was also turning down and increasing the number of bad loans and bank failures.

After a brief period of calm in the first half of 1930, a wave of problems arrived. The collapse of the Caldwell banking empire was followed by that of the Bank of the United States (despite the name, a private concern). Exposure to real estate was largely responsible for both going under.[17]

The panic was on.

The second wave of failures began in April 1931 in the Midwest, among local banks particularly exposed to the booms in Chicago and Ohio. A third wave came in June 1932. This time a large bank also collapsed in Chicago, soon followed by more in Detroit. In February 1933 a fourth wave, the deadliest, led to a general banking crisis when the Michigan authorities closed all banks in the state, precipitating bank runs everywhere.

The common thread to these failures was a high level of real estate lending during the boom. In total, 4,800 banks failed, and no one knew how large the losses would be. In 1931, the collapse of Credit-Anstalt in Austria added to the panic in the US as it demonstrated the problems were spreading throughout Europe.

All the while, the stock market was bearish. Large business conglomerates were collapsing, wiping out many thousands of small investors. Business failures mounted as bank credit disappeared. Adding to the gloom were new stories of the fraud perpetrated during the boom years, most notably by the 'Match King', Ivar Kreuger, who had succeeded in building a business empire on the back of a series of matchstick monopolies and then created one of the largest Ponzi schemes the world has ever seen.

The Rescue

The market and economy did not recover for a good four years. Authorities attempted to contain the problem but did not succeed until President Roosevelt declared, in 1933, an end to fear and instituted an immediate, nationwide bank holiday with no announced end date. Despite the economic hardship of the spring of that year, the public understood that the government was determined to act, and to do whatever it took.

From March, banking licences were reissued, and three-quarters reopened, capitalised by deposits frozen during the bank closures. New regulations were instituted, including a system of deposit insurance and measures to support urban and rural land values. To boost demand and provide support against the worst effects of the downturn, Roosevelt established his signature New Deal programme.[18]

In the depths of what has come to be known as the Great Depression, the Empire State Building opened. There were no tenants to be found: 'the Empty State Building' was how locals knew it in the early years. Many of the other icons of the era – the Chrysler, RCA, Los Angeles City Hall – also remained untenanted for a decade.

The US economy had contracted by 40%, and four-in-ten workers had lost their jobs. The stock market would bottom in 1932, having lost 90% of its value. The economic devastation was as severe in France and Germany. In the troubled atmosphere of the early 1930s, desperate German workers were only too keen to listen to those with an explanation for why things had become so bad, such as an Austrian by the name of Adolf Hitler.

The dark economic times that led to even darker political ones could not have been predicted.

Or could they?

The recurring pattern

In 1933, a doctoral student in Chicago, Homer Hoyt, completed a monumental study into the expansion of the city over the prior century. He charted the city's development but through a different lens: the change in its land values. It was the first instance of a comprehensive study of the development of a young, dynamic city. His dissertation was published as *One Hundred Years of Land Values in Chicago*.

This sober and unexciting title hides a work of breathtaking rigour and discovery. Over the course of those 100 years, during which a grand metropolis of some four million people emerged out of a village consisting of only a few log cabins on the shore of Lake Michigan, land values and, by extension, the price of real estate grew enormously.

But it was not steady growth. While over the very long term land values reflected the development of the city, there were many periods where prices were significantly higher (and lower) than they should have been. "Periods of feverish activity in which the whole city seemed to be possessed with a rage to reconstruct its business centre and to cover the adjacent prairie with houses or flats, were followed by periods in which the new growth was so slow as to be almost imperceptible."[19] Eventually, periods of slow growth would lead to another building frenzy, followed by a ruinous collapse and economic depression.

The Start of each cycle initiated a new era, powered by a new technology such as canals and railroads. New businesses would emerge and land prices would increase fairly steadily as the economy grew, people moved into the city and the authorities funded new infrastructure. But after the good times had been going on for a while, investment turned to speculation. Easy bank credit caused land prices to accelerate rapidly, even as the number of housing and commercial developments outstripped demand. Eventually, people would recognise that things had gone over the top and they would pull out. The land market would slump, real estate borrowers would default on their loans and some banks would collapse as their capital evaporated. This would be followed by a general panic, a run on banks and a wave of failures. The economy would be thrown into a major depression. But then, during the difficult times, there would be a rescue and a cancellation of debts, and the cycle would begin all over again.

It was not just in the years after 1929, when Hoyt was writing, that the latter had occurred. Collapses took place after each of the five great land booms that he had forensically studied, leading to the building and real estate highs in 1837, 1856, 1888 and 1907 and the panics shortly thereafter.[20] He was himself intimately acquainted with their destructive power, having acquired a piece of land on Chicago's Cicero Avenue in 1925, right at the top of the market. He lost a great deal of money on his investment and wanted to learn lessons from his mistake. His study gave him the answer. There was a regular pattern of boom and bust.[21] Here was the most remarkable finding of all: not only was there a common cause to each of them, but the time span between these periods of feverish speculation was highly regular. It was 18 years in duration, and it had run almost like clockwork for over a century. Had he known this in 1925, he would never have bought that land – for he was doing so exactly 18 years after the prior Summit in 1907.

The enduring 18-year cycle

Hoyt's observations for Chicago were true of other real estate markets across the United States.[22] At the time he wrote, this cyclical phenomenon had persisted for over 100 years in Chicago, but could be seen as far back as the founding of the United States.

The first major panic of the new nation was in 1798, following several years of speculation in the stock of the First Bank of the United States, government debt securities and titles to western lands. Thereafter, from 1800, the westward expansion was carried out through a programme of land sales. This was supposed to lead to orderly settlement of the west, through townships and homesteads, but soon became the means by which eastern speculators acquired large tracts of land and held or sold them on at (eventually) exorbitant prices.[23] There was a major boom in land sales coinciding with each building speculative peak documented by Hoyt for Chicago. Figure 2 shows that land sales peaked every 18 years on average between 1800 and 1908, after which the public domain had been largely sold off.

Figure 2: US public land sales, 1800-1923

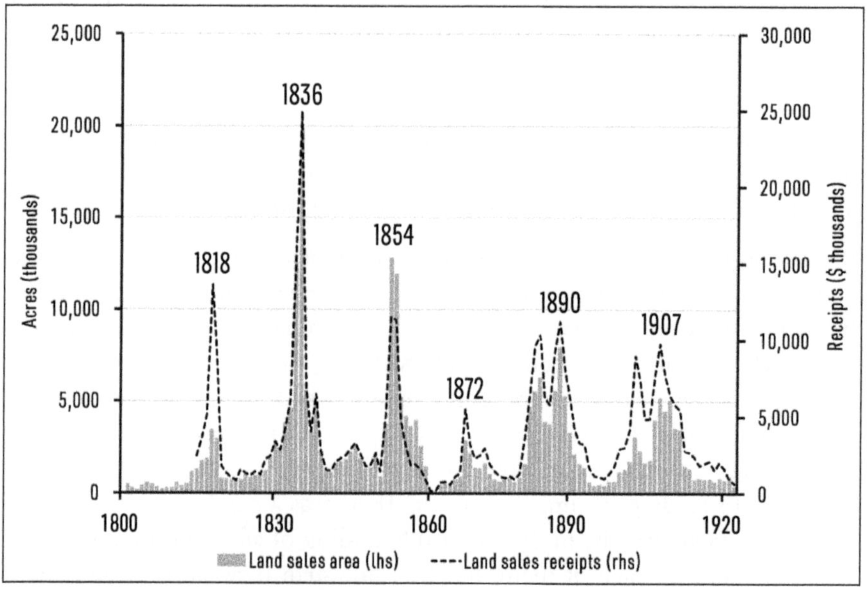

Source: Data taken from Smith and Cole, McCartney, Hibbard.

The dates of each cycle high and trough since 1800 were as follows:

Table 1: US cycle highs and major recessions, 1818-1930

Cycle high	Major recession (start date)	Years since prior cycle high
1818	1819	
1836	1837	18
1854	1857	18
1872	1873	18
1890	1893	18
1907	1907	17
1926	1930	19

Source: Dates derived from Anderson, Harrison, Hoyt.

After the 1930s it had seemed the cycle had disappeared. Hoyt himself was not sure it would continue. He had a point. The low in land prices in 1930 should have led to a cycle high around 1944, but this did not materialise. Hoyt wondered if the pattern only applied to new cities and disappeared after they became established. The world was focused from the late 1930s and early 1940s on the Second World War and economies were fully directed to fighting. A very different world emerged from the ruins of war.

So had the cycle been eliminated?

An English economist, Fred Harrison, resurrected Homer Hoyt's thesis in the 1970s and, in a brilliant piece of detective work, posited a new starting point: the completion of post-war demobilisation and reconstruction efforts in the mid-1950s. Western economies had boomed during the 1960s and there had been a frenzy of speculative activity in the early 1970s. And then there was a crisis.

The conventional explanation of those events was that they were caused by the oil shock of 1973. Not so, said Harrison (emphasis in the original),

> *Yet an economist, if he had used the cycle in land values as his predictive tool, could have predicted the economic contortions into which the UK economy would have spiralled in 1974* even if OPEC had never been established.[24]

Harrison had discovered that the cycle was alive and well. Though the world war had interrupted it, it had endured.

Harrison published his findings in 1983, in *The Power in the Land*. Tracking the cycle from the low after the crisis, he used Hoyt's thesis to predict a boom in real estate during the 1980s, culminating in a major economic recession to take place after 1990. He was exactly right, forecasting events fully seven years before they occurred. He did the same again in 1997, predicting the boom of the 2000s that would ultimately lead to the crisis of 2008.

These were not lucky guesses. They were based on a deep knowledge of the patterns of history. When the British Academy claimed it was difficult to answer the Queen's question, here was clear proof that it was not.[25]

The cycle highs since the Second World War are presented in Table 2.

Table 2: US cycle highs and major recessions, 1950-2008

Cycle high	Major recession (start date)	Years since prior cycle high
1972	1973	-
1989	1991	17
2006	2008	17

Source: Harrison.

Harrison identified the same 18-year pattern in British history since at least the late 18th century, albeit with an alternating rhythm to the USA until the 1950s. After the war, the two cycles synchronised. The pattern is evident in the history of other countries, albeit not with the same clarity as for the US and UK, given the political upheavals that many have experienced over the centuries. But, since the middle of the 20th century, this rhythm has been present in most of the major industrialised nations of the world and, over time, many developing ones as well. The evidence is clear: all of the most significant economic depressions in history have followed a boom and then a collapse in the land market.[26]

The roadmap for your 18-year journey

You now possess an overview of the cycle and an understanding of its enduring nature.

The internal dynamics of an 18-year cycle become clear through study of each historical cycle. It manifests itself as a clear definable pattern of 14 years of rising, then four years declining, land prices.

The 14-year rising phase of the cycle encompasses three Acts:

i. the Start of the cycle, an Expansion and a Peak. This lasts for six to seven years;

ii. a mid-cycle Recession, usually lasting a year or two;

iii. a Land Boom, Mania and Summit, for another six to seven years, completing the 14-year phase.

The declining phase of the cycle comprises the fourth Act and consists of:

iv. a Crash and a Rescue, lasting four years on average and bringing a full 18-year cycle to a close.

This is illustrated in Figure 3. This diagram will be your roadmap to guide your expedition through the cycle.

Figure 3: The roadmap to the 18-year cycle

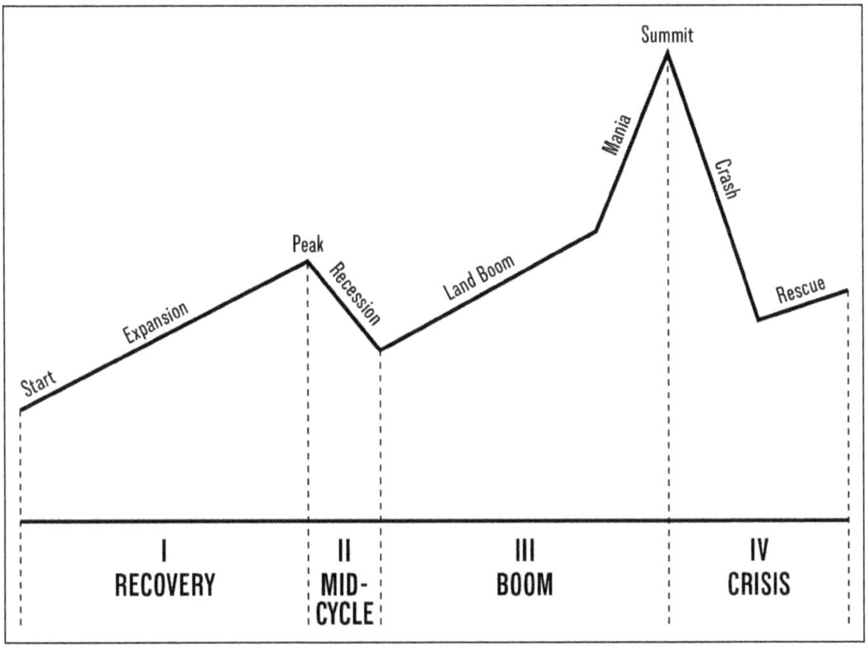

Source: author's own image.

We are now ready to begin our 18-year journey.

We begin, as with all journeys great and small, at the Start.

ACT I
RECOVERY

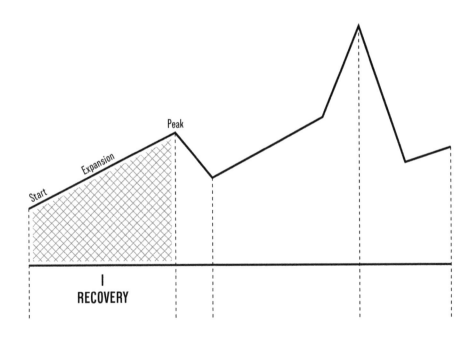

In this Act, the new cycle begins, and the expansion takes hold. It lasts six to seven years on average.

Chapter 1: The Start is where the cycle begins, driven by an exciting new technology. The stock and property markets recover. This is the best time to buy.

Chapter 2: The Effortless Return and the Law of Economic Rent explains why property and land are so important to the cycle. They are linked to the fundamental law of economics: that land takes all the gains of progress. You need to take advantage of this.

Chapter 3: The Expansion is the next stage of the cycle, where the property market grows and construction surges, especially in large cities. You should now expand your portfolios.

Chapter 4: The Effortless Return and the New Economy surveys the various forms of rent in the modern economy, such as licences, natural resources and technology. Buy companies with digital, natural and legal moats.

Chapter 5: The Corruption of Economics explains why most do not see or understand the cycle despite its long history. The role of land has been airbrushed from the economics discipline by those who control the economic rent as a way of preserving their power.

Chapter 6: The Peak brings the expansion of the first half of the cycle to a close. Do not get carried away now; it is time to get your house in order.

CHAPTER 1

THE START

During the past history of the world, following each depression some new discovery or some
new invention has stimulated business and progress and brought on another boom.

W. D. Gann, *45 Years in Wall Street*

A new cycle begins...

WASHINGTON, D.C. WAS in a festive mood. Despite the bitter January cold, the
crowds along the Mall stretched as far as the eye could see, basking in
the glorious sunshine and marvelling at the largest gathering for a presidential
inauguration in the history of the republic. This was a national moment like
no other. At midday, the young, eloquent senator from Illinois, Barack Obama,
took the oath of office and assumed the US presidency. He was the first African
American ever to do so. A new age had been born.

The brightness of that moment only briefly diverted attention away from the
deep gloom enveloping the world. The financial crisis was still raging. Swiftly,
President Obama took action to reflate the American economy, signing into law
the *American Recovery and Reinvestment Act* in February 2009. At $787bn, it was
the largest stimulus bill in US history. It funded unemployment programmes
and large-scale investments in infrastructure, health and renewable energy. This
followed hard on the heels of the Chinese response announced the previous
November which, at 4 trillion renminbi ($586bn), was – in proportion to the
Chinese economy – even larger than the American one.[1] China also directed
investment towards building rail links, roads and bridges to bind its vast
economy together.

The world's two largest economies, covering one-third of global economic activity, were in stimulus mode at the same time. Despite the scale of the crisis, this action brought it to a close. And it indicated a new development: emerging economies, led by China, would drive the new cycle forward, through their seemingly insatiable appetite for raw materials, food and energy; and their ability to marshal the entrepreneurial spirit of their peoples into developing high-quality products for export.

Later that year, the world's tallest building opened in Dubai. At a height of 828 metres, it was the centrepiece of a large downtown development designed to show off the city's economic might. The crisis, however, had killed the city's six-year construction boom, and half a trillion dollars' worth of projects were put on hold, leaving a trail of unfinished towers and unfulfilled plans across the city. This included a $100bn resort complex with four theme parks and an artificial island. The project's sponsor, a real estate developer by the name of Donald Trump, had declared it would be "the ultimate in luxury". It was never built. The emirate itself ran out of money and was bailed out by neighbouring Abu Dhabi. In return, the record-breaking skyscraper had to be swiftly renamed, opening as the *Burj Khalifa*, in honour of Abu Dhabi's ruler, Khalifa bin Zayed Al Nahyan.[2]

Two things happened in the first half of 2009 that signalled transition from the old cycle to the new was underway. The first was that the US and other stock markets reached a low on 6 March 2009, with the S&P 500 famously printing *666*. By this point it had lost 50% of its value, and even deeper stock market falls took place in Europe and Asia. As the economic news worsened that year and into the next – European countries threatened to default on their debt, which might have precipitated the collapse of the euro, and a number of financial scandals came to light – the second signal occurred. The stock markets started rising again, even though the American economy was still in recession. Stock markets were led higher by the Nasdaq, on which were listed many of the world's largest technology stocks. The Nasdaq had, in fact, bottomed in late 2008, and its upward turn indicated what would drive the new cycle forward: technology, and in particular a new device that would change the world.

...powered by a new technology

The ascetic-looking man in a black jumper began his talk. When he finished, about two hours later, the world would never be the same again. And he knew it:

> This is a day I have been looking forward to for two and a half years... Every once in a while a revolutionary product comes along that changes everything.... Today, we are introducing three revolutionary products...[3]

It was a bold claim. But Steve Jobs was right: his revolutionary invention was the iPhone, which combined a touch-controlled digital music player, a mobile phone and an internet communications device. Though the iPhone was launched a few years before the Start of this cycle, by the time it began properly – around 2012 – close to a billion people owned one (or one of the phones developed in its image). The world had moved onto the fast 4G wireless standard, and there was almost no industry untouched by its awesome power and utility.

Bankers are saved and the people ruined

Yet for all the boundless possibility of the new technology, the end of the old cycle and the Start of the new one followed a familiar course: bailing out the banks and foisting the costs of doing so onto the population.

Many governments enacted huge bailout packages which covered many types of support for ailing banks – loans, recapitalisations, asset purchases and state guarantees – on a scale that had never been seen before. Officially, the Federal Reserve response amounted to $7trn. In fact, the total commitment was closer to $30trn, almost half of the economic output of the entire world. The UK's package approached £1trn. Politicians, of course, did not have an interest in talking up how big the bailout really was. The European response could not be coordinated at the European Union level and so was done nationally.[4] The Irish government declared it would cover the liabilities of its bloated banking sector – a commitment that was seven times the size of its economy. Other countries attempted the same, though the lack of an overall EU response almost led to the collapse of the euro – until the European Central Bank stepped in and, like other central banks, declared it would do whatever it took to save the system.[5] We will later examine the mechanics by which banks are saved. The goal is always the same: to permit banks to resume their lending quickly.

Regulatory measures were introduced to shore up the system. The US government passed a new set of bank regulations in 2010 to increase supervision of the financial industry, particularly the large banks that had been deemed 'too big to fail' in the crisis. Other countries followed suit. Together with new international banking rules, which increased the amount of capital banks held in reserve, the goal was to ensure that the crisis the world was recovering from could never happen again.[6] One of the unintended consequences of these new rules was to restrict the flow of bank credit into the economy, which did not assuage the economic pain that most people were feeling. Furthermore, interest rates had been reduced, but this had not achieved a stimulative effect on growth. So central banks around the world came up with a new tool to get money flowing again: quantitative easing.

Quantitative easing and negative interest rates

The head of the US central bank, Dr Ben Bernanke, was a student of the Great Depression. He understood how government inaction in addressing the crisis of the early 1930s had allowed what might have been a recession – albeit a severe one – to become a deep depression, setting off a chain reaction of social and political events that brought the world to war in 1939. Bernanke was determined to avoid history repeating.

As the money supply dropped because banks were not lending, he devised what was regarded as a novel policy – one of swapping the assets on the balance sheets of banks and other finance providers for central bank reserves. While people saw this as an unconventional approach, the underlying principle was the same as in the aftermath of every real estate cycle: remove bad loans from bank balance sheets to free up capital – so they can resume lending.

The policy had a significant effect on interest rates. Short-term rates were already at record lows, and these in turn helped to push down longer-term rates. In many places, interest rates even went negative. Investors were pushed away from buying bonds in favour of riskier assets such as commodities and real estate.[7] This was given a name: 'the hunt for yield'.

From 2010 onwards, the price of real estate started recovering in most major cities around the world. This eased the pressure on banks. Behind the scenes they were quietly offloading all of the problem loans created during the boom of the 2000s. Wall Street 'vulture funds' swooped in to buy up huge swathes of European real estate and more – large portfolios of houses, offices, hotels, golf courses – at bargain prices.[8] America itself became a destination for overseas investors drawn to its cheap land. Because of the swift action in cutting interest rates and supplying the system with liquidity, the turnaround in property prices in many countries was quick.

The people were not so fortunate. Asset prices were recovering, but the real economy was not. What happened next made things much worse. The size of the bailouts had been large. The orthodox view – supported by some dubious analysis – was that when public debt reached a certain level in relation to the size of the economy (as measured by gross domestic product (GDP)) governments would face prohibitively high borrowing costs, so public spending had to be cut.[9]

We will soon see why this view of public spending is wrong.

After 2010, Western governments insisted on severe cuts to public services. This suppressed economic growth. The consequences were felt most keenly by the asset-poor working class, who were more likely to have lost their jobs and did not benefit from the rebound in stock and property prices. Predictably, it led to a sharp increase in economic inequality. But this too is a common pattern of each cycle: the bankers are saved and the people ruined.

It led to much anger.

The frauds, the cons... and the riots

Amid the Start it became clear that a huge amount of fraud had been taking place during the prior boom, further fuelling popular anger. A series of scandals emerged, as they always do when the crisis unfolds, reinforcing Warren Buffett's often-quoted quip that only when the tide recedes does one see who has been swimming naked. There was plenty of such nudity on display during those years. In late 2008, the world had already been shocked by the revelation of the largest Ponzi scheme in history, run by Bernie Madoff, at around $50bn.[10] There were plenty of others. It turned out that credit rating agencies, financially beholden to the companies whose products they were evaluating, were incapable of properly assessing their risks. Mortgage lenders, in the rush to lend and earn fees, had overstated borrowers' income and assets and ignored their liabilities. Bankers had hardly been models of probity when reporting the rate of interest at which they borrowed from one another. This rate – the London Interbank Offered Rate, or LIBOR – was rather important, as it was used to price around $350trn worth of derivative contracts, mortgages and US student loans. It turned out that over the past two decades, banks – in the absence of regulatory oversight – had been manipulating the rate so that they appeared more creditworthy than they were, or to profit from LIBOR-related trades. There had been suspicions of their deceit, but the turbulence of the crisis caused the scandal to break out into the open in 2012. There was seemingly no end to the violations of public trust.

Globally, banks paid $321bn in regulators' fines when the full scale of the mortgage fraud became apparent.[11] But very few bankers were imprisoned for their criminal conduct. The anger at the lack of punishment was palpable.

Economic depressions are times of despair due to the insecurity experienced by those at the margins of society. Youth unemployment in Ireland reached 30%; but this was lower than in Spain or Greece, where almost half of all young people were out of work. There was understandable rage that the support for banks and asset owners failed to trickle down to those whose livelihoods were at risk. This spilled out into the streets in many cities around the world. High commodity prices triggered the Arab Spring – a series of anti-government protests in the Middle East – in 2011. In north London, the police killing of Mark Duggan on 4 August 2011 sparked rioting around the city and spread to other British cities. In New York, a social movement, Occupy Wall Street, railed against economic inequality (under the banner *We are the 99%*). Three million Spaniards took to the streets, and protests in Athens in June 2011 turned violent.[12]

The market points the way

But the markets – particularly the American one – shrugged this news off. Trouble in Europe relating to the euro caused a sharp market sell-off between July and September 2011, but it bounced back. On 15 March 2013, the Dow Jones Industrial Average moved back into new all-time highs, five years and five months after it peaked on 11 October 2007.

That same month, the price of gold crashed, making it obvious that fears of the collapse of the financial system were unfounded. John Paulson, the world's most famous hedge fund manager, who had been lauded for correctly betting on the real estate crash and making billions, lost almost $1bn in two days, ironically because he had failed to anticipate the recovery in real estate prices.[13] Such are the trials and tribulations investors face if they have no knowledge of the 18-year cycle. The market was confirming what was happening. The system had been preserved and the new cycle had begun. And given the speed of the recovery, the market was suggesting it was going to be big.

The Start analysed

1. The cycle begins quietly

Out of the depths of the prior Crash, and around four years after the prior top, a new cycle begins. But few people see the beginning. The literature on financial bubbles and manias and panics is full of rich tales of fortunes made and lost, of conmen and fraudsters, of extravagant displays of wealth, of irrational exuberance or of the animal spirits unleashed.[14] They are about the final stages of the cycle. Very few discuss the Start because it occurs in rather less colourful and more austere times. Thus there are few guides on how and when it takes place.

For at least the past century, the American economy has led the world into and out of each real estate cycle – starting new cycles in 1907, 1933 (a cycle that was interrupted after the outbreak of the Second World War in 1939), in the late 1950s, after post-war reconstruction had been completed, in 1974, 1992 and 2011. The transition from the old cycle to the new is a process, and some of the factors noted below might occur before the Start (especially the stock market low). But the Start has definitely arrived by the time of the low point in land prices. This is typically around four years after the Summit of the prior cycle.[15]

2. Bank problems ease and new regulations are put in place

For the cycle to properly get underway, problems in the banking system have to be resolved so that banks can lend again. Bad debts must be moved on. The longer this takes to do, the more protracted the crisis of the prior cycle (as countries within the eurozone found out after 2008, as did Japan after the Summit of the cycle in 1990). New bank regulations are put in place to prevent the next crisis, or so the authorities believe at the time.[16] Yet new regulations delay the recovery by making it harder for businesses to access credit. As we shall see, when the cycle reaches its Summit these regulations do not prevent the crisis. No one ever looks at the land market as the destination to which all that bank credit goes and therefore as the cause of boom and bust.

3. Government stimulus reflates the economy

Alongside new regulations, governments typically introduce large stimulus measures to get the economy moving again. This involves fairly standard actions, such as lower interest rates to boost demand for credit, tax cuts or tax breaks. The government itself might attempt to stimulate economic activity by increasing spending, particularly on major projects.

Such measures eventually capitalise into the price of land (for reasons that will become clear in the next chapter). Governments that opt for austerity measures in response to a crisis condemn their economies to a period of stagnation, as European economies discovered after 2008. Which part of the private sector recovers best depends on the nature of the stimulus provided.[17]

4. The Start is powered by a new technology

Those who are watching carefully will notice a shift in activity. Indeed it was foreshadowed by President Barack Obama in his inaugural address when he said (echoing W. D. Gann's observation quoted at the start of this chapter),

> The state of our economy calls for action, bold and swift. And we will act, not only to create new jobs, but to lay a new foundation for growth. We will build the roads and bridges, the electric grids and digital lines that feed our commerce and bind us together. We'll restore science to its rightful place, and wield technology's wonders to raise health care's quality and lower its cost. We will harness the sun and the winds and the soil to fuel our cars and run our factories. We will transform our schools and colleges and universities to meet the demands of a new age.

Every new cycle begins with new investment and new technology, which profoundly reshapes the economy. Recent cycles furnish the following examples:

- the smartphone and 4G (2007 onwards)

- the World Wide Web and Netscape (1993)

- the personal computer (1977)

- interstate/motorways and suburbanisation/aviation (late 1950s)

- the Model T (1908)

- electricity (1881)

- railways (1830s)

5. New leaders come to power

A new generation of political and business leaders arrives on the scene with a promise of change, such as the 'third way' of Clinton/Blair (1993/1997), 'new monetarism' of Thatcher/Reagan (1979/1981); the New Deal of Roosevelt (1933).[18] The promises are sincerely made, no doubt, and in part are a natural response to the failure of the prior economic paradigm that resulted in crisis. But no new leader has ever demonstrated any knowledge of the 18-year cycle. In implementing their ideas, they merely preserve the system as it is.

6. The yield curve steepens

As a result of the lowering of interest rates, the yield curve noticeably steepens. When it is in this position, the Start of the new cycle is never far behind. It helps banks to recapitalise by giving them access to cheap short-term funding. A steep yield curve is the sign that the economy is moving beyond the problems of the past and is a reliable guide that the next two years (at least) will be expansionary for the economy.

7. The stock market bottoms first

Savvy investors should look to the stock market to see that the low is coming. The stock market is a discounting mechanism that looks beyond current news. The low in the stock market is always the first thing to look for at the end of the prior cycle. And how does one know it is the low? As we saw in 2010, it is when bad news brings in a higher low (see Figure 4). The same happened at prior cycle lows in 1908, 1933, 1975 (and 1978) and 1991.

Figure 4: The Dow Jones Industrial Average, 2007-2012

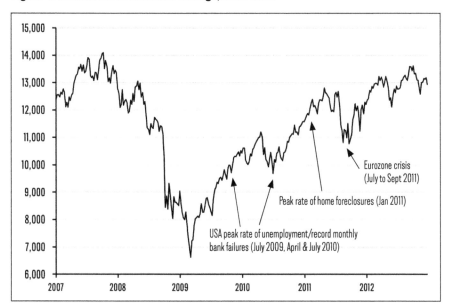

Source: Optuma (with author's own annotation).

8. Rents begin to rise; residential property recovers

Another sign is to be found in the land market. The economy might be in a dire position and contracting, scarred by high unemployment, with property prices depressed and an urban landscape blighted by shuttered businesses, empty high streets and half-finished buildings and yet, paradoxically, rents start to rise. The stimulus measures to reflate the economy and the new developments cited above are beginning to work. This leads to the formation of new businesses and the movement of people in search of jobs (usually into cities or across borders into larger countries), creating a new demand to rent space.[19]

Residential property recovers before commercial property. The shortage of housing in areas where people are moving to supports residential prices and rents. Commercial property is more closely linked to economic growth and takes longer to recover. Recessions also bring about a surfeit of commercial space, which takes time to be absorbed.[20]

The property market has now stabilised and, in some places, is recovering. The prior cycle has ended and is now consigned to history; the new one has started. From its low, land prices will go up for 14 years. Even if there are pauses along the way, there will not be a major collapse until then. On this one factor is founded your entire financial well-being. Possessing this piece of knowledge, and understanding its significance, is your wealth advantage.

Why should land be so crucial to our economies? Why does the recovery in land prices signal the Start of the new cycle? Is its importance applicable everywhere? These important questions need to be considered before we move forward on our 18-year journey, and so are the subject of the next chapter.

THE BEST TIME TO BUY

Stage: the Start

Approximate timing: years 1 and 2

Prevailing emotion: denial

Managing emotions

Denial is the prevailing emotion. Few believe that things might be turning around because there is a ceaseless flow of bad news. This fear holds investors back in cycle after cycle. The key to managing emotions at this stage is to tune out the noise and learn well the lessons this book gives you. This will gift you the most priceless emotion of all at this point in the cycle: confidence. There is a long expansion to come, and you must be ready to act.[21]

Managing investments

This is the best stage in which to buy stocks and property. The lows are in place and the economy is moving into a new cycle. Ahead of you is an economic expansion lasting 14 years, interrupted only by a mid-cycle Recession.

Now is the time to buy.[22]

1. Buy strong stocks, especially the US market and technology

The stock market follows the real estate cycle through periods of boom and bust. The stock market will often bottom before the Start in anticipation of a recovery in company earnings. Investors who can spot this early become very wealthy indeed. Let the 18-year cycle be your guide.

The main periods of earnings recovery take place at the Start (and after the mid-cycle Recession).[23] From the Start to the Summit of the cycle the stock market appreciates on average 450%; from the Start to the mid-cycle Peak the average gain is 233%.[24]

a. Stock investors should take advantage of the 'very good year' in the market. A very good year is one in which the market gains are 35% or more in a 12 month period. Such years take place when the markets have fallen considerably, and the government is in stimulus mode – pumping huge volumes of liquidity into the financial system. This invariably ends up being better for financial markets than for the real economy.[25] These are precisely the conditions that occur around the Start of the cycle.

b. Buy the US market, because the American economy leads the world into and out of each cycle. But the index of any economy in reflation mode could be bought at this time. Investors who are feeling cautious about buying right at the Start can invest at the sign of the first higher lows in the stock market.

c. Buy technology stocks. These tend to reach the bottom a few months before the broader market index as they lead the economy into the new cycle and appreciate to a greater degree during the first half of each cycle. For example, the tech-heavy Nasdaq index has outperformed the Dow Jones Industrial Average and has recorded a greater percentage gain in the first half of the cycle compared to the second (see Figure 5: it had relative strength into the first-half stock market peaks of 1981, 2000 and 2021, and mainly relative weakness into the lows before the Start of the cycle around 1976, 1991 and 2009).

Figure 5: Increase of the Nasdaq 100 relative to the Dow Jones Industrial Average, 1971-2022

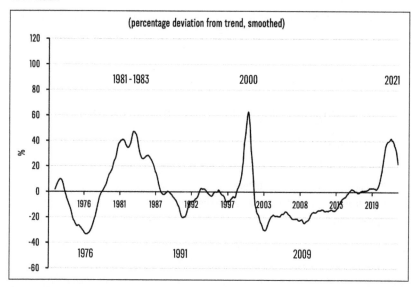

Source: author's own work.

d. Buy strong stocks. A strong stock is one that has fallen the least in relative terms in the prior Crash and finds its lows before the broader market. This is an indication that the selling pressure on the stocks is lower, and the buying power greater, than for the rest of the market.[26]

e. Do not buy stocks that look cheap in relation to the prices they traded at during the prior Summit, e.g., banks. Those that have fallen the furthest are cheap for a reason.

2. Buy good quality property

Despite the gloomy news and the depressed state of the property market, this is a good time to invest. There are good deals available because of forced sales and because there are comparatively few buyers.

a. Buy well-located residential real estate in or close to city centres and in central cities within a country or region. This will be the first to recover. This is the very best time to buy real estate, because the first feature of the new cycle is that rents will start increasing and so yields will go up. As we move our lives increasingly online, and as more activity is transacted in the metaverse, in future cycles we will see this dynamic with virtual real estate too.[27]

b. Buy real estate with development potential (e.g., which need to be modernised, or can be augmented with additional floorspace such as rooms or floors, or new buildings). As the cycle moves forward, returns will come from both the increase in land price and the enhancements made. These gains will be even greater if you buy in areas people are starting to move to, where new infrastructure is going in or which are adjacent to better areas.[28]

c. As interest rates are low, borrow to fund property purchases if possible. At this stage, bank lending for real estate may be curtailed, so you may need to use larger deposits or cash (this is why preparation for this stage is key). Buy land at the edge of expanding cities (or at the edge of important areas in cities).

d. For those with deep pockets and long time horizons, buy land at the edge of a city and hold it as the city expands.[29]

e. Buy cheap commercial leases. In the slump after the prior crisis, business conditions are often depressed. This causes the value of commercial real estate to drop. However, many businesses are able to ride out the difficult period and continue to pay rents which may have been locked in when rents were high during the prior boom. This means commercial leases may be available at excellent valuations.

3. Businesses that have reserves should expand

Businesses with cash reserves should be able to take advantage of the recovery because they have the resources to expand organically or through acquiring other businesses.

CHAPTER 2

THE EFFORTLESS RETURN AND THE LAW OF ECONOMIC RENT

Among material resources, the greatest, unquestionably, is the land. Study how a society uses its land, and you can come to pretty reliable conclusions as to what its future will be.

E. F. Schumacher, *Small is Beautiful*

T O UNDERSTAND WHY land is so important to the cycle, let us begin with a thought experiment. Imagine a country where a property boom could *not* take place. If this experiment is to reveal anything significant, this country should have a familiar market economy, where people can buy and sell things and move around in search of a place to live and work; but otherwise, it should share none of our advantages that lead us to speculate in property. After all, without speculation there would be no cycle.

Given that each property boom involves financial excess, let's make it a poor country, with many of its people living in poverty. There should be little prospect of improving this situation, so we will say that the economy is barely growing, wages are not rising and it is difficult to start a business. What about political leadership, you might ask: perhaps some far-sighted official could make wise investments to alter this sorry country's outlook. Indeed; so, let's give it a dysfunctional, corrupt government which is barely capable of delivering such benefits.

But, you might point out, one way out of its miserable situation could be to exploit the gifts of nature, such as minerals and energy: this could create an investment bonanza. True. Let's not endow it with any natural resources whatsoever, and give it only a small land area so it is unlikely to discover any in the future. Maybe it has a large population to draw in foreign investment to serve the local market? Alas, no. Its population is small.

Clearly, with its position so bleak, there is no imminent possibility of growth to ignite speculation in the property market.

Let's make its situation even more unfavourable. Let's introduce conflict. Say the country is being attacked by a much stronger neighbour. This is not a struggle where the country might be obliterated (after all, what would be the point of examining anything if everyone was soon going to die?), but one where bombing causes extensive damage to infrastructure and where its opponent subjects it to harsh economic sanctions. In such circumstances what incentives are there to invest and build for the long term?

This is quite the litany of problems to bestow on our unfortunate country.

So now, if you were to ask one hundred people: can this country, this small place, with a small population, no natural resources, beset by widespread poverty, low growth, weak government, and devastated by conflict – can it *ever* experience a property boom? Every one of those one hundred people, after considering this question briefly would answer you: no, such a country, in those circumstances, could never experience one.

And yet.

While in our minds we have loaded such problems on to this woebegone country to minimise *any* chance of a property boom, even here it can take place. Because the situation described above was faced by the West Bank and Gaza around 2012. In spite of the region's many challenges, including war and occupation, when not much worked well at all, the fundamental law of economics continued to operate – and it experienced a property boom.[1] To understand how this law operates is to understand why we *must* get real estate cycles.

To see this more clearly let us begin with possibly the world's unlikeliest real estate tycoon.

The unlikeliest real estate tycoon[2]

Nada spent his days working his family's farm in the south of Gaza, hard against the Egyptian border. His only possessions consisted of a few animals and, worthless as it possibly was, he also owned the title to his plot of land. It was a hard life. So meagre was the yield from his farm that he could barely afford to purchase cigarettes. But fate had something more in store for him.

Riches were to fall from the heavens – almost literally – and from an inadvertent benefactor: the Israeli military. It first started bombing the region in 2008 and returned in 2012. The accompanying economic blockade made the import of many goods illegal. To continue to source them, people tunnelled under the border with friendly Egypt, away from where the aerial bombardment was taking place. The gateway to one of those tunnels was on Nada's land.

Nada stopped working as a farmer and started renting access to the tunnels. These were not sophisticated structures, but they served to facilitate the flow of vital goods. A significant proportion of the region's goods came through these tunnels, and Nada collected a portion of this in rents. Soon, this impoverished farmer, now a rentier, became a millionaire.

It was not just Nada's land that became valuable. The bombing campaigns took place close to the Israeli border and caused many people to move to safer areas. The areas they moved to experienced a surge in property rents due to the new demand. Existing land and property owners experienced a windfall gain.

Contrast Nada's situation with another Gazan, Ahmed. Unlike the economically precarious life of a farmer, his was comparatively well off because he had a well-paid job as a policeman. As he had a young family, he dreamed of owning a place in a nice neighbourhood with good schools where he and his wife could raise their children. But when he began to search for a place to live, he found that property prices were escalating rapidly. He had a good job, but his wages were not rising at nearly the same rate. With each week of fruitless searching, the properties within his budget were getting smaller and smaller. He and his wife were forced to confront the desperate choice that many young couples face when buying their first home: sacrificing space to live in the right neighbourhood.

Difficulties were experienced, in a different way, by even wealthy business owners, such as Hatem. He was a member of the older business community, one that had good links with Israel. Before the war, he had made his fortune by importing electrical fixtures. Now his business was subject to fierce competition from traders who smuggled goods in through the tunnels. In the old days, he was hundreds of times richer than Nada; not so now, as his profit margins had fallen sharply. Property speculation was where the money was being made. The surge in prices led to a boom in construction of new housing. But the market had adjusted to higher prices and, despite the boom, these were not getting lower; except for temporary lulls as the market absorbed new supply.

The contrast in outcomes for the landowner, the skilled wage earner and the successful businessman was quite striking. The first became fabulously wealthy from mere ownership of land in the right location; the others, despite their hard work in respectable occupations, could not keep up. While the circumstances through which Nada became wealthy were specific, the dynamic that led to the landowner reaping a windfall profit while the worker and businessman were left behind is not. Indeed, we have seen the beginning of it already, at the first stage of the cycle. Though the economy was depressed, people were moving in search of work. This led to a rise in rents and the recovery of the property market. This dynamic is caused by the unique nature of land, and it operates at the heart of our economies.

We all need land and there is only so much of it

"Buy land, they're not making it anymore," said Mark Twain. We all need to occupy a bit of land in order to live and work, and there are only so many bits to go around.

There is no shortage of land in an absolute sense. Our world is vast. But there is a limited amount of land in areas where people want to settle. Our economies are a complex, cooperative undertaking; and we all come together to divide our labour to produce and exchange things. This takes place at certain locations, and it is in those places that the amount of land is limited.

Land is unique. It cannot be produced. If all the land in an area is occupied, and there is still demand for it, one is forced to pay more to acquire it or to find another location, which will not be quite as good. In the best locations, one has easiest access to employees, suppliers and customers; at less favourable ones, this is not as good. One piece of land is not the same as another. In fact, they can vary greatly in quality depending on location.

The difference in quality between the best and worst locations leads to a dynamic that is critical to determining who in our economies gets to be wealthy and who does not, as the following example shows.

The law of economic rent: locational value

In 1991, the social entrepreneur John Bird founded the publishing sensation of the decade, *The Big Issue*. Under its motto 'A hand up not a hand out', the magazine's route to market was unique: it was sold by those who were homeless, or at risk of losing their home, directly to customers on the streets. It was intended to help those at the margins of society with meaningful employment. Celebrities and politicians were enthusiastic supporters. The pop icon George Michael, for example, gave his first interview in six years exclusively to the magazine. In the 30 years since its launch, *The Big Issue* vendors have become a visible presence on busy streets in many cities around the world.

While the initiative was undeniably brilliant at bringing work to those struggling at the margins of the economy, sellers of the magazine soon identified a problem. They were organised around a city by being allocated a spot, or 'pitch', far enough away from each other that they would not directly compete for customers. Their pitch gave them the exclusive right to sell the magazine in that zone. But even though they were all working equally hard, some made more money than others by virtue of the pitch they had. On some, one could generate just enough sales to earn a wage. But on others, they earned a lot more: a wage and a surplus above that. The difference could not be attributed to any greater skill, it was simply a benefit of better location – some pitches were on busier streets than others. Naturally, those allocated worse pitches would envy those given better ones. In some US cities, sellers felt compelled to arm themselves to protect their locational advantage from others who might try to take their territory by force.

Imagine you were a researcher studying the locational value of pitches. You would gather data on the level of sales on a typical day on each pitch and could then plot them in order of best to worst locations. If you did so, it would look a bit like Figure 6.

Figure 6: The locational advantage or value of *The Big Issue* pitches

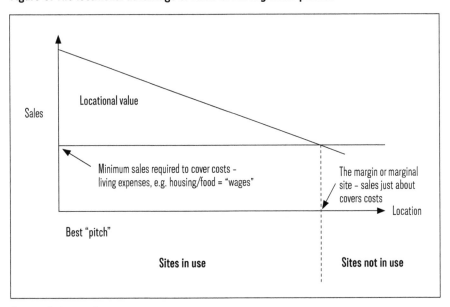

Source: author's own work.

The best pitch, plotted at the far left of the graph, would generate the highest level of sales. Likely it would be at the centre of the city on a busy street corner where footfall was greatest. The next best site would perhaps be a little further down the road, where not quite as many people came (but still enough to make a large, but lesser, surplus from a day's work). And so on with each pitch, as represented by the downward sloping line, until one got to a fairly isolated location which nonetheless would generate just enough sales to cover the minimum requirement for a vendor: a night's accommodation and food.

Let us call this location where the minimum sales requirement was just about met 'the margin'. Beyond the margin, it would not make sense to use a pitch because even though a seller might make some sales, they would not be enough to cover their living expenses. In other words, economic activity – selling *The Big Issue* magazines – takes place on all pitches up to the margin.

Pitches were allocated by granting them to sellers on a first come, first served basis. But if sellers had the opportunity to rent out a pitch, how much would they bid for a given location? The answer is supplied by Figure 6: it would be the full surplus value of the pitch. This surplus value is everything above the minimum sales requirement up to the maximum achievable sales for that pitch. Clearly, they would not pay more because to do so would mean they could not earn enough to cover living expenses. At the same time, competition would compel them not to bid less because someone else could come along and usurp their offer with a better one.

Two hundred years ago the economist David Ricardo had observed and generalised this phenomenon. In Ricardo's framework the surplus, attributable to the advantage of location, was called 'economic rent'.[3] On the best sites someone might get more income, but really this was split between a wage to compensate the worker and cover other costs of sales (such as working capital and materials) and a rent (which reflected the value of that location). This rent was the surplus earnings on the best site compared to the least viable one, the one at the margin. This phenomenon is the *law of economic rent*, and it is critical to understanding the economy and the economic cycle.

Ricardo also observed that the *most important* location in an economy is not its *best* location; it is in fact the marginal one. Why is this? Because this is where the level of wages is established. Take the example of *The Big Issue* sellers: at the margin it still just about pays to sell these magazines. But if that is the wage at the margin, it must be the same everywhere where people can move in search of work. Wages that are higher in one area are competed down until they equalise (for a given type of work) across all locations. This is also true of other relevant costs needed to produce things, such as capital equipment and materials. Everything earned above that level, the surplus, goes as rent and is paid to whomever owns or controls the site. Where there is a large pool of labour searching for work, wages get pushed down to the minimum that they can tolerate, possibly even to a bare subsistence level.[4] Earning by using your skills and earning by virtue of owning a location, it turns out, are quite different things – as was demonstrated in Gaza's property boom.

That location matters may seem to be an obvious point – but this insight unlocks the essence of our modern economies and the cycles of boom and bust that rip through them on an 18-year basis. Well-located land is fundamentally scarce and cannot be moved. It takes all of the surplus – because all excess wages and returns on invested capital are competed away.

We can see how the owners of land might take the full surplus from a location, but how does it arise in the first place? The value of a location arises from the presence of the surrounding community. It is created through the dynamic, competitive and cooperative practices of the economy – in other words, it is created together with (and is a reflection of) an economy's interconnectedness: "Land obtains value from the natural, social and cultural wealth that exists in the surrounding environment."[5] In the modern economy, this is generated by infrastructure, work opportunities, housing, public spaces, local shops, transport and so on. This locational value is not attributable to the actions of any one individual or enterprise. In the property market, much of the price of real estate is based on locational value. The price is set by whatever people are willing to pay for what they perceive that value to be, as the Gazan policeman discovered in his search for a better location for his family.[6]

But that is not the end of the story. Our economies are dynamic, productive, restless. Something is always changing. Businesses invest, introduce new technology and try to outdo their competitors. People train, learn new skills and try to improve their earnings. Governments improve the dynamism of economies by investing in infrastructure and public services. What happens then is a critical feature of the economy called the *law of absorption*. It is the counterpart to the law of economic rent and dictates how much land prices increase as an economy develops.

To see this law in action, let's take a look at the experience of Don Riley.

The law of absorption: land takes gains of progress

Don Riley came to Britain from New Zealand in 1962 with only £200 in his pocket: enough money to buy a cheap suit and cover one month's living expenses. He soon found a job in operational research, specifically in the use of large computers to solve management problems. Eventually, in the late 1970s, he set up his own firm close to London Bridge station, south of the Thames, purchasing a redundant electrical factory. The premises were larger than his company needed, so he rented spare space to other firms. As his firm expanded, he bought more buildings in the area and let out more excess space. But London Bridge in those days was not the favourable location it is now. It was surrounded by derelict warehouses and was not easily accessible to the wealthier residents on the north bank of the river. As Riley observed, in those days he "had to drag people by the scruff of the neck to view the offices and become my tenants."[7]

Everything changed in 1993. The government announced the extension of the London Underground's Jubilee Line to London Bridge. Until then it had linked such famous areas to the city's northwest, such as Baker Street, to the luxury shopping district on Bond Street and Green Park and the area close to Buckingham Palace. The extension would take people under the Thames to Waterloo Station and then along the south bank of the river through London Bridge right up to the new financial district out east in Canary Wharf.

The effect on the value of Riley's property was immediate. "I found myself aboard a gravy train. In the autumn of 1995, I let 13,000 square feet and some vacant land to Costain Taylor Woodrow, the contractors for the Jubilee Line extension London Bridge contract." This was only the beginning. The value of his properties – and what he could charge – soared, courtesy of the taxpayer-funded infrastructure.

Riley decided to track this in real time and work out the exact benefits to landowners like himself, because "Frankly, I was outraged at what I regarded as the insane economics of public investment." He examined how the value of the land changed before and after the extension opened and calculated increases in the site value at different distances from each new station, as shown in Table 3.[8] For our purpose this focus on land itself (unlike other studies) is important: property (as in buildings) consists of both land and capital, and our interest is to demonstrate how *land* absorbs the gains in a dynamic economy.[9]

Table 3: The law of absorption - land value gains from the Jubilee Line extension

Distance to station	Total area (square feet)	Site value increase per square foot	Estimated total land value increase due to JL extension
Up to 400 yards	4.5 million	£100	£450m
Up to 800 yards	13.5 million	£50	£675m
Up to 1,000 yards	10.2 million	£20	£204m
Total	**28.2 million**		**£1,329m**

Source: Riley.

The new line had the effect of increasing demand for land around each station, which drove prices up. Even as far away as 1,000 yards, the increase in land values was of the order of £20 per square foot; but within a 400-yard zone the increase was five times as great. These were averages for each zone; the closer to the station, the more site values went up.

To avoid being accused of exaggerating the scale of the gains, Riley was deliberately conservative in his calculations, but around each station he estimated the total increase to be just over £1.3bn. Multiplied along the ten stations of the extension, this came to an enormous £13bn, which was almost four times the cost of the entire project. Riley exposed to the world in real time the law of absorption in action: that site owners take the gains from all improvements to the surrounding area.[10] In fact, they benefited far more than the cost of the infrastructure that generated these gains.

In a dynamic economy, such improvements are happening all the time. They include building large-scale infrastructure, such as rail schemes, and minor ones such as enhancing the quality of roads and traffic flows or beautifying the urban environment. They also include measures to reduce costs, such as introducing new technology or management techniques. Look at the updated locational value diagram shown in Figure 7. As costs reduce (because of the development of, say, the internet) the margin extends, because lower costs mean that sites that were not viable before are viable now. Similarly, improvements that draw businesses and people into an area and increase the size of the market – such as the Jubilee Line extension – increase the revenue-generating capacity of a site. The effect of both is not to increase wages or returns on capital investment – these are still subject to being competed down – but to increase the amount of locational value. This will be reflected in higher property prices and rents on existing land, which induces new building at the margin. Thus, when an economy improves there is more building going on.

Figure 7: The law of absorption: how improvements increase locational value (economic rent)

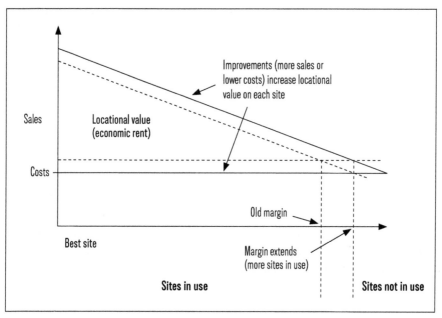

Source: author's own work.

Figure 8: Increase of house prices relative to wages (percentage), 1977-2016

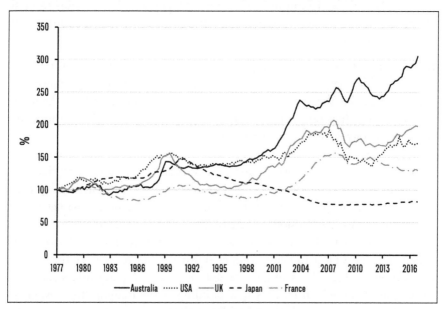

Source: Bank for International Settlements, Federal Reserve (and author's calculations).

Similarly, you can see how much more house prices have increased over wages during the last few decades in Figure 8 (with only the exception of Japan in the aftermath of its post-1990 housing market collapse). The difference is clear. As our economies improve, it is land that takes the gains.

This is why land is the ultimate speculative asset. Landowners take enormous benefits from such improvements, at zero cost to themselves.[11] This is reflected in the value of their land: global real estate is worth over $300trn, by far the most valuable asset class.[12] These benefits are paid for by taxpayers everywhere, even those who will never get to enjoy them. People and businesses who then move into the area end up paying for the same benefits a second time – through increased rents or property prices.

The land market and perverse incentives

With a scarce asset, any additional scarcity benefits the asset owner. So in the land market there is a perverse incentive to increase such shortage. Riley gave a good example. Across the road from his property was a building that had been bought for £100,000 in 1980. Thereafter it lay empty for 20 years, providing nothing by way of services or taxes to the public purse because it was closed off to businesses that might have been able to make productive use of it. Its only contribution to the local economy was to create an eyesore. In January 2000 the building's owner sold it for £2.6 million, earning 26 times the initial investment.[13]

The problem was not site owners – like anyone, they wanted to make money. If that meant holding a piece of land out of use, so be it. But the tax system deliberately made that a more lucrative activity. For while Riley had done well out of his plot of land as the site owner, earning an enormous increase in its locational value, he also worked hard and invested money to make it a pleasant place for businesses to occupy. The owner of the derelict land had none of the difficulties of finding new tenants, maintaining and improving the building, dealing with service providers and insurance agents and the rest. The owner only reaped a massive gain in locational value with no effort whatsoever. Why wouldn't any rational owner do more of this, particularly given that the scarcity of sites they are contributing to increases prices?

Indeed, landlords make this very calculation. The percentage of vacant buildings in cities is typically in the region of 10–20%, an enormous proportion given the generally acknowledged shortage of sites.[14]

This feature of property ownership is not simply 'how things work'. In fact, for most of human history, societies had practices that better reflected the public nature of locational value; whether land was formally owned by the public or had rules in place such that there was a way of returning this value back to the community. The means by which this flow of value ended up privately owned is a long tale of theft, violence and alienation, in which humanity's darkest impulses are revealed.[15]

The economy's law of gravity

These simple relationships – that land is a scarce resource (fixed in supply), that it is an inherently locational asset (fixed in space) and that as a result it absorbs the gains of progress – are key to understanding the dynamic of the 18-year cycle. As the economy recovers and grows, rents increase and so do land prices. This encourages new building but does not lower prices, which reflect the increased productivity of the economy. This induces speculation; land held speculatively out of use can still provide a return and this further increases prices. Banks lend, raising the purchasing power of borrowers. Prices go up more. Higher prices provoke a construction boom. This greater activity boosts economic growth, which further feeds into the land market. High prices and rents ultimately squeeze businesses and cause a major crisis. The process by which this happens will be laid out fully in the chapters that follow. This is the reason why each economic cycle is ultimately a land story, subject to bouts of wild speculation and excesses – particularly, as we will see in a future stage of the cycle, when banks get involved.

The law of economic rent is utterly inescapable, even in places where life is difficult, such as the West Bank and Gaza. It is the economy's law of gravity: invisible and universal, applying at all times, in all places, to all participants. You are subject to it from the moment you are born, and its hold on you is dissolved only at the moment of your death (and if your remains are buried in a plot of earth which you purchased while you were alive, you are bound by it even after you die).

———————— - ▪ ■ ▪ - ————————

As you now understand the central role that land plays in the economy, you have a critical insight with which to observe what is going on around you as you progress on your journey. The rhythm of the property market determines the pace of the economy.

It is time to return to the cycle. It has been going on for a year or two. From the first shoots of recovery we saw at the Start, the property market is now growing strongly. Let us see what unfolds next.

TAKE ADVANTAGE OF THE LAW OF ECONOMIC RENT

Chapter 2 explored the unique nature of land and how it absorbs the gains of economic progress. Understanding this, and ensuring that you are able to take advantage of it, is key to your financial health.

Key lessons

1. Land takes all the gains of progress

Over the course of a cycle these are enormous. Therefore, to build wealth you must have some exposure to rising land values.

2. Buy land where future value is yet to be priced in

This is particularly true when you buy in good locations, early in the cycle.

a. Buy land where infrastructure is being built and where people are moving to. The best time to buy is around two years prior to the infrastructure going in.

b. Those with deeper pockets and longer time horizons can buy land at the edge of growing cities and wait for the city to spread out. This can deliver extremely high rewards over time.[16] The holding period may be a decade or two, and the initial investment is large and is typically made with cash, so this strategy is not for everyone (note that some countries may also impose land holding costs that make this strategy difficult).

3. Avoid buying land where future gains are already priced in

Buying land where future gains are already priced in will limit capital growth. This means that you should avoid buying late in the cycle and in locations where there is a lot of available supply.

4. Always do due diligence before buying

Look carefully at the quality of the location (new infrastructure, amenities, inward investment) and what the typical buyer in that area demands (e.g., family homes with a garden). Projections of future demand often rely on optimistic or unreasonable assumptions. Buying in areas where there is a lot of building taking place might limit capital gains, for example.[17]

CHAPTER 3

THE EXPANSION

There is a tide in the affairs of men,
Which, taken at the flood, leads on to fortune.

William Shakespeare, *Julius Caesar*, Act IV, Scene 3

To the (real) victors, the spoils

THE OPENING CEREMONY of the London Olympics in 2012 was a uniquely British celebration: traditional pageantry, edgy and innovative artistry, a musing on the country's past and a large helping of its famous sense of humour (even the Queen was in on it, appearing to parachute into the Olympic stadium from a helicopter escorted by none other than James Bond). The ceremony inaugurated two weeks of spectacular sport, and Britain's athletes played their part by slugging it out at the top of the medals table with such sporting heavyweights as the United States, China and Russia.

For all their excellence, they were not the real winners of the Games. These were the landowners. The Olympics were hosted in Stratford, east London, formerly the home of such attractions as 'Fridge Mountain' (Europe's largest pile of discarded white goods), 'Waterworks River' (a heavily polluted waterway, full of old tyres) and an open space optimistically called 'the Greenway' (a field of abandoned and burnt-out cars). But the awarding of the Games had put Stratford at the centre of a £9bn regeneration scheme that created an entirely new London district served by new rail and road connections, major retail schemes, new commercial space and the large Olympic Park.

After the Olympics there was a burst of activity in the property market in London, with the greatest growth in the six London boroughs that had seen the most inward Games-related investment. It was also a sign that the next stage of the cycle – the Expansion – was now fully underway. The surge in property prices was also seen in most major cities of the world as the land market responded to the new technology and infrastructure investment initiated at the Start.

The US markets continued upward, assisted by the easy money conditions established by the Federal Reserve. These existed elsewhere and so other markets followed suit, including the German Dax, the Japanese Nikkei and the Indian Sensex. After 2013, all of these broke above highs established at the top of the last cycle.

The mood changes as home prices rise

Slowly, the mood around the world shifted. The denial and fear of the cycle's early years were dissipating, replaced by a certain optimism. The world was changing, and technology led the way. For example, the range of possibilities open to users from applications on their smartphones grew exponentially. One could access the world's entire online knowledge base on these devices; hail a taxi; carry out banking services and invest savings; shop for practically anything; book holidays; and even run a business.

House prices in major cities started increasing quickly. Rising prices induced construction of new housing, and there was a mini boom. As prices went up, there was a renewed concern that not enough housing was being built – just a few years after overbuilding had collapsed the property market. Even Ireland, which at the height of the boom in 2007 had enough housing under construction to meet demand for a full three years, was experiencing a shortage. Not that more housing led to lower prices. Housebuilders drip-feed completed dwelling units into the market so as not to put any pressure on prices. At best, more supply will stop prices rising rapidly, and, even then, the price of housing is at the mercy of rapidly rising land values.

In 2014, the International Monetary Fund's deputy managing director, Min Zhu, warned about the unsustainable growth in housing markets because prices were rising in 60% of countries and had done so for the last couple of years. The IMF launched its *Global Housing Watch* to track what was happening. It appeared that some lessons from the 2008 crisis had been learned, six years too late. It was also a clear sign that some were still looking back to the prior crisis, rather than forward to the new cycle.[1]

Figure 9: US housing construction (percentage of GDP) and US home price index, 2002-2021

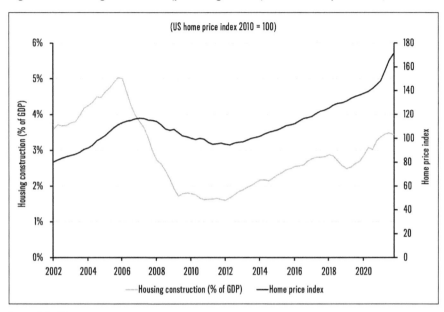

Source: Federal Reserve.

Zhu made his speech in Berlin. Germany had been one of the few countries that did not have a property boom in the 2000s, so it did not suffer much of a bust (though its banks had helped to blow bubbles elsewhere in Europe); and it had not been shy about contrasting its 'responsible' economic management with that of its profligate eurozone and Anglo-Saxon neighbours. Yet with interest rates low, its export-oriented economy had benefited hugely from American and Chinese stimulus and was now in the middle of a property boom. Between 2010 and 2019, house price gains in Germany's largest seven cities outstripped even those in London and Manhattan.[2]

As the Expansion progressed, prices accelerated in most of the largest cities in the world, in both developed and developing countries. Emerging economies were rapidly urbanising, creating huge demand. Capital was flowing around the world and looking to be placed somewhere. Prime housing in Western cities became the bank vaults of the global rich, from Auckland to Vancouver. Often the owners would not even bother renting their housing out, so those prime areas became 'zombie' districts, quiet zones where nothing much seemed to happen. High house prices in central areas pushed resident populations further out, increasing prices where they went.[3] There was a rise in homelessness, the constant companion of expensive housing. The sorry sight of desperate people forced to beg on city streets became ever more common in the advanced countries of the world.

Bank lending returns – with some changes

As construction surged, banks exited bailout schemes and offloaded their loans books, then started lending again. The share prices of housebuilders and banks began to perform strongly. New banks were formed, aided by changes to rules and by the widespread use of mobile technology. In the UK, just £1m capital was required to establish a bank, and by 2013 five new banks had been granted licences. "In any sector, newcomers to the market bring fresh thinking and challenge established firms to consider how they can offer a better deal or improve the service they offer," said Martin Wheatley, head of the UK's Financial Conduct Authority.[4] Quite right. What he did not say was that new banks and finance houses always have the edge over established rivals because they have lower overheads and younger, more energetic managers. Once they discover how to lend efficiently for property, they drive the boom of the second half of the cycle, as we shall see.

Innovation was not just confined to the banking sector. Companies used the internet to create peer-to-peer lending (or P2P) platforms where smaller sums of money could be pooled to invest in businesses and real estate. The most significant change that would take place in this respect was outlined in an innocuous post on 11 February 2009 on the P2P Foundation website, utilising a novel technology called the blockchain to create "a new open source P2P e-cash system called Bitcoin." The author of the post was an anonymous computer programmer going by the name Satoshi Nakamoto. Some people acquired his bitcoins in the hope they might be worth something one day.

In May 2013, Ben Bernanke, chair of the Federal Reserve, remarked that quantitative easing might stop at some point. This spooked markets, especially in emerging economies, as they were busy loading up on dollar-denominated loans at low rates. There was a spike in bond yields. But this was simply history repeating. In February 1994 – at the same point in the last cycle – an unexpected hike in US interest rates had caused a minor market panic. This tightening was reversed a year later; and so it was this time too: asset purchases did not stop until late 2014, and interest rates were only raised incrementally from late 2015 onwards. The UK also started raising rates, while Japan and Europe doubled down on easy policy to ward off the threat of deflation, including instituting negative interest rates on bank deposits.[5]

The American economy recovered first, at least among the world's wealthiest countries, and the US dollar surged. As markets adjusted to this, there were a number of strong moves, including a significant fall in the value of the euro against the dollar: it eventually approached parity. The price of oil crashed in late 2014.[6]

As a consequence of the ongoing low interest rate policies pursued by central banks, the hunt for yield continued and asset prices appreciated quickly – and with markedly lower volatility. The spread between yields on low-grade (or junk) bonds and high-grade (or investment) bonds narrowed significantly.[7] It baffled commentators because prices kept going up despite the many political events that might ordinarily have been expected to rattle markets, such as the rise of the Islamic State in Iraq, the 2014 Russian invasion of Ukraine, a Syrian refugee crisis and much more.

Much of the flow of money was coming from China. The authorities had put in place capital controls, but people found ways to circumvent them. Sometimes this involved straightforward bribery: bank officials were paid to take deposits which were wired overseas across several borders so that the taxman could not track them. Other times it might involve driving truckloads of cash over to casinos in Macau, where notes were blended with others and 'winnings' were taken out in another currency. In the 12 years to 2014, it was estimated that $1.4trn had flowed out and been used to acquire Western property assets and art.[8] Their prices rose dramatically. It was yet another example of China's influence on the global economy. On a larger scale it was an old story: new money flows around the world and ends up in rent-based assets.

Generation Rent

As the Expansion continued, young people struggled to get onto the property ladder because wages did not keep pace with rising house prices.[9] They were forced to buy later and to borrow more money over longer periods, or to buy with a partner. Plans for saving for a deposit, buying property and making the best of mortgage rate rises became common, if rather unromantic, topics to broach on first dates. The UK soon discovered a new, entirely unregulated, lender was now a key part of the mortgage market: Bomad, or, to give it its full name, the Bank of Mum and Dad. Prices had become so high that even small deposits were beyond young people's ability to raise, and their parents helped out by releasing equity in their own homes, guaranteeing mortgages or parking money in a bank account as security for additional borrowing. As most people did not have parents with spare cash, an increasing number were forced to remain renters and came to be known as 'Generation Rent'.[10] Governments tried to address this through lending restrictions, measures to reduce demand by penalising overseas buyers or second-home owners. None of these measures had much success. Prices continued to rise.

As they did so, cities built upwards. It was unusual to see so many supertall buildings appear in the first half of a cycle. But this was testament to high urban land prices and low interest rates.[11] This was not just in the largest cities. The port of Rotterdam in the Netherlands, for example, was dubbed the 'Manhattan on the Maas' for its soaring skyline. The aim was to increase the density of inner-city locations (always a code for higher land prices).

Political winds change

China, too, faced rapidly rising property prices. Land sales and a surge in construction had been key to its recovery from the crisis. Property prices had their lows in 2012 and then began surging in 2013. By 2014 the authorities deemed them problematic enough to institute price controls in the market. Prices fell. So the government introduced a different scheme to build household wealth: declaring it was patriotic to own stocks and encouraging stock market speculation. Thirty million new retail accounts opened in the first five months of 2015, and many were used to trade on margin (a practice that the government now permitted).[12] A bubble quickly formed, which the alarmed authorities then tried to diffuse by restricting margin lending. Over a three-week period in June, this resulted in a ferocious crash as almost $3trn was wiped off the Shanghai and Shenzhen indices, equivalent to the entire GDP of the UK. The leadership had to reverse course: interest rates were reduced so that house prices could rise again.

China's new leader, Xi Jinping, had a very different approach to governance to his predecessors. This was China's moment: no longer would the country follow Deng Xaoping's prescription to bide its time. It would be assertive abroad and deal with the US as an equal. It swiftly started building artificial islands in the South China Sea. His signature policy was 'One Belt One Road', later known as the 'Belt and Road Initiative'. It was to result in ports, rails and roads criss-crossing the Eurasian landmass. The aim was to secure supplies of vital resources for the vast Chinese population and enable the export of Chinese goods to the rest of the world in a way that was not dependent on the protection of the US Navy. We know from Chapter 2 what happens when infrastructure goes in: land values increase rapidly. Commentators dusted off their copies of Sir Halford John Mackinder, a 19th-century British strategist who had noted that whoever controls the world island (Eurasia) controls the world. The US was not going to accept this challenge to its hegemony lightly. President Obama declared that US foreign policy would "pivot to Asia". A clash between the rising and the incumbent power, often a feature of prior cycles, seemed likely. We will return to this in Chapter 11.

At home, President Xi instituted a crackdown on corruption, which was rife at all levels of the Chinese communist system. No doubt a worthy initiative, it had the helpful side effect of removing any potential rivals for power and naysayers to his edicts. In 2018, he would be effectively allowed to remain as leader for life when the National People's Congress abolished the two-term limit on the Chinese presidency. Two (brave) delegates (out of 2,964) voted against the motion. The lifetime rule and lack of dissent in the world's second largest economy will become significant as the Summit of the cycle approaches.

Economic and political turbulence are present in each cycle and serve to distract people from the underlying forces (the law of economic rent) at play. This Expansion phase served up plenty of such instability. As the benefits of growth were unevenly distributed – a consequence of new banking regulations and austerity measures that many governments had imposed in the aftermath of the crisis – this greatly increased political turmoil in Europe and the United States.

Europe remained caught in its own economic trap. Greece elected a government that promised to break loose from austerity imposed upon it by its eurozone creditors. But despite its popular mandate, the EU institutions forced the government into submission, threatening an ejection from the euro. That was the least of Europe's worries. Britain had a similar referendum, but this time it was an in/out decision on EU membership. On 24 June 2016, the British people ordered its government to leave the EU. It was a seismic moment in international relations, on par with the Suez Crisis some 60 years before. Britain became the first country to quit the bloc since its founding in 1957. The precise terms of the exit would absorb the energy and attention of the political class for at least the next five years. Many millions of words have been written about why it happened. Though such things have many causes, it was at least in part a protest vote against the complacency of politicians presiding over a system that delivers crushing periodic crises and rising inequality.

Similar forces influenced politics in the United States and delivered an even bigger shock: the election of Donald Trump in November 2016. His campaign was controversial, but effective. He was voted in on a promise to 'drain the swamp', meaning to get rid of the vested interests that profit from boom-and-bust economy and the excesses that they perpetrate. History has given us few greater examples of irony than a real estate mogul, who had grown rich exploiting the cycle, claiming to act on behalf of the people it had so badly damaged. Even more ironically, he was backed by banking interests to whom he had promised the unwinding of regulations that fettered their lending (for real estate). Once in office, Trump seemed most interested in undoing much of his predecessor's work reforming banking and environmental regulations. He even made a couple of attempts to do so with healthcare. He claimed to want to 'Make America Great Again', which (in his eyes) meant undermining international alliances and beginning a trade war with China.

Markets continue rising

Needless to say, markets again taught investors that they ignore ideology and climb walls of worry. George Soros, the man who had made a billion dollars betting against sterling during the real estate-led downturn of 1992, lost a billion shorting the US markets after Trump's election victory in 2016. The lesson is clear: understand where we are in the cycle and learn how to read what a price chart is telling you. Trump had promised his Republican Party colleagues tax cuts, and markets rose on the prospect of higher profits. Pass-through companies, such as those Trump himself owned, also benefited handsomely. The Nasdaq was in the lead: 17 years after its prior high in 2000 (before the dot-com bubble burst), it broke above it and surged some more. Apple led the charge, as it had done since the Start of the cycle. On 2 August 2018, it became the first American company to be valued at over $1trn. It then took less than two years to add the next trillion.

Property prices in all major cities continued to rise, especially in areas with large tech sectors, such as Silicon Valley. Soon, even billionaires such as Peter Thiel were complaining about how high real estate prices had become. The capital he was investing in start-ups was effectively going, via the inflated housing costs faced by their employees, straight into the pockets of landlords. This was evidence, at the very frontier of our technological world, of the law of economic rent in action. It simply cannot be avoided.[13]

Trump had replaced the head of the Federal Reserve, Janet Yellen, with a man made in his own image: experienced in business and – apparently crucially for him – tall. (When it came to considering Yellen for a second term in office, Trump felt that, despite her impeccable credentials, she was too short to be a central banker.[14]) Jerome Powell began to raise rates. Rising rates meant that the yield curve went flat. Hardly anyone was watching. For all the chaos of the Trump years, the US economy continued the Expansion that had started under President Obama. In fact, by 2018 the mood was euphoric. There were signs of lavish investor behaviour, indicating that this stage of the cycle was drawing to a close.

The Expansion analysed

The Expansion stage starts approximately two years into the new cycle and lasts until around year six. The signs of economic recovery and growth are now apparent to all.

1. Construction expands

The Expansion increases the demand for new space. The rising rents seen during the Start now translate into higher prices of existing buildings in the main centres of population, wherever people are moving to and new businesses (especially technology companies) are forming. Higher prices induce new construction. In turn, this boosts demand for land and increases economic activity. The construction industry is home-grown, a large buyer of capital goods and raw materials that employs many people. Suddenly, two to three years into the cycle, scaffolding and cranes, and the clanging sounds of building construction, are commonplace.

Housebuilding leads the way, but as the economy is growing again there is increasing demand for commercial property too. This stimulates the building of new offices, retail, logistics hubs and other premises needed to serve the economy in this new age.

2. New areas become trendy

As the property market recovers, new parts of old cities suddenly become hotspots. After 2012, it was areas such as east London. New cities within countries also become attractive, such as Manchester or Austin, Texas. Many people want to move into the new buildings being created. New technology and industries will increase the demand for space, and that is where the new property market goes. Suddenly, site owners in previously derelict areas reap windfall gains. Property investors that get in early do so too.

This is how the cycle begins and spreads out to new sites, leading to increased building and growth.

3. Government investment leads the way

Stimulus packages initiated at the Start typically involve infrastructure investments. By the Expansion these are being made or have been completed. We know from Chapter 2 what the result will be. If well-targeted, they will increase the efficiency of the economy by (for example) reducing travel times and making new locations desirable. They will also increase land prices for the benefit of landowners.

4. Bank lending increases

By now, the economy is back on its feet and there is a new confidence. The steep yield curve of the Start has helped banks to recapitalise. Property portfolios can be sold, freeing up capital. Banks reduce costs, closing branches and laying off staff. As property prices rise, banks come back to the market and bank credit supports new business growth. Within the limits of new bank regulations, available credit supports property purchasing; increased demand pushes prices up further; as the economy grows and wages rise, prices increase.

First-time buyers worry that they are getting further away from the property ladder and do what they can to find a place. This burst of interest further pushes prices up. There is a lot of talk about a housing shortage and the need to build more. Generational equity issues come to the fore.

Regulations imposed at the end of the last cycle to prevent the next crisis are increasingly seen as a barrier to bank expansion. It may take some time to unwind them because the memory of the prior crisis is still strong, but this is now an issue being discussed openly. A few years in, towards the end of the Expansion, politicians running for office can cosy up to banking interests by promising that these restrictions will be reduced or lifted.

5. Vacant land begins to be absorbed

There is strong growth, particularly at the centre of cities or in the main cities that have been the focal point of the expansion (those where jobs are being created, especially in relation to the new industries powering this expansion). Prices here are now too high. As the prime areas get built out, construction firms move on to new ones. Often they follow infrastructure investment and business and household relocations, so the property boom begins to move outwards from the centre. Even though more housing is built, it never comes on to the market at lower prices than before.

6. The yield curve flattens

The cycle moves forward, and after a few years the yield curve flattens. This is because the economy is growing robustly and there is an expectation that short-term interest will rise to moderate any inflationary pressures that might be starting to build (though central bankers will hold them as low as they can for as long as they can, and often for too long).[15]

7. The stock market

The stock market, by now well off its lows, will typically rise for at least four years, if not longer. Bank stocks take longer to recover than other sectors because they are unwinding the bad loans from the prior cycle, and a condition of government support in the last crisis may be that dividends are cut or stopped for a time. The revival of property prices enables banks to address the problems in their loan books and, once completed, bank stocks start to trend upwards. While technology stocks continue to lead the way, as the Expansion takes hold there will be strong growth in housebuilding and consumer stocks.

If the first moves off the lows are longer than four years and the stock market breaks above the prior cycle highs quickly, the bull market will last the entire first half of the cycle, as it did in the 1950s to mid-1960s, 1990s (and 2010s).[16]

8. Strong dollar

The US dollar is typically strong relative to other currencies during the first half of the cycle, a consequence of the fact that the US leads the world (so far) into and out of every real estate cycle. It goes first through the Expansion, boosting demand for the dollar. Flows of investment capital to the centre of cities are mimicked on a global level: to the economic centre of the world, leading to an appreciation of the dollar relative to most other currencies.[17] A strong dollar can also put pressure on commodity prices (which are priced in dollars).

———————— - ▪ ▪ ▪ - · ————————

The cycle is now ticking along. The land market is driving the tempo and direction of economic growth. You may well be wondering by now whether land will continue to play such a central role in the cycles of the future, given how technologically advanced our societies are becoming. Might this not diminish the importance of location and physical space? If so, how does the law of economic rent play out in this technologically advanced world? Is it still as foundational as claimed in the previous chapter?

These are valid questions. So, while the Expansion continues in the background, let us turn aside from our journey to consider them in the next chapter.

EXPAND YOUR PORTFOLIO

Stage: the Expansion

Approximate timing: years 2 to 6

Prevailing emotion: optimism

Managing Emotions

While there may not be the outright fear and denial of the Start, even as the economy turns around many may still be looking backwards to the past crisis. However, there is some optimism at the economic expansion and rising asset prices, even if there is a lingering hangover from the prior crisis (such as high, though falling, joblessness), especially in the early part of the Expansion. The importance of this stage to your overall financial wealth is high. If one can excuse any caution at the Start given the relentless negative news, one cannot do so now. This is the time to be optimistic and act. Expand the range of your investments.

Managing investments

1. Buy a broader basket of stocks

a. While technology stocks continue to lead the way, the share prices of companies across a broader range of sectors break out and appreciate. Buy those that are trending up. As the Expansion moves forward, stock markets will experience normal corrections, sometimes in response to external events such as political crises or the withdrawal of stimulus packages and rising interest rates. During this period, if markets are turbulent (as they were during the late 1970s, for example) remember the bigger picture: rare is the cycle where markets do not eventually reach higher highs than the previous one.[18]

b. As the bull market expands, there will be a rotation of money into different sectors, such as consumer staples, materials and energy stocks; and then into cyclical sectors, such as housebuilding and other real estate stocks. These can be bought as they move up.

c. Banks tend to lag as they offload bad loans and, if under public ownership, will be prevented from paying dividends. In addition, they will have to adjust to stricter capital requirements which tend to reduce earnings. A few years in, they will start recovering and trending up – at this point they can be bought.

d. If you are invested in a US tracker fund, continue to hold this; but you can branch out into other markets as they follow the US into the Expansion stage.

2. Build your property portfolio

a. As the property market returns to growth and lending recovers, now is a good time to borrow money, taking advantage of still-low interest rates, and to continue to build your property portfolio.

b. Buy in new property hotspots.

c. If you want to build, you can find good development opportunities, especially in newer locations where land is cheap and buyers returning to the market show increasing interest.

d. As the economy expands, you can invest in commercial real estate in growing sectors.

3. Buy commodities

As the recovery takes hold, focus in particular on industrial commodities, especially those related to technology or construction (e.g., iron and copper). Note that the appreciating dollar will act as a headwind for commodities, which are usually priced in dollars (see below).

4. Buy US dollars

The dollar tends to appreciate against other currencies during the first half of the cycle, so parking spare cash in dollars will at least ensure that such funds will appreciate relative to cash held in another currency.

5. Consider buying alternative assets

a. Devote a small portion of your portfolio to any asset that looks like it may enter into a bubble as investment excitement builds. This is usually an asset that has an exciting story attached to it and draws in newer investors, particularly one that represents a new paradigm in the way things are done. Often it will involve new technology (in the 1990s it was dot-com stocks; in the 2010s it was Bitcoin). It is worth participating in this with a small portion of your wealth, but this should not be a long-term, buy-and-hold strategy. Plan to sell it by the end of this stage or at the beginning of the next one.[19]

b. In recent years, there has been a broader interest in investing in 'alternative assets' such as fine art or wine. These are likely to appreciate during the Expansion phase and could be considered worthwhile, though it is important to understand fully what is involved (some investments may incur significant storage or insurance costs and may be difficult to sell easily).

6. Businesses should continue to expand

As the economy is growing, there will be opportunities for businesses to expand. Bank credit, usually with a favourable rate of interest, will be readily available to facilitate this. Now is a good time to do so.

CHAPTER 4

THE EFFORTLESS RETURN AND THE NEW ECONOMY

We are in the midst of enclosing the world, this time not in law, but in digits.

Katharina Pistor, *The Code of Capital*

WHEN THE SINGER Courtney Love arrived at Paris's Charles de Gaulle airport in June 2015, she did what anyone would do to get into town quickly: she hailed a cab. Though a renowned artist and the former wife of Nirvana frontman Kurt Cobain, her short journey should not have made the news. But it did.

Unbeknown to her when she got into the taxi, she was being ferried straight into the middle of a public protest that was about to get ugly. We know about this because Ms Love gave the world a running commentary on Twitter as events unfolded. Allowing for some artistic creativity as to the real level of danger she was in and who was responsible for sorting the mess out, it was clearly a harrowing episode:

> they've ambushed our car and are holding our driver hostage. they're beating the cars with metal bats. this is France?? I'm safer in Baghdad

> François Hollande where are the fucking police??? is it legal for your people to attack visitors? Get your ass to the airport. Wtf???

Eventually, Love was rescued by a couple of motorcyclists. Her driver was not so lucky: his car was smashed up with a metal bat and overturned, and he was taken hostage. He, rather than Love, had been the real target.[1]

Why was this? Because he responded to Love's request on the ridesharing app, Uber. Those protesting were drivers of the city's licensed taxis who were raging at what they perceived to be the unfairness of having low-cost competition Uber drivers did not have to obtain a taxi licence, which at the time cost 250,000 euros, and so they could charge customers lower fares.

In Chapter 2, we saw how land is key to understanding the cycle because of the law of economic rent. While physical land is by far and away the most important source of rent in our economies, it is not the only one. Rent is also generated by exploiting the gifts of nature, such as natural resources, or having privileged access to infrastructure, including the internet. Legal constructs, such as licences which grant monopoly powers to favoured entities, are also an important source. This was the fundamental source of Uber's controversy: it undermined the rent of existing licence holders. As the wrath of the cabbies illustrated, the holders were not happy about it.

To see this more clearly, let us take a look at the licensing system in New York City.

Licences and medallions

During the high unemployment of the Great Depression, many thousands of men turned to driving cabs around New York City to earn an income. But the market became so saturated with drivers that the industry quickly became unprofitable. There were over 30,000 cabs on the road, more than the number of passengers. Desperate drivers would work ever longer hours to make a living. The integrity of their vehicles and their health suffered because they could not afford to be away from the streets for long.

The city government introduced a licensing system to limit the number of cabs. Only 16,900 licences – or medallions – were issued, cutting the number of taxis by almost half. It immediately addressed the oversupply of taxi drivers; but soon, it created a much more significant problem: a cartel of medallion owners.

Medallions could be bought and sold, transferring ownership of the right to drive a cab. Over time, the demand for taxi services increased as the city grew, but the number of licences remained the same, and profits were much higher than you would expect to see in a properly competitive market. As a result, the price of those medallions increased sharply (see Figure 10).

Medallions were issued at a cost of $10 in 1937. Within a decade the price had risen 25 times to $2,500 and, by 2013, was $1.3m.

Figure 10: Number and price of New York taxi medallions, 1940-2010

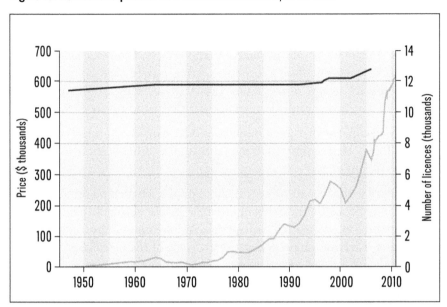

Source: luiscabral.net. Number of NYC taxis (horizontal line, right scale) and corporate medallion prices (rising line, left scale).

There is a similarity here with the real estate market. What Don Riley found with his property on the south bank of the Thames,[2] New York taxi licence holders found with their medallions: the growth of the city and investment in new housing and offices, transport links and other improvements drew in businesses and people – and increased the value of their assets enormously. This did not reflect additional risk-taking or effort on their part, merely ownership of a scarce asset that secured such rewards: it was a case of having rather than doing. [3]

It is unsurprising that those who owned the medallions did everything they could to prevent any more being issued, including lobbying politicians and contributing to their election campaigns. So successful were their efforts, that no new licences were granted until 1996, almost 60 years later.

Unlike the pitches used by *The Big Issue* sellers, you can see the stark contrast between locational value and wages. Many medallions came to be owned by people who did not even drive cabs, but who used them in other ways to become rich and lead plum lives. The Murstein family was one such example. Grandfather Murstein was the owner of a 1930s medallion and he bought several hundred more. His son then established a lending company to provide loans to cab drivers wanting to purchase medallions at inflating prices. By the time his grandson, Andrew, joined the family business, they had diversified into other business lines such as real estate, consumer loans and even car-racing team ownership and were fabulously wealthy.[4]

By contrast, wages earned by taxi drivers did not improve. The owner of the licence simply rented it out to someone who then had to work long shifts to ensure they made enough of a surplus to earn a decent wage. All the risk was with the driver, not the owner. As we saw in prior chapters, workers get low wages while the owner of the scarce asset gets all the additional value.

The high cost meant that most medallions were owned by a small number of people. This is because they used the rents from existing licences to purchase more medallions.

This changed with Uber and other ridesharing apps, which brought 50,000 new drivers on to the roads. These were unlicensed drivers who could be summoned via an app on a 4G-connected smartphone; and their lower fares reflected their lower costs. This innovation decimated the value of the medallions, and as of late 2021 their price had collapsed over 90% to around $100,000.[5]

One of the owners most affected was Gene Freidman, otherwise known in New York as 'the Taxi King'. Freidman owned somewhere between 800 and 1,100 medallions. He had borrowed against those to build a business empire that included a chain store selling high-end pyjamas and to buy a string of property assets, such as a 4,000-foot town house off Park Avenue in Manhattan, an estate in Bridgehampton, New York and a villa on the French Riviera. He was forced to surrender a number of licences to creditors to settle his debts as the value of his medallions collapsed.

Freidman got his drivers to protest. He himself used the courts to prevent reforms to the industry. A meeting with then-Mayor Michael Bloomberg resulted in a heated exchange that so irked the latter that he shouted, "I'm going to kill your fucking industry!" Freidman donated a large sum of money to the next mayor's election campaign. It is when the economic rent is threatened that you get to see the connection between money and power. We will come back to this point in the next chapter.[6]

It is easy to see why existing licence holders felt threatened by the new technology that brought more drivers onto the roads. This was why the protest in Paris was violent and why Courtney Love's driver was kidnapped.

Taxis are one form of licensing but there are many others: from gambling, fishing and forestry, to those relating to technology, such as intellectual property rights. Possibly the most important one in an economy is the banking licence, which grants to the holder the power to create the money supply. The crucial consequence of a licensing system is that it generates scarcity, which drives up prices. In most cases the law protects and privileges the holder's right to capture the flow of income, trade it, and monetise its value through borrowing.[7]

An inventory of rent

There are many other sources of economic rent. Natural monopolies such as airports or utilities generate rents. The gifts of nature, such as energy (oil, natural gas, uranium) or water resources are another. The importance of natural resources will be covered in Chapter 11. An inventory of the main sources of rent in the economy is set out in the table below.

Table 4: An inventory of the major rent-generating assets in the economy

Category	Examples of rent assets
Land	Residential, commercial, rural or other land
Natural resources	Energy – e.g., hydrocarbons (oil and gas), uranium, renewable resources
	Subsoil minerals – on and off earth
Natural monopolies	Water rights
	Taxi licences
	Airports
	Utilities
	Fishing and forestry licences
	Gambling licences
	Electromagnetic spectrum
	Satellite orbit rights
	Internet infrastructure
Licences and other sources	Domain name registrations
	Banking licences
	Corporate commons
	Patents
	Parking fees
	Public transport
	Alcohol or liquor licences (or other prohibited goods and services)
	Vehicle registrations
	Pollution rights
	Advertising
	Mooring rights
	Rights of way
Digital economy	Digital money and non-fungible tokens
	Digital platforms

The final row in the table above includes something that has become an increasingly important part of the modern economy: the digital platform.

Colonising virtual space: the digital platform

Platform rents in the internet age have become so important that some economic commentators now refer to a new variant of capitalism called 'platform capitalism'. Platforms are valuable digital locations established by companies such as Amazon, Google, Meta, Airbnb and Uber, where buyers and sellers come together to exchange goods and services.[8] They are commonly thought of as 'making the market place' in which e-commerce takes place.

An analogy might better describe what these platforms do: they are like the first colonial settlements of the vast new digital continent of the internet. Like the virgin savannah of some new world territory, in its early days the space of the internet abounded with possibility but was not particularly valuable. But, as with physical land, its value increased enormously through building high-speed broadband connections; licensing the electromagnetic spectrum; launching satellites; putting down the cables, pipes and other infrastructure of the digital network; establishing global standards; and providing access through highly sophisticated computers, tablets and smartphones belonging to billions of netizens (internet citizens). This collective endeavour made digital 'land' extremely valuable. These platform companies, then, were the first to enclose this digital space into quasi-colonies, and in doing so have become the rulers and rent collectors of the internet. They exercise vast control over people and companies operating in their territory.

While newer companies are free to create their own rival platforms, the original ones, by virtue of being the first, have significant advantages. These arise from:

- network effects (the more people using the service the greater its value, meaning that a competitor can only really be a viable alternative when it reaches the same scale)

- the need for rivals to incur very high upfront costs in order to achieve similar economies of scale and be genuinely competitive

- economies of scope (the ability to take an advantage in one area, for example, selling books and transferring it to another, such as selling household items).[9]

Incumbents also benefit from the advantages of digital proximity and default. Typical internet users lack the time or patience to spend hours searching for an alternative provider so use the services of those who are 'nearest' or most familiar; this is similar to the convenience of proximity in the physical world.[10] Their monopoly advantage is consolidated by acquisition of newer, more innovative rivals before they grow large enough to challenge them (and the new platforms' technologies can be absorbed or quietly discarded).[11] The huge revenues and cash balances such companies record in their accounts is evidence of their ability to extract value from their digital colonies.

The word 'platform' is neutral, but a platform company is not an impartial player within the digital economy. As anyone who has tried to sell through Amazon or advertise through Meta knows, platforms have a huge controlling influence on whose products get sold to whom and on what terms (particularly if they are a competitor to a product offered by the platform).

They are also able to exploit their dominance in the digital world in relation to employees or suppliers, by not even acknowledging employer obligations in some cases (Uber), or threatening the outsourcing of jobs, often overseas, to ensure that wages remain low even as profits skyrocket. This is the same as with the taxi licensing system, and is a consequence of the law of economic rent.

Another critical feature that generates economic rents is the ability of these companies to conduct surveillance and aggregate vast data sets on user behaviour for commercial exploitation. The value of the data is generated by the public, but is privately captured by the platform.[12] Some might argue that these platform services are typically provided for free, so surveillance is a *quid pro quo* ("If you're not paying for the product, you are the product," as the saying goes). However, in the physical world, no one generally has to pay to enter a building where they expect to do business and it is normally the business owner that understands the customers best, not the landlord. These companies exact a level of control over private transactions that former colonial powers could scarcely have dreamt of.

In the 19th century the celebrated industrialists Vanderbilt, Rockefeller, Morgan, Mellon and Carnegie successfully built industrial empires based upon private capture of rent. When the history of the 21st century comes to be written, the same tale will be told with new characters: Bezos, Branson, Gates, Mittal, Musk Slim, Zuckerberg.

———— · ▪ ◼ ▪· ————

As our economic life migrates into the metaverse making the outright ownership of digital spaces possible; as the blockchain secures property rights through unimpeachable records; as non-fungible tokens (NFTs) permit the trading of fractions of a greater variety of assets such as artwork, alternative currencies and even, through natural asset companies, Mother Nature herself; how vast will the economic rents of the future be? How many ways will we invent to speculate in them? Unless addressed, the cycles of the 21st century will be of a scale that we can barely believe, taking place simultaneously in the digital universe, on physical earth and perhaps even in the settlements and operations of outer space.

Are we doomed to live this endless cycle of boom and bust? This is a critical question indeed. Now that you have seen its causes, you may well ask why no one else sees the cycle. There is a puzzling blindness among our most learned experts. If they cannot see the cycle, how can it possibly be solved? And if unresolved what might the consequences be?

The answers to these important questions are the subject of the next chapter.

BUY COMPANIES WITH DIGITAL, NATURAL OR LEGAL MOATS

Key lessons

This chapter has expanded our treatment of the law of economic rent. The lesson from this section of the *The Handbook of Wealth Secrets* is that this law can be applied to a broader range of investable assets.

Legendary investor Warren Buffett looks for companies that have 'moats' which, because of their product or standing within their industry, insulate them from competition. This protects their earnings and gives them financing to expand. The best type of moat is owning or holding exclusive locations and licences, because moats of these types are defended by the government and are much harder to bridge.

1. The value of digital rents reflects control of cyberspace

There has been much discussion about how expensive the share prices of technology companies are – typically at high multiples of current earnings. Some of this concern is valid but needs to be set in context. The value of their assets derives from economic rent, which does not necessarily materialise as a flow of income but as a capital gain.

This is, again, similar to economic rent in the physical world. Think about owning an empty plot of land in the middle of a growing city, as Riley saw with his neighbour near London Bridge. It will not generate any rental payments, but the value increases substantially as the economy around it develops. If this appreciation is even declared, it accrues on the company's balance sheet rather than being reflected in its profit and loss statement. A similar process applies to rent in the digital world. Investors are paying for their effective control and privatisation of digital space. Think of them as settlers in frontier territory appropriating vast lands that will accrue in value immeasurably as the population moves out to settle.

2. Invest in digital, natural or legal moats

As the rent can be generated by digital, natural or legal means, you should invest in companies that:

a. own or control digital space, which will assume an even greater importance in the coming decades

b. benefit from natural resources, including minerals extracted from the earth and asteroids, and have exclusive access rights to space (e.g., orbital pathways)

c. possess licences to deliver services in areas where economic activities are growing.

It is quite likely that merely owning a portfolio that tracks the stock market index will give you exposure to such companies anyway because the largest companies (by market capitalisation) on stock exchanges are now essentially rentier companies.[13]

CHAPTER 5

THE CORRUPTION
OF ECONOMICS

It is the world that has been pulled over your eyes to blind you from the truth.

Morpheus, *The Matrix*

A S HE WALKED into the famous triangular Flatiron Building on Manhattan's Fifth Avenue on the morning of 19 March 1935, Charles Darrow had a spring in his step. Parker Brothers, the famous games manufacturer, wanted to sign a deal. They were offering a fee of $7,000 and a share of future profits in return for the right to market and sell his real estate game.

Darrow did not need much time to consider the offer; it was simply too good to turn down. Work had been difficult to come by in the Great Depression after losing his job as a radiator repairman. Nothing he had tried to make ends meet had worked out, not even dog walking. To his shame, he had barely been able to provide for his family, relying on his wife's needlework for a small income. Those desperate days would now be over.

He could not have anticipated what came next. He had always suspected his game would be commercially successful but not the bestseller it suddenly became. Within a few years he had earned millions in royalties and the world had been introduced to the game of *Monopoly*.

Parker Brothers was keen to protect its investment and applied for a patent. Darrow was asked to explain how he had come up with the idea for the game. It had come to him, he told the company, after some friends described a university course where the professor had given students fictional money to create investments. Later he would tell a local newspaper that the invention was a "freak of inspiration and entirely unexpected." His unemployment meant he had time to try his hand at refining the board game. Parker Brothers used this rags-to-riches tale in its marketing campaigns because it fitted well with the game's concept. Every player would begin a game of *Monopoly* with a small endowment of cash and one player would end up extremely wealthy indeed.

But Darrow's story was a fabrication. It was not his invention at all. In fact, the game had a far more interesting backstory. And while created as an amusing pastime, it also had an educational purpose.[1]

We are probably all familiar with *Monopoly*. It is one of the world's most enduring and popular games. But why we play it and the lessons we take from it are dramatically opposite to the purpose of its creation. As this chapter will demonstrate, the reason why its key lesson is no longer known is, in fact, the reason why no one ever sees the boom-bust cycle. Moreover, the failure to learn its essential teaching has had tragic consequences ever since.

Monopoly's real inventor: a social activist

Darrow had himself been introduced to the game by his neighbours, the Todds, a few years before. As Mr Todd explained, players were to start with the same amount of cash and they were to move their pieces around in a clockwise direction. Darrow was immediately intrigued by this innovation, because at the time a circular board was unusual. When they landed on a space, named after a local street, they could purchase a title deed to it, drawn out on a playing card, if they had the cash and if it had not already been bought by someone else. Each time players completed a circuit of the board – representing a period in one's life – they earned an additional amount of cash, which were their wages for that round. If another player landed on a site already owned, they had to pay a rent for the right to occupy that space for a turn. Paying rent was unavoidable, because you had to land somewhere. The periodic infusion of wages was designed to cover this rent as well as other living expenses and taxes which a player would incur to varying degrees each round. With any money left over, players had a decision to make: hold it as cash or invest it either in buying utilities or acquiring land.

The best strategy, said Todd, was to acquire as much land as you could as quickly as you could. The game really got going when all the land was owned. If you owned sites adjacent to one another, marked with the same colour, you created a land monopoly situation. You could build houses on the site and charge much higher rents to any guests that happened to visit. Suddenly the game flipped. Before all the land was privately owned, players were cash-rich; when all the land was owned, while most were asset-rich they were cash-poor. Then the race was on to see which land monopolist would end up bankrupting the other players by charging them enough rent to relieve them of their cash and forcing them to sell their properties.

It was a complicated game, but one which Darrow immediately saw mimicked real life. There was some judgement involved in terms of what to buy and how much to build. As the game progressed it reinforced the old business adage that 'cash is king'. But it was also a game of chance. The first player to build a land monopoly would control the game and this was down to luck (perhaps, again, not unlike the real world).[2]

Darrow asked about the game's inventor, but Todd did not know: he too had obtained his copy earlier that year from his friends. In fact, at the time, the game was being played all over the northeastern United States. With some local variations to place names and certain rules, all players had hand-made copies of an original – one that had already been patented by a most interesting and remarkable woman, Elizabeth Magie.

Magie was brilliant, creative, highly educated; a suffragette, a poet, an essayist, an actress and an inventor. In 1893, at the age of 26, she filed an application for a device that would feed paper through a typewriter more efficiently – at a time when less than 1% of all patents were owned by women.

She had observed the growing middle-class fashion for playing board games after dinner as houses acquired electricity and so could support family entertainment after sundown. As an activist for social and economic justice, she alighted upon the idea of creating a game that might simultaneously amuse and educate people. This was why she had invented her real estate game, which she called *The Landlord's Game*. It was the first ever board game to be patented, in 1904, and while she attempted to sell it to a company to manufacture, to popularise it she allowed copies to be made. By the time Darrow passed the game off as his own, it had had over 30 years of testing and refinement. Darrow reaped the benefit of this to the tune of millions of dollars in royalties. Magie, on the other hand, while not destitute in her later years, was not wealthy – nor did she see her vision realised. Though *Monopoly's* subsequent success showed clearly that she had developed a brilliantly entertaining game, her real purpose for doing so was to bring to life the ideas of a prominent 19th-century economist and social thinker by the name of Henry George.

The most famous economist who ever lived

Henry George grew up in a religious household in Philadelphia in the 1840s and left school at the age of 14. He had no university education or formal training in economics, but he became the most famous economist who ever lived.[3]

As a young man, George had drifted. He had wanderlust, working on a ship that voyaged to India and Australia. He then ventured west to California to seek gold and fortune. His early life was one of hard graft, interspersed with periods of unemployment. Like Darrow, he also knew the desperation of struggling to support a family.

Eventually, George committed to a career as a writer, having had some early experience in journalism. Throughout his youth he had been a voracious reader, and economics was his special focus. He grew up in the Gilded Age, a time when the pace of economic and social change was fierce, bringing with it enormous inequality and upheaval. It was natural that his inquisitive and restless mind would try to solve the puzzle of the times: why amazing economic progress seemed always to be accompanied by backbreaking poverty for large swathes of the population, and why such progress turned so often into economic depressions.

He puzzled over these questions for many years from the rapidly expanding city of San Francisco. It was not until a trip to New York in 1869, at the exact midpoint of his life, that in a flash of inspiration the pieces fell into place.

George later wrote about the moment it happened:

> Once, in daylight, and in a city street, there came to me a thought, a vision, a call, give it what name you please. But every nerve quivered…
>
> … and I saw and recognised for the first time the shocking contrast between monstrous wealth and debasing want.

So he made himself a promise:

> And I made a vow from which I have never faltered, to seek out, and remedy, if I could, the cause that condemned little children to lead such a life as you know them to lead in the squalid districts.

He was to be fired up by this solemn undertaking for the remainder of his life. In the late 1860s, the United States was booming due to the construction of the railroads. The first transcontinental railroad was completed in May 1869, but George had already seen one of its effects. One day, as he was riding outside San Francisco he enquired about a piece of farmland and was told that it could be purchased for $1,000, at a time when the average price was around $5 per acre. Land speculators had preceded the railroad into the state and were reaping massive windfall gains as each passing mile of track was laid. At this moment, the mystery resolved itself:

> Like a flash it came upon me that there was the reason of advancing poverty with advancing wealth. With the growth of population, land grows in value and the men who work it must pay more for the privilege…
>
> Crystallised, as by lightning flash, my brooding thoughts into coherency… I there and then recognized – the natural order – one of those experiences which make those that have not had them feel that they can vaguely appreciate what mystics and poets have called the "ecstatic vision".

His 'ecstatic vision' was realising how Ricardo's law of economic rent was playing out in the development of the United States, and that the application of this law was the reason for poverty amid progress and for the periodic paroxysms that racked and wrecked the industrial economy. The insights from Chapter 2 have their origin in George's thinking. George's flash of inspiration came at an opportune moment. The railroad had been completed at the Summit of the real estate cycle. Soon after, the United States would enter an economic collapse during which half of the railroad companies went out of business, 54,000 businesses failed and 5,000 banks collapsed. It became known as the Long Depression and lasted most of the 1870s.

It was this very process that Magie's game was designed to show. As each player passes the board space marked 'Go', they obtain a wage with which they pay their rent. As the game progresses and players build houses on their sites – that is, as this economy develops – rents increase dramatically, far more so than wages. The only option a player has is to become a rentier and land speculator, even if only to survive in the game a bit longer. Over time all spare cash gets sucked into the property market. The differences between the players emerge quickly thereafter: the largest landowners, having been the lucky ones to get the best sites first, become disproportionately wealthy – to the detriment of the other players. No player is safe. One round, a player might be flush with cash and the next, after landing on a well-developed site owned by another, he or she is penniless. The economy, as George showed, is inherently unstable.

If there were any doubt about the importance of land in this process, Magie dispelled it in the instructions provided with her game:

> *The Landlord's Game* is based on present prevailing business methods… that the land monopolist has absolute control of the situation.

To emphasise the point she said:

> If a person wishes to prove this assertion – having first proven that the principles of the game are based on realities – let him do so by giving

to one player all of the land and giving to the other players all other advantages of the game. Provide each player with $100 at the start and let the game proceed under rules with the exception that the landlord gets no wages [i.e., is not entitled to $100 as he or she passes 'Go']. By the simple method one can satisfy himself with the truth of the assertion that the land monopolist is monarch of the world.

George's Remedy

But George had vowed to find the 'remedy' to these problems. He had a genius for synthesis: rather than addressing the problem of inequality and cyclical boom and bust separately, he found one solution to both. Since the problem was land speculation, based upon the private capture of publicly generated value, George's remedy was that this value should be returned back to the public via a service charge or a land tax. This would remove the incentive to speculate in land because no one could benefit from the unearned income from the rising value of land.[4] Such value was created by the public and should be returned to it. And this would be the fund to provide for investment in infrastructure and public services that make our economies highly productive. On the other hand, George said that people's incomes and business profits should be free of any distortionary tax because this represented privately generated value. To tax it amounted to confiscation.

In other words, he wanted to correct the system where public value was siphoned off by a few private individuals – because land ownership was, and is, highly concentrated; and where a portion of private value – generated by all members of the vast economic system – was seized by the taxman. This would solve the problem of poverty because businesses and households would be able to capture their due share of a growing pie. Classical economists, such as Adam Smith, understood the benefits of this approach very well, but none had articulated it with the clarity and vigour that George did, nor in a way that could be understood by the common man, everywhere.

George's remedy was the key lesson of Magie's game and was the ultimate reason for its creation. The game had two sets of rules: the first, the ones described above, showed up the inequality and instability in the system. The second kept everything the same except for one thing. Instead of players paying the full rent to the site owner when they landed on a space, they had to pay a ground rent into the public purse and a house rent to the owner reflecting any housing that had been built on the site.[5] At first the house rent would be greater than the ground rent, but as the game developed the ground rent increased.

Under the second set of rules, the public treasury's takings were to be used on improvements, including building public utilities, then providing free education, and increasing the wages players earn as they passed "GO". As players had no other taxes to pay, over time they would build a surplus which they could use to develop lots and earn house rents. The result: every player ended up sharing in the wealth that was generated as the game progressed. Crucially, no one player could use a land monopoly to bankrupt the others, however long the game was played. This was George's remedy in action: greater fairness, no unearned profits for the land monopolists, and no inherent instability in the system, demonstrated through an amusing after-dinner board game.

George had fulfilled his vow. He had found the cause and the remedy. That the latter should be enacted was for him self-evident: a matter of universal moral law which said that all should be granted an equal chance to thrive in life, including equal access to the common wealth.

When he published his findings in his 1879 book, *Progress and Poverty*, George electrified the world.[6] While he had been forced to self-publish with an initial run of 500 copies, the book was soon taken on by a publisher. The big break came when it was released in the United Kingdom and instantaneously became an economics bestseller. It was not a tome confined to the musty halls of the academy. It spoke directly to the concerns of the masses. Every major economist in Britain felt compelled to respond to George's ideas, even if they disliked engaging with a non-academic. They tried to patronise him. The remedy launched movements across the world, advocating for social and economic reform and in time led to the progressive movement in the United States.

George's renown brought him to Great Britain for a number of lecture tours during the 1880s. He became the most talked of man in the country after William Gladstone, the grand old prime minister. It is said that, in that era, the only two Americans more famous were Mark Twain and Thomas Edison.

By the end of the decade, George was an adviser to the British Liberal Party. His moment of triumph came in 1891 when it formally adopted his remedy as the key part of its economic platform. The great prime minister himself, though initially sceptical, was persuaded of the value of George's ideas by his daughter, Mary, among others.[7]

By now, George was a global celebrity, and he ran for public office in the United States. But his health was failing. He suffered a stroke in 1890 and, though he recovered to remain active, he suffered a second, fatal, one in 1897, while campaigning to become the mayor of New York. He was afforded funeral honours befitting a statesman. As his coffin lay in public in Grand Central Station, more than 100,000 people came to pay their respects, the largest gathering of mourners for any American figure since the death of President Lincoln in 1865.

The restless, focused, uneducated, erudite Californian had produced a work for the ages. *Progress and Poverty* sold three million copies in the 1890s, more than any book other than the Bible. By 1933, John Dewey estimated that "it had a wider distribution than almost all other books on political economy put together." There has been no book in the history of the economics discipline that has come close to this. Even today, it remains the most widely read economics book in history.

Given his great renown and the strength of his political influence, it was inevitable that George's ideas would come up against deeply entrenched financial and landed interests. This did not stop with his death. The remedy, to which George had devoted the second half of his life, would be taken on by an unlikely pair of champions and led to an almighty conflict, one that would shake the very foundations of the British constitution.

The People's Budget

This is a War Budget. It is for raising money to wage implacable warfare against poverty and squalidness. I cannot help hoping and believing that before this generation has passed away we shall have advanced a great step towards that good time when poverty, and the wretchedness and human degradation which always follow in its camp, will be as remote to the people of this country as the wolves which once infested its forests.

With this declaration, the Chancellor of the Exchequer, David Lloyd George, concluded his speech to the House of Commons putting forward the Liberal government's budget of 1909. This was the piece of legislation that contained the first provisions for a change to the tax system along the lines set out by Henry George. It was called the 'People's Budget'.

Lloyd George might have declared war on poverty, but his real enemy was the country's aristocracy that controlled much of British public life. In the bicameral British Parliament, the lower chamber, the House of Commons, was fully elected; the upper, the House of Lords, was stuffed full of hereditary landowners.

The political battle now began. At Lloyd George's side stood a brilliant young orator. His name: Winston Churchill. They made an unlikely pair, Lloyd George a working-class Welshman with a deep distrust of hereditary privilege, Churchill a patrician Englishman, descended from a long line of noble land-owning forebears. But they had found common cause in wanting to see George's remedy enacted. For Churchill in particular this fight was personal. He had crossed the chamber to sit on the Liberal benches for this issue, but the wrench must have been great given his family's aristocratic roots.[8] Different as Lloyd George and Churchill were, they were a formidable team and were known on the opposition benches as the 'Terrible Twins'.

It was clear that the battle would be fierce. The Lords, the rentier class, were overwhelmingly on the Conservative benches and opposed to the Liberal government. And they had their lackeys in the elected house to make the government's life difficult. The Conservative opposition fired off amendment after wearying amendment at the government's legislation, over the course of a long, hot summer. Every tactic to delay was used, including late-night debates about whether a late-night sitting should be permitted. So interminable were they that on one occasion Churchill was rebuked for attending in his pyjamas. It was only after six sapping months of debate that the Liberal government passed its budget in the Commons.

The moment of triumph was now at hand. Though he did not live to see it, George's remedy was poised to become law in what was then the most important country in the world.

The counterattack

The Liberal government had a strong popular mandate for the reform. Under the delicate system of convention and precedent that makes up the British constitution, the House of Lords was required to pass any money bill that had the support of the elected House of Commons. Anticipating the possibility of constitutional defiance from the Tory lords, the government also made it clear that rejection of the bill by the upper house would result in legislation to formally remove their privileged powers.

What would Lord Lansdowne, the leader in the House of Lords, do? To even consider vetoing the bill alarmed many of his own colleagues. As much as they hated the reform, they pleaded with him that the loss of formal political power was not a price worth paying.

Lansdowne knew better. As there was nothing enshrined in law to prevent the rejection of the money bill, he ordered the veto to be deployed; thereby effectively detonating a bomb underneath the fragile structure of the constitution.

The result was political chaos. Two general elections were held in 1910, where the removal of the Lords' powers was on the ballot. And so the House of Lords' ability to veto a bill was formally abolished by the 1911 Parliament Act.

In these elections the Liberal government lost its large majority in the House of Commons. While a land value tax was subsequently introduced, its implementation was interrupted by the outbreak of war in 1914. After the war, it was repealed by the Conservative government. It should have been the moment of triumph for the movement started by George and championed by Churchill. But it was cut short. The taxes were even paid back to the landowners, surely one of the few times in all of human history that a government has voluntarily returned taxes legitimately collected. It was the final insult.

Magie was right. Formal political power was secondary: the land monopolist was the real monarch of the world, and Lansdowne knew it: "the landed aristocracy and the government are one – the latter being nothing more than the organised means of preserving the power and privileges of the former."[9] From the perspective of his narrow interest, he made entirely the right call.

Landowning interests had prevailed. They successfully blocked what they thought was an utter revolution to the natural order. Yet George was no revolutionary – unlike Karl Marx whose works were also circulating at the time. His genius was that he showed that the highest aspirations of the current system, the free market economy, could be realised.[10] This was the key lesson from Magie's game: you only needed to make a simple tweak – pay the ground rent to the public treasury and keep all other rules the same – and almost *everyone* would be better off.

The political counterattack had worked, for now. But the rentiers had a problem. Only a desperate act of constitutional vandalism had stopped George's proposal from being implemented in Britain. And before he died, George himself had been a hair's breadth from winning the mayoralty of New York City, one of the most influential elected executive offices in the United States. His ideas had an enormous hold over progressive politicians and activists the world over.[11] George's remedy was popular, and it was right. As Tolstoy, a prominent follower, pointed out, "People do not argue with the teaching of George, they simply do not know it. (And it is impossible to do otherwise with his teaching, for he who becomes acquainted with it cannot but agree.)"[12]

In a democracy with a well-informed citizenry who understood George's argument, it was an ever-present danger to rentier interests. And so to permanently undermine his remedy, a deeper, more insidious strategy was required because, somehow, they had to finagle a win in the battle of ideas.

The intellectual corruption

Almost every economist in the 1880s had felt obliged to write about George's diagnosis. Some academics were quite in favour of George's ideas, but a good number were not, whether by choice or necessity. Business schools and economic faculties tended to be conservative in their outlook and, in the United

States, relied heavily on the generosity of wealthy men, whose benefactions were conditional: they could not publish or be associated with views that ran counter to the financial interests of their wealthy patrons.

The most prestigious universities of the day were supported by some of the most prominent rentiers in the country: the University of Chicago (John Davison Rockefeller), Columbia (John Pierpont Morgan), Pennsylvania (Joseph Wharton) and Cornell (named after its founder, Ezra Cornell).[13] Their wealth had become engorged on the lands granted by a pliant Congress during the rail boom of the late 19th century and the awarding of other monopoly rights. So George's remedy was a direct attack. Clearly such proposals could not be tolerated, as Scott Nearing, an economist at Pennsylvania, found to his cost. He supported George's ideas and introduced Magie's game as a teaching device in his classroom. But this, and an article in a Georgist publication in 1915, led to his dismissal. As a trustee of the university explained:

> Men holding teaching positions in the Wharton School introduce their doctrines wholly at variance with those of its founder... and talk wildly and in a manner entirely inconsistent with Mr Wharton's well-known views and in defiance of the conservative opinions of men of affairs...

It would not have been too hard to work out what might constitute a 'variant view' given, for example, Wharton's 100,000-acre New Jersey estate. Dissent could not be tolerated.

Suppressing academic freedom of thought was one thing, but a permanent solution was needed, lest George's ideas emerge again after each new crisis. To do so, the remedy needed to become taboo. A culture of silence was needed. The strategy to create this was brilliant: recast the economics discipline; shape it in such a way that few people from the mainstream could ever propose George's remedy again. This remoulding was led by a pair of Columbia economists, J. B. Clark and E. R. A. Seligman, whose influence on their profession and tax policy has been significant and enduring.[14]

George's argument for a service charge on the value of land as opposed to wages or profits was based on the uniqueness of land as a factor of production and the fact that tax distorted or undermined economic activity. So the first intellectual device was to attempt to show that land was somehow not unique. If it were not unique, then it should not be treated differently to wages and profits. And since tax on wages and profits was bad, a tax on land was also bad.

But how did one argue that capital, as in capital equipment used in production, was the same thing as a piece of ground or space? You could not, not in a subject devoted to studying the real world. But the enterprising Clark found a solution: take the discipline into the realm of fantasy. In this world, capital was given a kind of eternal presence which meant it always existed, flowing or 'transmigrating', like a Platonic soul, from one object to another, from factory to machinery and into land. His argument boiled down to: you have to pay money to build a factory and you have to pay money to acquire land, so they must be the same thing. Since a factory is a type of capital, so must the piece of land be, and both are permanent.[15]

While having some superficial appeal to the uncritical mind, these arguments were all spurious. Nonetheless, they were repeated often enough that they caught on. In a genius of marketing, these changes to the discipline were dubbed 'neoclassical' to give them credibility as having their origin in the classical economics of Locke, Hume, Smith, Ricardo and the French physiocrats while being updated for a modern age. Really, it was more of a hostile takeover of the discipline.[16] The goal was not to replace the precision of George's diagnosis with something equally exact, albeit different. In fact, the more imprecise the better: all they needed to do was sow enough confusion that no logical arguments or proper diagnosis could be made.

In the final analysis, the intellectual corruption was brutally effective. "[It was] one of the most heinous episodes in the history of the development of scientific knowledge."[17] Economics as studied today evolved from this engineered mutation and now operates with two main factors of production, not three, with land being treated as a form of capital. We live with the confusion in language today. If you sell a house that has appreciated in value, we talk of it as a 'capital' gain, rather than the reality, which is an increase in the value of the land on which the house sits.[18] We measure almost every economic variable you can think of: economic output, employment, trade, prices of commodities, final goods and services; interest rates and even the density of light in cities. Our tax authorities know intimately what we buy and sell. Yet hardly anyone, anywhere, shows the remotest interest in measuring the most valuable asset of them all: land.

The world of economic models that drive government policy today is a fantasy one where location does not matter. For all their mathematical sophistication, it is hard to exaggerate the crudeness of their representation of reality (which after all is the purpose of a model). Humanity learned over 2,000 years ago that the planet it inhabited was spherical, but it seems that this lesson has yet to be absorbed by the orthodox high priests of the modern economy. Because a world where location does not matter is effectively a flat plane.

As most generalised economic models were produced from this foundation, professionally trained economists today are ignorant of the role of economic rent in driving economies through periods of boom and bust.[19] Hence, no one can see the cycle, let alone forecast it. This is the real answer to the question posed by the Queen.

Further, explanations of inequality, particularly prevalent today as it becomes more and more obvious, are muddled. Any number of studies have diagnosed the problems of modern capitalism: climate change, environmental degradation, social and economic inequality and all the rest; but none focus on land, and the way we treat it, as the root cause of these problems.[20] In fact, because they accept the forced marriage of land with capital, these studies have been co-opted into the defence of the corrupt economics that the neoclassicals created.[21]

The foundations of the entire discipline of economics were subverted so that Georgist ideas could not challenge the financial interests of a wealthy elite. The remedy never returned as a serious proposal in any large, developed economy after 1909, despite the continued episodes of boom and bust that wreaked havoc on people's lives and livelihoods.[22]

In a final twist, when Darrow stole Magie's *Landlord's Game*, the second set of rules – the ones designed to educate the world about the effect of sharing the rent – was eliminated. Given *Monopoly*'s immense popularity – "no other game, except maybe chess, has so imprinted itself on the world's collective consciousness" – the game she had designed to educate people about the dangers of uninhibited property speculation became, ironically, the very celebration of it.[23]

People reap what they sow. In addition to the inability to understand or forecast the economic cycle, this ignorance inculcated in universities, and perpetuated by modern economic policy, has come back to haunt the West in a big way.

The bitter harvest

November 1989 saw one of the most significant events in world history: the fall of the Berlin Wall, which brought to an end seven decades of brutal communist repression. The effect of the events that took place that day were far-reaching and well-documented. Among them, but little acknowledged, was an illustration of the very corruption of our economic thinking.

The nations that emerged from the Soviet Union hold vast natural resources. If anywhere there were a set of countries that could have developed along the lines set out by George and championed by Churchill, it would have been these – and the time was right. The system of economic governance that could have been built would not, unlike in the United Kingdom, have needed to be constrained by existing institutions and systems. And there was political will: the peoples of those newly created republics had never lost hope that one day they too might choose how to live and earn a fair reward for their labours, something denied to them under communist rule.

An open letter, sent on 7 November 1990, urged President Mikhail Gorbachev to introduce policies to capture the flow of land rent in order to smooth the Soviet Union's transition to a market economy:

> The movement of the Soviet Union to a market economy will greatly enhance the prosperity of your citizens... It is important that the rent of land be retained as a source of government revenue... Social collection of the rent of land and natural resources serves three purposes. First, it guarantees that no one dispossesses fellow citizens by obtaining a disproportionate share of what nature provides for humanity. Second, it provides revenue with which government can pay for socially valuable activities without discouraging capital formation or work effort, or interfering in other ways with the efficient allocation of resources. Third, the resulting revenue permits utility and other services that have marked economies of scale or density to be priced at levels conducive to their efficient use.
>
> A balance should be kept between allowing the managers of property to retain value derived from their own efforts to maintain and improve property, and securing for public use the naturally inherent and socially created value of land. Users of land should not be allowed to acquire rights of indefinite duration for single payments. For efficiency, for adequate revenue and for justice, every user of land should be required to make an annual payment to the local government, equal to the current rental value of the land that he or she prevents others from using.[24]

Despite the intellectual corruption described above, not all were ignorant of the importance of economic rent and this letter was signed by 30 of the world's most prominent economists, including three Nobel laureates: Franco Modigliani, Robert Solow and James Tobin. William Vickrey, another signatory, subsequently went on to win one.

A team of experts, including Fred Harrison,[25] worked at the Russian Academy of Sciences to organise congresses and seminars in the federal Duma to describe this model for the benefit of Russian policymakers. With land tax experts from Denmark and the UK they also worked on a pilot study in Novgorod, the old Russian capital, to demonstrate how a rent-collecting tax system could be quickly established even in the absence of a property market.

From their initial reception, it was clear that the Russian people in general were enthusiastic. But as Churchill and Lloyd George had discovered more than 80 years before, the forces arrayed against the sharing of the rent were formidable.

On the one hand, the theft of Russia's natural resources was already underway. In the years prior to 1989, the KGB had foreseen the end of the Soviet Union and had taken steps to siphon off wealth and maintain its networks of influence. They needed friendly Western firms and corrupt (or financially fragile) businessmen to absorb the flow of money. On the other, Gorbachev's market reforms in the late 1980s had made things worse. They allowed young entrepreneurs to access the surpluses of large Soviet firms and convert them into foreign currency at a price well below the black market rate. This gave them access to enormous pools of wealth, which they used to acquire enormous industrial firms. In addition to this, they were permitted to set up banks to finance their operations.[26]

By 1989, Gorbachev was concerned about the reforms he had unleashed and made efforts to limit the profits such firms could make. But by now the genie was out of the bottle and these new entrepreneurs switched their support to the Russian president, Boris Yeltsin. Soon after successfully facing down a hard-line coup in August 1991, Yeltsin became the new leader of the country. The coup failed in part because it was not supported by the KGB, who did not want to stop the theft.

Harrison and those who supported the views expressed by these 30 prominent economists were also totally overwhelmed by a strong push from Western institutions, especially the IMF and World Bank, to privatise all of Russia's natural resources – including of course, all of the land – and to shift the burden of taxation onto Russian companies and citizens. When that was done, it opened up vast new lands and natural resources – never before mortgaged – for Western banks to be able to securitise ever more rents.

Because of these two forces, Yeltsin presided over the biggest giveaway of land and resources the world has ever seen. As with the game of *Monopoly*, the winners ended up with all of the spoils. Winners that were intimately connected to those at the centre of power. For the rest, the people, the result was chaos. The West advocated 'shock therapy' to introduce 'market reforms', in other words, to replicate the Western system of land monopoly. This was a reflection of the intellectual corruption described above, but perpetrated in a country which had no social welfare safety net to ameliorate its worst effects. The result: plummeting life expectancy, a rise in infant mortality, an increase in the rate of suicides and alcoholism, to name but a few.[27] The deadly consequences of the political and intellectual corruption of the West could be seen on a terrifying scale in the opening up of Russia.

Worse was to follow. As the Russian government approached bankruptcy in 1995 amid all the chaos, a handful of Russian businessmen lent the state the money it needed to keep functioning. As collateral, they received stakes in state-owned businesses. When the state failed to repay the loans, the businessmen, now known as 'oligarchs', simply sold the stakes to themselves at advantageous prices and acquired the remainder through the rigged privatisation auctions being run at the time. Mikhail Khodorkovsky, for example, took ownership of the state-owned oil company, Yukos, for just $300m.[28] Since he had also founded the bank Menatep in the years before, he did not even have to dip into his own pocket to finance the purchase.

By 1996, the oligarchs knew that the permanently inebriated and deeply unpopular Yeltsin was a liability. So they hatched a new plan which they called 'Operation Successor': install a new man in the Kremlin, someone they could control to ensure that the system they now presided over would be preserved for their benefit. In a little-known career bureaucrat, they found their man. His name: Vladimir Putin.

Putin had gained a reputation as a fixer and someone who was loyal to those who supported him. He had worked as the deputy to the mayor of St Petersburg and was chairman of the Council of Foreign Economic Relations. This gave him insight into the value of the vast resources of Russia, and he had reputedly been party to some shady practices whereby these resources were sold abroad and the money deposited in bank accounts he controlled. It seemed he would be the right man to cultivate; he would be a steady hand at the tiller, would be beholden to his wealthy patrons and would ensure they could go about building their business empires without interference.

How wrong they were.

Putin turned out to be anything but a patsy. In fact, as a former KGB officer, he retained strong links to his former colleagues while working his way up the Russian political establishment. He was intimately involved in their plans to maintain a war against the West. He turned against his patrons. He marshalled the political, judicial and law enforcement arms of the state to bring them to heel. To do so he made an example of the biggest of them all, Mikhail Khodorkovsky.[29] Then he consolidated power and helped himself to his own cut of Russia's wealth (and is now allegedly the world's wealthiest man by far).

In turn, his Russia became increasingly hostile to Western interests. In the early stages, Russian wealth was squirrelled away in Western firms. Later on it was used to buy influence, particularly if it helped to support businessmen who might prove useful contacts in the future – on whom they might also have *kompromat* (compromising material). The fallout from the 1990s real estate cycle was significant and there were many such candidates. Perhaps the standout example of business failure in that decade was a New York real estate developer by the name of Donald J. Trump. Russian money helped reduce his debts at a time when no bank (other than Deutsche Bank) would do business with him. Lucrative licensing fees at well above market rates helped him recover his standing. And given his predilection for erecting tall buildings with his name displayed prominently on them, the possibility of building a Trump Tower in Moscow, to be potentially Europe's tallest, was repeatedly dangled in front of him.[30]

Trump would have been one of a number of such contacts cultivated in the early 1990s. He was a small bet at the time, but what a pay-off it gave. At the Putin-Trump press conference in July 2018 in Helsinki, the influence of the creditor (and one of the world's foremost rentiers), Vladimir Putin, over the debtor (and one of the world's foremost real estate moguls), Trump, was plain to see. Both of them had made political careers out of exploiting the pain and anger of those who suffered in the aftermath of a real estate cycle they were partially responsible for perpetuating. This must surely rank as one of the most bizarre spectacles in modern Western history. Here was yet another direct consequence of political and intellectual corruption.

———————— · ■ ■ ■ · ————————

This chapter should help explain to you why those who wrote to the Queen in 2009 could not answer her: most have been trained not to see the cycle. Even if they could, there is little political will to address it. This is why the cycle endures and why you can rely on your understanding of it to make major investment and business decisions for the foreseeable future.

We must end this brief detour and now return to our cycle journey. In the meantime, the Expansion has continued. We are now around six years in, and are close to a short-term peak, as we will see in the next chapter.

WHO CONTROLS THE RENT CONTROLS THE WORLD

Key lessons

The law of economic rent explains why we must get real estate cycles, even in the digital age. Follow the rent and you will understand the direction in which the economy will move.

This chapter shows you why they endure: because they can neither be diagnosed nor solved. It is only when the economic rent is threatened that you learn who really controls your government. The focus of government is then to preserve and enhance the current system. This should give you certainty that the cycle will repeat.

1. Follow only those who understand rent

Few people understand the law of economic rent when analysing markets and the economy. Pay special attention to those who do. Only selectively engage with the views of those who do not.

2. Acknowledge and obey the law of economic rent

While the system remains as it is, based on land monopoly, you must understand the law of economic rent properly and manage your affairs accordingly. At present, the cycle cannot be avoided, and you *will* be affected by it.

3. Support reform whenever it is proposed

However, we are all citizens. Most of us would probably prefer to live in a fairer society where people earn rewards in proportion to their efforts and do not take out that which they have not earned. Therefore, while fundamental reforms that would solve the boom-bust cycle will be difficult to enact, they are possible. Seek out and support those leaders who are prepared to take on the powers that be and propose measures that lead to the sharing of the rent. Our economies and societies will be much stronger and more prosperous, and we will all benefit from that.

CHAPTER 6

THE PEAK

Today, I'm proud to declare that the United States is in the midst of an economic boom the likes of which the world has never seen before.

Donald Trump, 21 January 2020

Bins, bitcoins and super-tall buildings

GIRL WITH BALLOON, a work by the British street artist Banksy, has just sold for a record £1m at Sotheby's in London. As the sale is confirmed, a switch is activated remotely and the painting starts to shred itself on blades concealed in its garish gold frame. "It appears we just got Banksy-ed," says the (delighted) auctioneer, referring to the street artist's inexhaustible capacity to surprise. The artist later authenticates the mutilated work and gives it a new title: *Love is in the Bin*. The stunt is intended to make a statement about the folly of the big money art world. That might be. But what is now being referred to as "quite possibly the biggest prank in art history" reveals folly of another sort: excessive investor behaviour.

There are many other examples. The price of bitcoin is in bubble territory, as seen in Figure 11. When launched it was worth fractions of a cent, but now the price – which breached $10,000 in 2017 – has risen a further 70% into the start of 2018. As it does so, those who used it as a form of money in the early years are left aghast when they work out how much their purchases have cost them. Matt Hanycez, a computer programmer, used some of his coins to buy pizza. "I wanted to do the pizza thing because to me it was free pizza," he later claimed. As the price peaks at $17,500 in January 2018, the bitcoin he paid for two Cheese Supremes from Papa Johns are now worth $175 million.

Figure 11: The price of bitcoin, 2010-2018

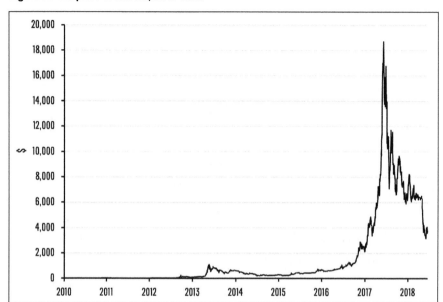

Source: Optuma.

Excess is apparent elsewhere. The 2019 Monaco Yacht Fair is the biggest yet. One hundred and twenty-five super-yachts are on display, with a combined fleet value of $4.3 billion, the highest ever assembled.[1] The long stock bull market is entering its tenth year, the longest ever in American history, driven by low interest rates and record corporate profits – in aggregate $2.4 trillion.[2] Market ebullience is everywhere. There has been a boom in cannabis stocks, so much so that some companies are buying entire towns in California in anticipation of tourism. The news is full of stories about the testing of driverless cars, flying taxis or transportation in vacuum tunnel via a pod – a 'Hyperloop' system. Facebook announces it is launching its own currency, Libra, while the large technology players, leading the market charge, are moving wholesale into consumer finance.

The global construction boom has continued, and humanity is building upwards more than ever before. 2019 is a banner year for the opening of skyscrapers: 26 open, and a further 37 are due in 2020. Half will be in China.[3] House prices in most advanced countries are back into all-time highs and are still rising.[4] The American government has created 'Opportunity Zones' for rich stock investors. They are sitting on $2 trillion of unrealised profits and can now invest them (tax-free) into former rust-belt towns to earn a further tax-free return. What are the chances that most of this enormous flow of money does not end up in the land market? Global wealth has now topped $360trn, reflecting the high prices of assets.[5] Almost a third of this – more than $100trn – has been created in just the last three years.

Given the boom, the Federal Reserve is raising interest rates. The flat US yield curve of the late Expansion phase now briefly inverts in August 2019, around seven years after the Start. Where the American economy leads, the world will follow. Other indicators suggest a slowing global economy.[6] And so, encouraged by a sharp market sell-off in 2018, as well as a Twitter tantrum by Trump, the Federal Reserve reverses course and begins reducing interest rates again.

Record deals and the 'greatest boom in history'

Investors pay no heed to the warning signs and jump in enthusiastically. The private equity firm Kohlberg Kravis Roberts wants to set a new record for a leveraged buyout, with its proposed $70bn acquisition of Walgreens Boots Alliance, a pharmacy chain. This would break its own global record set in 2007, the Summit of the prior cycle. In October 2019 the S&P 500 crosses 3,000 for the first time ever. The mood at the World Economic Forum meeting in January 2020 is very bullish.[7] Trump boasts that the US is experiencing a boom like never before, of course all down to his wise management of the economy. "Cash is trash," declares Ray Dalio on 22 January. Dalio is the head of the world's largest hedge fund, Bridgewater. His CFO claims that the business cycle as we know it is over. Americans are taking the hint: with unemployment at low rates not seen since the 1960s, households have money to invest. Bloomberg reports that 'mom and pop' investors, who have sat out most of the 11-year bull market, have been on a stock-buying frenzy.[8] The S&P 500 surges a further 13%.

It will clearly take something significant to wake up investors, great and small, to what is really going on. It often does at this stage of the cycle.

The Peak analysed

Business has been good for several years, unemployment is low, the property market strong and the stock market is at all-time new highs. It is much easier at this time to make big decisions – for example to expand production, buy assets at high prices or engage in risky behaviour – because the news is generally positive. You should look out for the following at this stage.

1. Extravagant behaviour

Watch carefully for extravagant behaviour (e.g., purchases of luxury items or art) around six to seven years after the Start. Often this is accompanied by a grand statement by a prominent person about how well things are going and suggesting that people should be buying (see below).

2. The long bull market

The stock market has likely been going up for some time now and is usually at or back into all-time highs.[9] The Expansion and Peak stages of prior cycles involved lengthy bull markets (for example, those of the 1950s and 1990s). The average stock market gain from the Start to the mid-cycle Peak since the 1950s has been 233%.[10]

3. Property markets reach all-time highs

By the Peak stage of each cycle, the property market has got above where it reached at the top of the prior cycle.[11] There are renewed calls for more housebuilding as the market surges up, because first-time buyers struggle to get onto the property ladder. As housing gets more expensive, there is more building on new sites in new locations. Vacant land in the major cities gets absorbed, and buildings in cities get taller. By the Peak, there is plenty of construction going on. Large housebuilders report record revenues and profit growth, but their share prices fall. This is because all the cheap land acquired at the Start of the cycle has now been built on. In the future, they will have to build on more expensive land and move outwards to secondary and tertiary cities in search of profitable developments.

4. Bank lending

Bank lending assists the construction boom and surging property market. In most places, lending is back to normal; this boosts profits, and bank share prices should have recovered (though this is dependent on how quickly they have been able to offload the bad loans from the prior crisis). The cycle is now fully in gear.

5. The yield curve inverts

Economic indicators are generally bullish, but there are some warning signs pointing to a coming economic slowdown or recession. This includes an inverted yield curve, which is the most reliable advance indicator of a slowdown.[12] But because times are good, many of these negative signals are explained away and not heeded.

6. The grand statement

In this context, a grand statement by a prominent politician or businessman about how good things are (or how different they are to before) inadvertently reveals that the mid-cycle Peak stage is about to end. For example, in October 1999 of the last cycle, a well-publicised book claimed that the Dow Jones Industrial Average, then trading around 10,300, was severely undervalued and would appreciate to 36,000 within three to five years.[13] The Dow peaked two months later and then fell almost 40%.

———————— - - ■ - · ————

We have now completed the first Act of our 18-year cycle: the Recovery. Times are good again, defying the gloom and fear with which we started our journey. Along the way we have seen how new technologies have brought our economies into a new age. We have watched new businesses start and flourish. The property and stock markets have recovered to such an extent that they are now at higher levels than ever before.

There has been plenty of change; but as we have also seen, in the most fundamental way our economies are just the same, subject to the law of economic rent which drives them through periods of expansion (as now) and (eventually), after a boom, into a crisis and a bust. That is all to come. We now know why most will not – cannot – see the repeating cycle.

So, we must go on into the next Act, the Mid-cycle. Soon things will not look quite so rosy, because the Recession is about to commence.

DON'T GET CARRIED AWAY, AND GET YOUR HOUSE IN ORDER

Stage: the Peak

Approximate timing: years 6 and 7

Prevailing emotion: overconfidence

Managing emotions

The mid-cycle Peak arrives around six to seven years into the cycle. As the Expansion stage matures, its optimism eventually turns into overconfidence, and investors and businesses engage in some excessive behaviour. You will see this in the high prices paid for assets, the opening of glitzy corporate office headquarters, the launch of a new range of exorbitantly priced luxury items, the well-attended yacht/car/private jet fairs and so on. This is the time to remain level-headed and not over-reach. The good times will not last forever.

Managing investments

The key at this point is to get ready for the next stage of the cycle. Get your house in order; ensure you can survive what may soon turn into a difficult period. The value of having some foresight about the direction of the economy, which understanding the cycle gives you, really comes into its own now.

1. Make no further stock market purchases

a. As the stock market continues up, you should not commit more capital into it. Instead, build a pool of spare cash. This is in preparation for the Recession, during which you can take advantage of falls in asset prices.

2. Ensure property portfolios have a margin of safety; act with caution

a. Property investors should ensure that their portfolio is earning sufficient cash to absorb any problems, such as reduced rents and arrears, that may occur in the next stage of the cycle.

b. If you are looking to reduce the size of your portfolio, now is the time to sell; otherwise, you may have to wait a while.

c. Property developers should ensure that they have sold stock prior to the end of this stage, or plan to hold stock during a recession.

d. Do not load up on debt, even if it is readily available.

3. Take profits on alternative assets

a. If you have been speculating in other assets, especially those that have entered into bubble territory, take profits now. Do not try to time the top of the market. The price of assets that have low or no earnings can fall very significantly. Assets in bubbles are vulnerable to a crash whenever the broader market corrects and when the story powering the investment turns out to be not quite so positive. The best time to take profits is when the rates are low, and the news is still full of stories of how much higher prices can go.

b. The very latest you should sell is when central banks begin raising interest rates, because invariably this will cause the bubble to burst at some point. If you have missed out on the large gains over the last few years, do not buy now, even if upward price momentum seems (and everyone says it is) unstoppable. It is not.

4. Business owners: time to rein back, develop contingency plans and manage costs

a. Business owners should build up reserves of cash, have control of costs (including workforce costs), and be prudent with borrowing. Exercising such restraint during a period when business is growing strongly, and opportunities are abundant, can be difficult. The trade-off is to endure a high short-term opportunity cost, i.e., forgoing business, against the medium-term gain of surviving the recession in good shape and having the chance to expand when your competitors are facing difficulties. A balance needs to be struck between shorter- and longer-term strategies. It is important to use your knowledge of what is about to happen and make decisions with foresight. Any business expansion at the Peak stage should be done prudently, rather than aggressively.

b. Owners considering selling their businesses should do so now – and do so quickly.

ACT II
MID-CYCLE

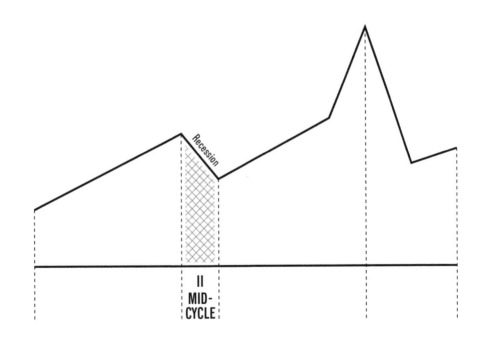

In this Act, the economy goes through a slowdown or a recession. The length of this part of the cycle can vary but lasts a year or two on average.

Chapter 7: The Recession sees the economy slow down and the stock market crash. By contrast, the property market and banking system hold up. This is the time to hold steady and get ready to buy.

Chapter 8: The Magic of Money explains what money is and the role of banks in creating it out of nothing. Banks are efficient at exploiting the rent and amplifying the boom. You should own one.

Chapter 9: The Magic of Money, Part 2 shows that governments also create money (when they spend) and destroy it (when they tax). Government investment, especially on infrastructure, pushes up land prices and creates the boom. Follow it and invest accordingly.

CHAPTER 7

THE RECESSION

The shock to the global economy from Covid-19 has been faster and more severe than the 2008 global financial crisis and even the Great Depression.

Professor Nouriel Roubini, 25 March 2020

The return of fear

WITH MARKETS SURGING into all-time highs and politicians only too eager to make grand statements, what can puncture the general confidence? Clearly it is going to take something big.

Though little noticed at the time, on 31 December 2019 the Chinese government informs the World Health Organization of a cluster of pneumonia deaths caused by a virus of unknown origin in Wuhan City, Hubei province of China.[1] Prior to this point, the authorities had gone to great lengths to suppress this information; but now a concerned doctor, Li Wenliang, has posted news of the outbreak on social media. Police from the Wuhan Public Security Bureau immediately accuse him of spreading false rumours and disturbing the peace. Tragically, Li dies a few days later, having been infected by one of his patients. As cases appear outside China, it becomes clear that the virus will pose a significant problem, one for which most countries are ill-prepared. The US stock market peaks on 19 February and then starts to drop.

Soon the virus breaches 100,000 cases worldwide, and its rate of growth is accelerating. Health systems are overwhelmed in a matter of weeks. The supply of vital equipment – such as oxygen and protective apparel – becomes severely restricted. On 11 March 2020, the World Health Organization declares a pandemic. Governments panic. Borders are closed in a desperate attempt to reduce the rate of transmission. Businesses are ordered to cease operations, and people to stay at home.

The global economy, already slowing down, is now frozen. There is widespread panic in the financial markets. On 9 March, all hell breaks loose: the interbank market – the market that lubricates the wheels of international finance by providing financial institutions with access to liquid assets, such as dollars or bank reserves – seizes up. Large funds need dollars to meet investors' demands for redemptions, but there is a shortage. Not even US Treasuries – the largest, safest, most liquid asset on the planet – can be easily sold. If no one is buying American government bonds, everything else is potentially unsaleable. This leads to a run on all assets. The US markets fall faster than they have ever done in their history.[2]

The lockdowns are causing the global economy to contract sharply. The price of oil collapses after OPEC, the cartel of oil-producing nations, fails to agree on production cuts. With demand for fuel dropping sharply because of severely curtailed travel, on one manic day in April the oil price collapses to negative $40 per barrel on the spot market. Economies are entering a recession that some predict will be more severe than the Great Depression. News headlines around the world reflect investors' worries: so bullish only a few weeks ago, there is now a real fear that we are in the midst of a new global financial crisis.

Slaying the boom-and-bust monster and reflating the economy

With markets crashing everywhere, the world needs a saviour. One duly steps forward: Jerome Powell. His Federal Reserve will supply dollars in whatever quantity the financial system needs to satisfy demand for them. In a matter of weeks, it acquires 5% of the entire $20trn Treasury market and provides access to dollars to any other central bank that requires them to cater to local needs. The Fed becomes the lender of last resort to the entire world.[3]

The selling of US Treasuries and other assets stops. Next, the Federal Reserve addresses the stock market panic. As there is a sharp drop in output, it introduces measures to ensure that credit continues to flow to banks, large businesses and municipalities; the latter are on the front line of fighting the virus and are in desperate need of additional funds.

The measures work swiftly. By 23 March, the market panic is over. Governments move quickly to stimulate their economies. Over the next few months, they enact stimulus measures of over $14trn, covering a large variety of policy measures: job support schemes, bank guarantees, bond purchases, tax deferrals and easing of bank regulations.[4] Given how fast they are rolled out, it is unlikely that they can prevent widescale fraud, but that is not important right now. They talk about 'building back better', code for a massive increase in infrastructure spending. There is an unprecedented level of public investment put towards the development of vaccines for Covid-19, as the virus is now identified. It takes less than nine months to have the first one approved for use. The great vaccination rollout begins, soon to be followed by the great re-opening of the economy.

This time politicians are only too eager to talk up how decisive and important their actions have been in saving the economy. In dollar terms, the rescue packages seem to be much larger than the response to the global financial crisis. In fact, they are not, but in the dark days of the financial crisis, when the entire system might have collapsed, the goal had been to obfuscate and downplay the size of the response.[5]

Crashing markets also reveal the frauds and the cons that were perpetrated over the past few years and hidden by the bull market. 2020 furnishes many such examples, such as Wirecard, Greensill and Ant Financial. A common feature among many of those engaged in deceptive activities is how well-connected they are to those in power.

As stock prices have dropped almost 40% and central banks have flooded the financial system with liquidity, 2020 is primed to be one of those very good years in the stock market.[6] And so it proves. Markets, particularly in the US, make an astonishing recovery. By June the Nasdaq 100 is back above the February high and closes the year an enormous 46% up. Commentators are bemused as markets keep on rising. Surely this is just down to central bank largesse in the face of such a severe recession?

In the event, the recession in the US lasts a mere two months, the shortest in its history.[7] China's economy even grows in 2020. What explains the speed of the recovery? For all the worry fuelled by the relentless barrage of negative news coverage every day, this is not a financial crisis. Governments were not faced with a collapsing property market and banking system. Both hold up well, because we are at the mid-cycle Recession and they are in a comparatively sound position. The government response is unexpectedly effective.[8] So, might the stimulus have been overdone? There is plenty of worry about its affordability. That concern is misplaced, because governments do not have an affordability constraint. The more important issue is the volume of new money injected into the economy. The amount of stimulus is far larger than it needs to be. Inflation will inevitably result.[9]

Things are different now

As the world emerges from recession, some things give us a clue about how the remainder of the cycle will play out. The long lockdown days force people to review their living arrangements, and many decide a change is necessary. They harness their savings, now at record levels owing to reduced spending on consumption and travel, and take advantage of low interest rates (and other property support measures, especially for first-time buyers) to make a change.[10] There is a spate of home renovations and a huge surge in buyer interest in the property market. The priority is outdoor space, such as gardens, and proximity to a nice high street and other amenities, such as parks. Across the world, where they have the option to do so, people leave the largest urban areas and move to smaller cities or the countryside. Governments promise to make infrastructure investments in such places.

High levels of saving also lead many, particularly younger people, to invest in the stock market and cryptocurrencies for the first time. New investing and trading platforms, accessible via smartphones, make this easy and cheap. Soon there is an investment craze, leading to a number of bizarre incidents and even coordinated buying.[11] Meanwhile, the price of Bitcoin reaches a high of $68,000, up 17 times from its March 2020 lows. If anything, this is the conservative end of the crypto-boom. During this mid-cycle people learn about non-fungible tokens, SPACs, meme stocks and meme coins (the most notorious example of which is Dogecoin, created by two tech people to poke fun at Bitcoin. Following some tweets by Elon Musk, it appreciates 68 times in the first five months of 2021, then promptly collapses).

After an initial adjustment period, many sectors of the economy are able to function during lockdown as workers connect to central office servers via home broadband. This immediately boosts local retail (after the severest restrictions are lifted) and coffee shops. The young parents and prams of pre-pandemic life are now replaced by casually dressed office workers and rows of laptops.

For a time, the bustling business districts of city centres are ghost towns. And as the economy opens up, it becomes clear that the era of the big corporate office, cramming as many people into small spaces as regulations will allow, is now over. More space and better facilities are required, offsetting a fall in demand for space from companies also moving to less expensive locations.[12]

Commodity prices follow the stock market up as construction booms: lumber, copper and lithium in particular. So does the price of gold, as fears of inflation start to take hold. Bond yields are low on account of the stimulus measures, so their real rate of interest is negative. Gold prices tend to move inversely to real yields.

External and internal turbulence

2020 is notable for a remarkable increase in tensions and conflict, both internationally and domestically. Geopolitically, as the world is distracted by the response to the pandemic, the US and UK take the opportunity to send warships into Russia's exclusive economic zone within the Arctic.[13] The tension between Russia and the West is slowly building, not just in the high north but elsewhere, such as in central Europe. China uses its security law to further suppress democracy and dissent in Hong Kong and flies fighter jets past Taiwan in ever-greater numbers to remind its people that reunification with the mainland is coming. In June 2020, there are high-altitude skirmishes between Indian and Chinese soldiers in the region of Ladakh, along the disputed eastern border between these two giant nations. As we will see in Chapter 11, these incidents are part of a longer-term cycle of conflict that has started to accelerate.

Domestically, 2020 sees some of the worst protests in years. These things are closely tied to the cycle, given that one of its consequences is an inexorable rise in economic inequality. While at first the virus appears to be the great leveller – one that affects presidents, prime ministers, princes and paupers alike – it soon becomes apparent that this is not true. In fact, its effects reflect, and indeed exacerbate, the deep fissures in the economic and social structure of Western countries.

The location where you live determines key social and health metrics, such as income levels, life expectancy, obesity and general physical health – and, unsurprisingly, affects the chances of catching the virus and the recovery rates of those infected.[14] While the pandemic is a genuinely universal experience, people's lived realities vary significantly across different locations, especially at the economic margins.

In our economies, there is an underlying hotbed of resentment at the many injustices of the system. But in the summer months of 2020, as many people face unemployment and extreme uncertainty, anger is threatening to erupt on to the streets. All that is needed is a spark. That arrives on one warm Minnesota evening, 25 May. Police officers are called to a local convenience store by a teenage employee who identifies a counterfeit $20 note. Suspecting it might have been a regular customer – an African American man – one of the white police officers arrests him as he sits in his car a short distance away, oblivious to the charge. There is a brief argument, after which the customer is handcuffed face-down on the street. He does not attempt any further resistance, yet one of the officers nonetheless deploys a controversial technique to subdue him by kneeling on his neck for more than nine minutes. With his face pressed into the unforgiving tarmac, the prisoner pleads in vain for the pressure on his neck to be released. He cannot breathe. What passes through a person's mind in those final moments before the end? In the case of George Floyd, he calls out to his mother, who died two years before.

Captured by the camera of the by-now-ubiquitous mobile phone, the technology that has driven the first half of the 18-year cycle, this incident reveals yet another example of the tough-justice approach to policing in America. Recent years have furnished many such examples in which black men die at the hands of white police officers. In the context of the recession – which lays bare the precariousness of economic life – it ignites a bonfire of protest and leads to the largest racial justice marches since the US civil rights movement in the late 1960s.[15] Protests occur around the world, because the issues of economic disparity, race and government heavy-handedness trouble many nations, particularly where they are linked to historical grievances. Governments, of course, do what they can to stop the protests or make them difficult, citing public health concerns.

There may be many factors behind these protests, but all are linked in some way to inequality engendered by the law of economic rent. This is the reason that they flare up now – as they have done in the past – at a key turning point in the 18-year cycle.

Meanwhile, Trump has spent most of 2020 raging against the damage lockdowns are doing to his electoral chances and is voted out of office, to be replaced by Joe Biden. As the recession ends and the world returns to a new normal, it soon becomes clear almost nothing has been unaffected – whether socially, commercially, or politically. It has been a recession like no other, it seems. As we move into a new decade, things really *will* be different this time. Won't they?

The Recession analysed

The Recession at the midpoint of the cycle is often a chaotic and confusing affair. There is surprise when it first arrives, then a return of the fear that characterised the Start of the cycle. But it passes more quickly than the crisis at the end of the prior cycle. It typically consists of the following sequence of events.

1. The slowdown or recession

The yield curve inversion that occurred before the Peak stage generally forecasts the coming mid-cycle Recession. Sometimes, the Recession ends up being a period of slow growth rather than a technical recession.[16] The slowdown or recession is made worse, at least for a time, by an external shock which causes a crisis of confidence and then panic. The mid-cycle of the 1920s coincided with a commodity price collapse and the Spanish flu pandemic; 1981 saw record high short-term interest rates as the Federal Reserve battled to control inflation; in 2001 the mid-cycle was rocked by the terrorist events of 9/11. These events were seismic in their influence over the subsequent decade, but they did not alter the course of their respective cycles.

2. The stock market crash and the frauds

Adding to the general panic is the stock market crash or bear market. Since the Second World War, the average fall at this stage of the cycle has been 38%. The average time to recover is two years. As markets crash, the reckless behaviour of the Expansion and Peak stages is unearthed. The financial press is full of stories of large-scale fraud, which only add to the sense of gloom – scandals such as those involving Enron, WorldCom and Arthur Andersen occurred in the wake of the dot-com bubble that burst in 2000.

3. The swift (and effective) response

The authorities are swift to react to the slowdown. Stimulus measures might take the form of tax cuts (as happened in 1921 and 2001) or a reversal of tight monetary policy (e.g., 1981) and stimulus investment in favoured sectors, such as agriculture or infrastructure (e.g., 2001 and 2020). As a result, the economy makes a comparatively swift recovery irrespective of how significant the events of the Recession appear to have been. What everyone seems to miss is that the recovery takes place because the property market holds up and land values do not drop, particularly if interest rates have been cut in response to the slowdown.

4. Banks and property remain stable

Similarly, bank lending remains buoyant. Economies in which banks continue to supply credit and land values are stable do not enter crisis. Even in the mid-cycle Recessions of 1921 and 1981 which, for different reasons, were extraordinarily difficult times economically and socially, there was no general banking crisis. The banking system was not overleveraged, and the economic woes of the time did not lead to balance-sheet problems or a general run on banks.

5. People go on the move

The disruption of the Recession often leads to people moving, especially as the stage comes to an end. Often, they move to cheaper locations. The reasons for wanting to move might be different in each cycle, but the underlying dynamics are the same. The cycle begins at the centre of cities and then moves out as rising prices force people to search further afield or for more space. This sets up the next stage of the cycle. The 2020 pandemic exacerbated this process.

6. The 'new era' begins

The changes wrought by the mid-cycle Recession and the comparatively swift recovery lead to a feeling that we are entering a new era, that there are new practices to take into account and new social movements. As we move forward, it feels like times are changing.

It is a paradox of the mid-cycle Recession that the deeper and more severe the difficulty during it, the more effectively it erases the memory of the prior crisis; and the more it strengthens the speculative forces to be unleashed in the next stage of the cycle. The mid-cycles in 1921, 1981 and 2001 – all periods of significant disturbance – achieved this. This willingness to speculate is enhanced by the fact that the authorities are seen to have acted swiftly and decisively to deal with the Recession and its after-effects; they appear to have a measure of control over the wild gyrations of the economy.[17]

———— · ▪ ◼ ▪ · ————

And so the first half of the cycle swiftly fades from memory. A new era will soon begin. Before we proceed further on our journey, we need to resolve a few puzzles: why it is that the Recession at the mid-cycle does not lead to crisis? Why does the property market remain sound? Why is the second half of the cycle typically so much bigger than the first? Up to now we have considered the law of economic rent and seen why land – in all its forms – causes the cycle to occur and to repeat over and over. To answer these new questions we need to examine the role of banks and government, as well as a longer-term cycle linked to commodities.

In the next chapter we will see how banks have a particularly important role in creating an economy's money supply, and therefore in amplifying both the boom and the bust.

HOLD STEADY AND GET READY

Stage: the Recession

Approximate timing: years 7 and 8

Prevailing emotion: fear

Managing emotions

The Recession takes place around seven to eight years into the cycle. After the overconfidence of the mid-cycle Peak, the economy moves into decline and the positive emotion quickly disappears. People and markets panic. Do not follow the emotion. You were well-prepared. Remember: the second, bigger half of the cycle, is still to come.

Managing investments

1. Sell stocks at highs and await market lows to buy back in

a. Stock investors can sell at highs, cash out and await the low to buy back in. At the very least you should have built a pool of spare cash to take advantage of the fall in prices. If the markets have crashed and central banks are pumping liquidity into the system, the result will be a very good year in the stock market.[18]

b. The stock market will lead the way out of the Recession.[19] It will tell you what is likely to lead the charge into the second half of the cycle. Stocks that fall the least during the crash or bear market, and stocks that find their low before the rest of the market, are indicating they are in the strongest positions. However, this time there will be a difference: real estate and banking stocks should also hold up, as there is no land crisis at this point, so their earnings are comparatively insulated. This is a good time to buy into the stock market, as history proves (for example, 1962, 1982 and 2002 were excellent years to buy into stocks following their respective Recession stages). The gain from the low of the Recession stage to the Summit of the cycle has on average been 227%.

c. The recovery will also demonstrate which businesses are likely to lead during the second half of the cycle, which sectors of the stock market will be strong and where the demand for space and new employees will come from. There will also be signs of where the new financing flows will go, both in terms of sectors of the economy and countries of the world. If you follow stock markets, you do not need to do much detective work. Look at the stocks that break first into new all-time highs, especially if they have gone sideways during the mid-cycle. Stocks that break out first tell you which sectors and companies investors have been actively buying up. This should guide both business owners on where to pursue new business opportunities and investors on where to invest.

d. Those who do not want to sell stocks at the top can hedge the value of their portfolios and ride out the crash. They can also rotate capital into 'defensive' stocks, the demand for whose products tends to remain steady even in a crisis (e.g., utilities and healthcare) and into other stocks that are likely to continue paying dividends. The prices of these stocks will fall during the bear market, but the fall should be less, and they should still generate income.

2. Property investors should hold; and buy at the point of maximum fear

In general, the Recession is not the time to sell property if you have prepared well by ensuring you have sufficient cashflow. Property prices tend not to go down much, if at all. Further, recessions will result in higher property rents for residences as people are forced back into the rental market during the slowdown. Then, as the economy recovers, these higher rents will capitalise into higher property prices.

a. Look for lower valuations and distressed properties. It is a good time to buy, given that the stronger half of the cycle is to come. Prices will never be this low again.

b. Buy in locations where the government stimulus is going in. This is where new infrastructure will be built, people and businesses are likely to relocate and property prices will go up.

c. The banking system remains in a good position, so bank credit will be available cheaply as interest rates are reduced to combat the recession. Buying property with the bank's money is a sound strategy if carried out at the right point in the cycle. Now is that right point in the cycle. Rents will cover costs and finance; the gains from the increase in land price will accrue to you. Inflation is also higher in the second half of the cycle, thereby eroding the value of the debt in real terms.

d. Typically, the first half of the cycle involves stronger growth in residential than in commercial real estate. Commercial real estate is stronger during the second half, because it is more closely linked to economic performance and the economic boom is still to come. This is the time to consider investing in commercial real estate. But be selective. The Recession is difficult for certain sectors, so careful appraisal is required.

3. Business owners: stay safe to survive

If you are a business owner, recessions highlight the importance of timeless business lessons.[20] These may be fairly simple and obvious – but their value lies in applying them at the right point in the 18-year cycle. This is why knowledge of the cycle is key. Businesses are only as strong as their customers. If you serve other businesses then ensure that they have sound operations, strong business models (especially those that will hold up when the cycle turns down) and deep pockets (this also applies to those who invest in businesses).

a. The first rule for any business is to survive the recession and make it to the recovery point. It is important not to panic. Things will recover more quickly than they did during the prior crisis. But in recession businesses need to draw on spare cash; those that have overleveraged during the prior expansion, or made large staff and other investments late in the first half of the cycle are the most vulnerable, because they will have the lowest free cash flow. Recessions are difficult times for any business, but those that have built up a reserve and been prudent in the expansion can ride out the storm.

b. Businesses should take a look at their expenses and reduce them as far as possible.

c. They should also avoid laying off staff: reduce working hours and introduce other measures as a preference. Larger companies should rely on local knowledge of local managers and give them the flexibility to adapt to local business conditions.

d. Finally, this is a good opportunity to invest in leaner operations. Companies that can survive the recession will be well-placed to rapidly expand once the economy turns around and to take advantage of the bigger expansion of the second half of the cycle. They will also be able to gain market share from companies that are still dealing with the fallout from the mid-cycle Recession.

CHAPTER 8

THE MAGIC OF MONEY

The study of money, above all other fields in economics, is one in which complexity is used to disguise truth or to evade truth, not to reveal it... The process by which money is created is so simple the mind is repelled.

J. K. Galbraith

ONE OF MY earliest childhood memories is of being taken by my mother to watch a showing of *Superman*. I could barely contain my excitement as we took a bright red London bus over to this place called 'cinema' where I would get to see my hero fighting 'the baddies'. But my eager anticipation was to be dashed when we got there: instead of seeing him, I had to stand next to my mother in a queue (even my three-year-old self knew what those were) which seemed to stretch forever across the patterned carpet of the foyer. This was very confusing.

After a while we got to a counter. I gazed upwards with some curiosity as my mother opened her wallet and handed over a round, gleaming token to the attendant. This act, simple though it was, initiated the magic. We were led into a dark cave, and it was there that I finally got to see my azure-clad, red-caped friend saving a reporter from a helicopter accident, repairing an earthquake and even reversing time itself. What a triumph he enjoyed! And all it took to witness it was my mother's shiny token. On this day of fantasy and wonder, was that not the most astonishing thing of all?

Money.

We all talk about it. The pursuit of it occupies the greater portion of our lives. When plentiful, it brings with it a life of ease and sometimes notoriety. But most of us could do with more of it. When it is scarce, it creates enormous anxiety because without it we cannot fulfil our most basic needs. When we want to start a business or buy a house, we often have to borrow it from our bank manager. The government spends much time figuring out how to tax it away from us (without our knowing about it). We save it (usually too little). We invest it (often too late). Conmen prey on our desire for it (sometimes far too easily). We are jealous when our neighbours have more of it than us. It brings us together, and it drives us apart. When you think about it, its role in our world is quite ubiquitous; and yet also profoundly mysterious.

There is much truth to the saying that money makes the world go round. But despite its obvious importance to our lives, it is hard to define; and it seems that those with professional expertise have given up trying. An intellectual, A. H. Quiggin, once quipped that everyone except an economist knows what money means. Until recently, orthodox economic models did not even include banks or consider money beyond the fact that the wheels of commerce are lubricated by its exchange. But understanding what money is, and how it is made, is key to understanding the 18-year cycle. In this chapter we will look at what money *really* is. We will look at the role of banks in creating it and their proper role in the economy. We then look at how this role has become distorted and, consequently, how bank lending is a key determinant of the size of the boom in the latter stages of each 18-year cycle.

The typical discussion of money focuses predominantly on what form it takes or should take, whether it be gold, paper, digits on a computer screen, or, more recently, an encrypted digital token. But the nature of money is more fundamental than this. Its essence is not its form, which merely gives physical effect to something more fundamental, that is, its relationship to a system of production.

To better understand this, let us pay a visit to the indigenous people of the island group of Yap. Despite the lack of formal education, awareness of the outside world or anything resembling a modern economy, they had a sophisticated understanding of money that would put many modern experts to shame.[1]

Stone coins and the deep blue sea

Yap's total land area is only 100km². Now part of the Federated States of Micronesia, it lies approximately 800 miles east of the Philippines in the western Pacific, ringed by coral reefs that are home to an abundance of manta rays and sharks.

Its remote location meant it was virtually cut off from the outside world, its inhabitants living in a paradisal bounty just as their ancestors had for a thousand years. This island people only began to impinge on the world's awareness relatively recently. In the 17th century the Kingdom of Spain, which had claimed Yap for a couple of centuries, sold it to Germany. This action led to the arrival of anthropologists keen to study the ancient customs of the islanders uncontaminated by contact with the outside world.

Yap had a very basic economy, consisting of the exchange of only a handful of products. Western scholars who came to Yap would have expected to find a barter economy, as it was a received truth dating back to Adam Smith that our system of money had evolved to solve the problem arising from the direct exchange of products. By this thinking money was a token, such as a shell or a piece of gold, that was used for exchange in increasingly sophisticated economies.

The anthropologists were somewhat taken aback to find a rather different monetary system on Yap. At first glance, it appeared the islanders had coins, which they called *fei*. These were large stone wheels, ranging in size from around 1–12 feet in diameter, with some of them weighing up to a tonne. The fei had a central hole into which a pole could be inserted, enabling the islanders to carry them. As a type of money, the fei appeared to be pretty useless. Money ought to be portable, so one can actually hand it over to the person one is doing business with. But these coins were difficult, or in some cases impossible, to transport. Their size and weight were out of all proportion to the rudimentary goods that were being exchanged, such as fish.[2]

The researchers were in for another surprise. One wealthy family owned a particularly large fei. One day, as it was being transported from one island to another, it fell overboard as the boat capsized. Under a standard view of money, this should have been an economic catastrophe for the family, whose wealth was now fast disappearing to the bottom of the sea. In fact, it was not. To their astonishment, the researchers discovered that this had no bearing at all on the family's economic status. That their fei was at the bottom of the sea was irrelevant. They were still able to use it in exchange for products, requiring only that others acknowledge who its current owner was. Possession of the stone was unimportant, as it was clearly irretrievable. What was true of this large fei was true in general: the coins were hardly ever moved. Clearly, the physical transfer of a token was not central to the process. At least not on Yap.

This is a profound example of the underlying process that gives rise to money. The form that money takes is not relevant; it can take any number of forms – shells, cigarettes, large immobile stones or even gold. Whatever form money takes, it is only a representation of something more fundamental and essential: a system of trust, or credit.

Some might argue that the fei backed the monetary system on Yap, in the way that gold has periodically backed systems in Europe and elsewhere over the centuries. But even this could not be true. In the case of the large fei at the bottom of the sea, the nominal possessor of that stone had no chance of retrieving it. It had physically disappeared from the economy.

What the episode illustrated was something more essential to the heart of the exchange economy: that is, the giving and receiving of credit bound together by trust. The word 'credit' derives from the Latin *credere*, 'to believe' or 'to trust'. "Credit is the belief that the other party to the exchange will complete the bargain."[3]

Production and credit

In exchange for a product, say a coconut, one islander owes another goods of equivalent value. The first, the coconut gatherer, would be owed something by the second, say a fisherman. This claim (or credit), symbolised by the fei, can be used with a third islander to acquire goods or services that he or she might be producing, for example, extracting a sea cucumber (which happened to be a luxury item on Yap). In accepting the obligation, or credit, from the coconut gatherer, the third islander trusts that the fisherman will fulfil his promise to supply an equivalent amount of fish. The exchange of these credits facilitates the trade of goods so that all parties get what they want. The fei reflects this underlying system of production – rather than brings it into being.

Herein is the key to understanding money: it is a way of representing the trust between parties that are exchanging things they have produced. Trust, as represented by the credit, is needed in every single exchange.[4] We all want things such as food and shelter, clothing, entertainment and so on. We are also skilled in producing specific things. By dividing our efforts and specialising, and then trading, we accomplish far more than we could alone. But the timing of satisfying our needs and wants and producing things to meet them is different. It takes longer to build a house, for example, than it does to mill wheat for our daily bread.

Credit facilitates the transfer of this variety of goods that have different production timescales. The builder will have a debt to the baker for the bread eaten during the time it takes to erect a house. The baker can use this debt (from his perspective, his credit) to obtain clothes and shoes. The clothes-maker and the cobbler, in turn, use their credits to obtain the materials they need in production and will sustain themselves on the bread bought from the baker. Very quickly, even in as simple an economy as this, the number and variety of exchanges taking place becomes large.

At any point in time, there is a balance of something owed to someone by another. In a small economy such as Yap's, the islanders were able to keep track for themselves and did not require anything else to settle claims. This is not the case in larger economies because there is a greater variety of products, and they are exchanged by parties not personally known to one another. Keeping account is difficult, so the exchange of a token solves these problems by helping to settle claims immediately. It also plays a role in calibrating one credit against another, i.e., how many loaves of bread will satisfy the debt owed to the housebuilder for creating shelter, by reference to a common standard or measurement.[5] The token itself is not the key thing; the credit behind it is.

What money needs to be, to adequately support the exchange of credits within society, is a universally acknowledged and accepted means of settling a credit balance. The intrinsic value of the token used as money has nothing to do with it: "It is not the intrinsic nature of the thing, but the use to which it is applied that gives its essential character to money, and constitutes the distinction between it and other things," said Henry George.[6] Whatever has this universal acceptance can serve as money. Sometimes this role can be played by gold or another precious metal, but it does not have to be. Its critical feature is acceptability and ease of transfer: that you can easily pass it to someone else who will accept it in settlement of your debt to them.

In this sense, money is really nothing. It is not itself a valuable thing. Our modern obsession with discussing forms of money is akin to discussing the type of paper a great novel is written on rather than the literature itself. Money is no more than a claim on something of value. It is the production and exchange that comes first, then the money to settle obligations owed by one party to another. All money is therefore credit.[7]

The trusted intermediary

Another problem arises in a larger economy where parties to an exchange are not known to one another. On Yap, everyone knew each other and had a high degree of confidence in their assessment (implicit though it might have been) that other producers would make good on what they had promised. With such confidence the first producer knew it would be worth his time and effort to, say, gather coconuts to use in exchange. It would have been straightforward to use the resulting obligation to acquire something else.

In a more complex setting, it is impossible to have this confidence without some help. A trusted intermediary is needed to assess whether the production will take place as promised and the goods be delivered. Whoever or whatever plays the role of intermediary must be well known within the community, know something about its members and be able to set aside preference and prejudice to make a sober assessment that a person is worthy of credit. Their judgement must be accepted. While there are several parties who might facilitate this role

– and perhaps one day, a technology based upon artificial intelligence and the blockchain might do it – in our current system the role of trusted intermediary is played by a bank.

Banks assess people's creditworthiness and their ability to deliver. Should a person pass that test, a bank will make them an advance. That advance, the banker's note, can be used to pay for things needed as part of the production process – because the bank is a trusted intermediary in the exchange. The bank advances credit, which is then spent by other parties. The bank's credit is the money upon which commerce takes place. As long as the bank's note is generally accepted, it serves as money for the entire production process and the entire economy.

This is the intrinsic role of the bank: to create and maintain that trust between two parties who might not be known to each other. But this role could be played by others, as an example from Ireland in 1970 demonstrates. The late 1960s and 1970s were a time of great union activity, as in many advanced economies, largely around negotiating pay increases that kept up with rapidly rising living costs. Banks were not immune to these pressures, and, in May 1970, after failing to agree a pay deal with the unions, they were forced to close. People and businesses had prepared for the closures by hoarding cash, but the strike lasted several months – far longer than anticipated – and the hoarded cash was insufficient to meet the banking needs of the economy for that length of time. This was no problem, however. Cheques made by people against their bank accounts still circulated as means of payment, even though there was, for the time being at least, no ability to deposit or cash them. The status of banks was such that their cheques continued to be the means of settling obligations. The system was, of course, open to abuse: people could write cheques that would ultimately bounce due to lack of funds. But the system worked because another party stepped in and was able to provide assurance of creditworthiness: the proprietors of that most vital of community institutions, the public house. As the Irish economist Antoin Murphy wittily observed: "one does not after all serve drink to someone for years without discovering something of his liquid resources."[8] Trust and judgement were once again key to the whole process.

In the early modern period, the note of a large trader who was known overseas vouched for the delivery of goods by smaller merchants. Their credit was the equivalent of money for the counterparty.

The alchemy of money

Banks used to issue their own notes, but in the UK this function died down after the 1844 Bank Charter Act. In the US, the first moves to end the practice began after the Civil War.[9] But in the modern economy this does not matter.

Their own notes are not needed. Instead, they mark up the accounts of those to whom they are advancing credit. If this is used in production, the recipient's bank account will be marked up by the amount of the payment made and the original account marked down. In other words, banks will settle the matter between themselves. Bank money, in the form of bank loans, is by far the largest proportion of money in any economy.

Such money, as on Yap, is created out of nothing.

No one, other than regulators and central bankers, pays much attention to the dull, dry tables that make up the balance sheet of a bank. But this is where the alchemy, out of which the modern economy is generated, is represented in rows of numbers. The balance sheet of any commercial enterprise records its assets, which it uses to generate sales and economic benefits, and its liabilities – the money it owes to other entities. In the case of a bank, when it extends a loan it records it as an asset (for which it will earn a fee and interest) and a corresponding liability (in the form of a deposit to the borrowing party). That deposit is then spent by the customer in the economy. And, hey presto, with the wave of a banker's magic wand (or more likely, the click of a mouse button), money comes into being. Until the loan was made, that money did not exist. Figure 12 depicts the monetary magic.

Figure 12: How banks create money

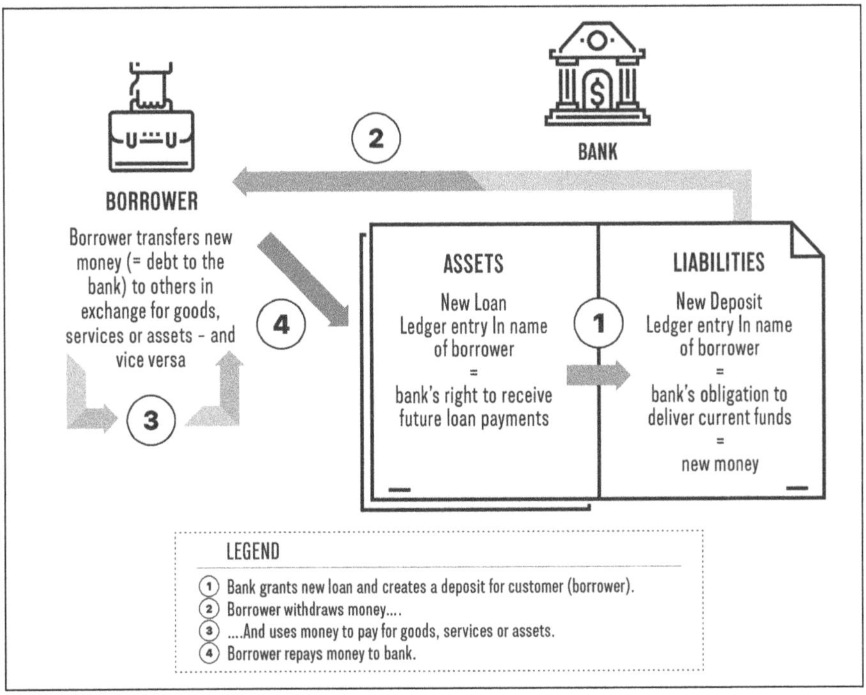

Source: Adapted from *Finance & Development*, vol. 53, no. 1, International Monetary Fund.

The money received in payment for goods and services is then credited to the recipient's bank account as a deposit. The money in bank accounts largely came from loans originated elsewhere in the banking system. In the beginning, there was the banker's advance. In the modern economy, banks create the vast majority of the circulating money supply.

This reality blows apart two common misconceptions about money in the economy. The simplest one is that banks take money from savers and channel it to borrowers. The slightly less simple one, taught in economics textbooks, is that money starts with savers but that banks are able to multiply it up because at any given point in time only a fraction of the saved money sitting in the bank vaults is needed.[10] So banks multiply existing deposits through a process called 'fractional reserve banking', named after the fraction of money held back to meet people's demands for it. This gets a little way towards the idea that banks create money, but it nonetheless perpetuates the falsehood that there is a pre-existing stock of money from which loans can be made. On the critical essence of money – as a form of generally accepted, transferable credit – it misses the point entirely. An example of how influential this misconception has been can be seen on Satoshi Nakamoto's original bitcoin post (my emphasis):

> The problem with conventional currency is all the trust that's required to make it work... **Banks must be trusted to hold our money, but they lend it out... with barely a fraction in reserve.**

One of the most important monetary developments in recent history reveals the mistake in this statement's founding premise.

Bank money creation was a secret known only to a few people in the banking world. "I'm afraid that the ordinary citizen will not like to be told that the banks or the Bank of England can create or destroy money," said Reginald McKenna, a former chancellor of the Exchequer, in 1928.[11] It was not until 2014 that the Bank of England admitted to what seemed like the first official, clear statement of financial reality.[12]

Banks are not intermediaries between savers and borrowers, or multipliers of money deposited with them. The bank creates the money when it lends; the loan comes first, then the deposit. When someone repays a loan to a commercial bank, the opposite happens: money is dissolved.[13] Loan, repayment; creation, dissolution. In an economy, private banks pump money into and out of the monetary system like a beating heart pumps blood into and out of the body's circulatory system. This is why Joseph Schumpeter called bankers "the ephors of the exchange economy". The ability to create money is what makes banks special and quite different from the stock or bond markets, which can only re-allocate already existing money between people.

This money creation is the magic of our economies. The alchemists of the Middle Ages searched for the process whereby gold – the means to acquire wealth – could be created out of base metals. They never found the special catalyst for this process. Where the alchemists failed, modern banking has succeeded. As I discovered that day when I watched *Superman* at the cinema, and as every one of us sees every waking second of each day, what a world of splendour we have created using this magic.

'Sound money' and the limits of banking alchemy

Money arises to fulfil the economy's need for credit, upon which the entire productive process rests. Money is not itself wealth, but a claim on wealth. The alchemy of the banking system is sound if the money created by banks leads to real increases in production by creditworthy, reliable borrowers. This is 'sound money', not because it is backed by gold or any other commodity but because it is backed by production.

Banks do not have an infinite capacity to create money. They operate under banking licence. While this grants them the power to create money, accept deposits, have an account at the central bank, settle payments and conduct other banking activities, they are in return subject to banking regulations and are required to meet certain standards. As we saw from Chapter 4, licensing generates economic rent, while the power to create money is enormously profitable – which is one of the reasons that the shares of banks are a significant presence on most stock exchanges.

Banks need to be able to meet depositors' demands for cash at any moment in time and so must have enough cash and liquid assets to be able to do this. When an advance is taken out of a bank by a borrower and then paid over to another party who deposits it in their own bank, there is a corresponding transfer of money between banks to settle the transaction. In this way all accounts remain in balance. This is done directly between them or between their accounts at the central bank, by transferring central bank reserves (see Figure 13).

Figure 13: A simplified illustration of banks' payments and settlement process

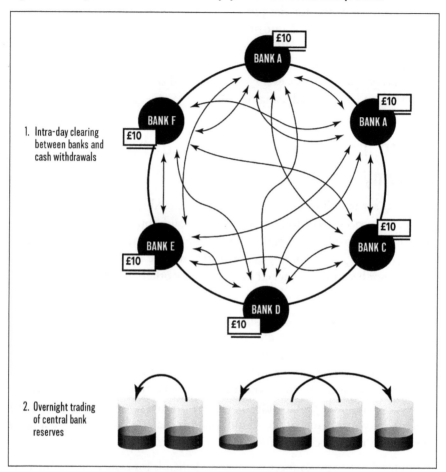

1. Intra-day clearing
   between banks and
   cash withdrawals

2. Overnight trading
   of central bank
   reserves

Source: Adapted from Ryan-Collins et al. (2011), p. 68.

As banks settle with each other virtually instantaneously, they need to possess sufficient cash and central bank reserves. If a bank has a shortfall, it can borrow from the central bank or from other banks via the interbank market. The central bank attempts to maintain some influence over the banking system by influencing the rate of interest at which banks can borrow from it or the rate that banks borrow from each other.[14] This in turn influences the interest rate on loans that banks extend to borrowers, which affects the demand for credit and the level of investment taking place in the economy.

Central banks also set a reserve requirement – the level of reserves a bank must hold as a proportion of the loans it has extended – to ensure that the system retains enough liquidity to function smoothly.[15] They can also step in to lend funds to banks that have a shortage of liquid assets. The other main way in which central banks influence bank lending is to establish capital adequacy requirements. This is to ensure the bank has a sufficient buffer to maintain operations even if some loans turn bad.[16] These requirements are established internationally and updated periodically, usually after a major financial crisis. [17]

Banking regulation is a topic of bewildering complexity, and the treatment above covers it in only a cursory fashion. The specifics of these arrangements are not our concern. The key point is that banks create money and are subject to regulations. It is a sound process when focused on production.

The problem is that, often, it is not.

The problems with money creation: unsound money (money created to acquire land)

Around 90% of the money circulating in the economy is created by banks.[18] As we have learned, this is sound money when used for production, to meet the needs of businesses. Over time, a growing economy needs a greater volume of money to facilitate exchange, so over time the money supply should go up.

But when banks create money for other things, it becomes unsound. Nowadays, most money created by banks is not for productive business but for securitising land. This happens when banks advance a loan to acquire property. [19]

This is an entirely different process to the one just described, which relies on banks making sober assessments of viability and creditworthiness for production. This lending is profitable but requires effort and carries the risk that their judgement is erroneous. But banks, as with other enterprises, want to maximise profits and minimise risks and costs. In the current system it is far more profitable to extend loans for mortgages.[20] So rather than using judgement about borrowers and their projects, they mainly lend with security against real estate. If the loan goes bad, they have recourse to the security. Banks have substituted their assessment function for one of securing their lending against collateral. This means that sound judgement is not required, nor is prudence, particularly during an economic boom when real estate prices are rising rapidly, giving their lending practices the appearance of soundness. Furthermore, it exacerbates the divide in an economy between those who already own assets, and can easily start a business, and those who do not. Business formation is hampered as a result.

Mortgage lending is the main activity carried out in the modern banking system. It does little to increase the productive capacity of the economy. As land prices absorb the gains of economic development, banks mortgage this increase and, with each passing cycle, debt levels must rise. Every real estate boom for which we have data has seen a rise in the ratio of private debt to GDP in the years leading to the Summit of the cycle (see Figure 14).[21] As land has no cost of production and operates in a non-competitive market, the price that people are willing to pay largely depends on how much they are able to borrow.

Figure 14: Private debt as a percentage of GDP, United States, 1805-2017

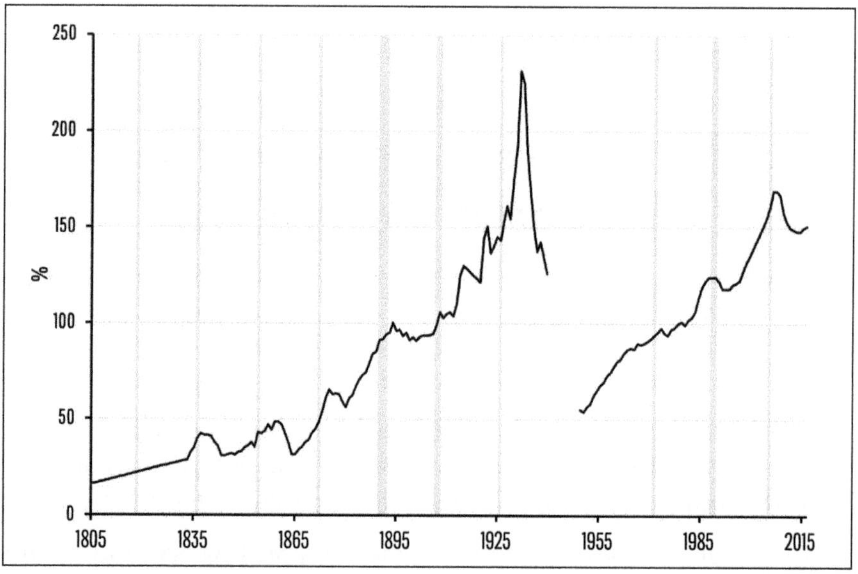

Source: bankingcrisis.org; data missing for the years 1940-1950; vertical lines represent cycle Summit years (see Appendix 1).

This becomes self-reinforcing. As the price of land rises, more money is created to acquire it. The margin extends and brings new sites into the economy, requiring further borrowing for construction and more mortgages for purchase. Banks create new business for themselves at will and, during a boom, it becomes increasingly lucrative for both borrower and lender.[22] Speculation can easily get out of hand. This is why credit conditions amplify the Land Boom and why what some people call credit cycles are so closely related to financial crises.

This is also why bank regulations ultimately do not work: because money, as with every other aspect of the economy, becomes chained to the land cycle and is bound by the law of economic rent, neither of which are a focus of regulations. With banking being such an abnormally lucrative profession (the banking licence represents a form of economic rent, and through their lending activities banks earn interest (and profits) from monetising the increasing value of land), regulators and regulations do not stand a chance of keeping things in check during a boom. There is invariably a build-up of leverage and risk across the system.

How problems in the real estate market transmit through the banking system

Scaling lending quickly – the interbank market

To meet reserve requirements banks need either liquid assets or to obtain reserves; but banks essentially have a choice in terms of borrowing from the central bank or acquiring reserves in the money markets. This is known as 'borrowing short to lend long'. The business model works because banks can borrow at a lower rate than they lend: the difference is the net interest margin.

The interbank market is the foundation of banks' ability to scale up lending quickly, especially during a Land Boom. There is fierce competition to extend mortgages, because the market attracts the attention of new lenders eager for a share of the profits. The interbank market is happy to supply growing banks with short-term loans to scale up their operations because they appear increasingly healthy. This is because the value of collateral against which most of their lending is secured is rising. Furthermore, lending is profitable, and banks' profits are high.

But underneath it all, the banking system becomes increasingly vulnerable to a crisis of confidence. As we will see later in the cycle, a boom requires an *increasing* flow of capital to keep it functioning. When this slows, the system is on the brink. Market participants eventually wake up to what has been going on. The interbank market seizes up.[23] As property prices come down – as they must eventually, because they have gone over the top – some debts will become bad. Problems in one area spread quickly throughout the system because no one knows how widespread these problem loans are. This causes all lending to cease and creates a broader crisis in the real economy – which is only arrested when the government steps in.

Innovations and new providers of finance, and the competition for real estate lending

Every cycle sees the introduction of new technologies and techniques that make banking more efficient. In the 1920s it was the widespread adoption of telephones, typewriters, calculating machines, Dictaphones and the rest that made operations vastly more speedy. The international banking system was enhanced by the development of the SWIFT payments system from the 1970s onwards. In the 2000s, it was automated credit assessment on the back of the novel internet technology.[24] These innovations make money cheaper to create.

Further, new banks are established and tend to have a lower cost base (smaller staff, leaner operations and a technological edge). They aggressively take real estate business from incumbent banks. Their presence is particularly prominent during an overheated property market. Competition may also come from 'shadow banks', i.e., from entities that are not commercial banking houses. These do not create money *per se* but channel money into real estate. Because they are not banks, they are not subject to the same regulations. As they lead to increased competition within the marketplace, they push incumbents to loosen standards so that they can continue to find profitable lending opportunities. Banks also use their considerable influence over the political system to have regulations changed. They need to increase earnings to keep their shareholders happy; they pay their staff large bonuses for bringing in new business. This causes the locus of lending activity to move outwards to peripheral areas as the cycle progresses. During a boom, this inevitably leads to more real estate lending than is prudent as banks maximise their loan books to the limit of regulations (and, if they can get away with it, even beyond that).

Less credit for productive businesses and rising interest rates

As most lending goes to real estate, the amount of credit available to productive business goes down. Despite the high volume of lending activity, the financial system becomes less liquid because real estate lending has longer payback periods.

Over time, this pushes up the rate of interest at which banks lend. Towards the end of the boom, businesses are squeezed in two ways: from rising rents and the rising cost of loan interest. This reduces investment in the economy and has a direct effect on large sectors, notably the construction industry where the largest input costs are the rate of interest and the price of land. As construction slows, this reduces employment and demand, which leads to a crisis.

When the crisis occurs bank balance sheets are clogged from all of the property loans, but they are incapable of offloading them without realising major losses that would make them insolvent. As my family found out in 2009, they will address this by calling in loans from small businesses, leading to a wave of business failures and unemployment. The process of freeing up bank balance sheets takes years and occupies much of the Start and Expansion stages of the cycle. But eventually it happens and, once returned to financial health, the credit creation process can begin all over again. It has ever been thus.

———— ·-■-· ————

Banks propagate a real estate boom, an inevitable consequence of the diversion of their money creation power into property lending and chasing excess profits. Regulations do not adequately limit how much banks can lend before the economy becomes dangerously overleveraged and vulnerable to a crisis.

We will see that play out in due course. In the meantime, the economy recovers quickly from the short and relatively mild mid-cycle Recession because the property market and the banking system are resilient. In fact, it is their very resilience at this point that encourages lending to a greater degree in subsequent stages of the cycle.

Before we return to our cycle journey, we need to consider a second main actor in the story of money. Banks are permitted to create money under licence, which is granted to them by the state. As we shall now see, the state is the ultimate manufacturer of money in an economy.

BANKS EXPLOIT THE LAW OF ECONOMIC RENT; OWN ONE

Key lessons

Money is always manufactured – and is drawn into real estate speculation

Banks are exceedingly efficient at exploiting the economic rent, particularly the rent of land. It is a good strategy to own one in your stock portfolio, particularly in the second half of the cycle when it is earning high profits from lending activities.

The financial system is highly interconnected, and problems can spread like wildfire

This is particularly important to remember at the end of the cycle. Somewhere, bank-created money will be going in large quantities into something speculative, that increases the leverage within the system and makes it liable to collapse. You may not always know where that is, but it will be happening.

Borrowing to invest is a sound strategy – if done properly

Borrowing money to invest in real assets supported by robust earnings is a strong strategy, if it is done at the right time in the cycle. Borrowing money simply to earn a speculative capital gain is rarely a good long-term strategy, and it is extremely hazardous to your financial health if carried out in the run-up to the climax of the cycle (which is when it will be easiest to carry out).

CHAPTER 9

THE MAGIC OF MONEY, PART 2

Interviewer: Is that tax money that the Fed is spending?

Dr Ben Bernanke: It's not tax money. We simply use the computer to mark up the size of the account.

Ben Bernanke, chairman of the Federal Reserve, *60 Minutes*, 2009

IN 1271 A young Venetian began what would become one of the most famous journeys in history. Together with his father and uncle, he journeyed through the fabled Orient. After four years of travel, they ended up at the court of the Great Khan, the ruler of the vast Mongol Empire.

A talented young man, the Venetian was adept at learning languages and a keen observer of local custom. He soon found employment as the Khan's official envoy and later became his trusted counsellor and administrator.

The young man did not return to his native land for 24 years, and his eventual homecoming was troubled. Conflict broke out between Venice and neighbouring Genoa, as was common among Italian city states in those days, and he was taken prisoner during a skirmish in the Mediterranean. But personal problems were to become posterity's profit. In jail the Venetian encountered another prisoner of war. During the long hours there, they discussed his eastern adventures. His companion, a writer of some renown, committed them to paper and upon release published a set of travel writings called *Il Milione* or, as we know them today, *The Travels of Marco Polo*.

The author, Rustichello da Pisa, otherwise known for his medieval romances, embellished many of Marco Polo's stories in order to thrill an audience eager for tales of the exotic east. In the burgeoning east-west trade of the era, such stories accompanied the luxury wares brought to Italy by merchants, justifying their high prices.

Yet the most fantastical tale of all those contained in the travel diaries was in fact completely true. Set in the city of Khanbalu, the predecessor of modern Beijing, Marco Polo observed the following curious piece of magic:

> In this city of Khanbalu is the mint of the Grand Khan, who may truly be said to possess the secrets of the alchemists, as he has the art of producing money by the following process. He causes the bark to be stripped from those mulberry-trees the leaves of which are used for feeding silk-worms, and takes from it that thin inner rind which lies between the coarser bark and the wood of the tree. This... is made into paper... when ready for use, he has it cut into pieces of money of different sizes, nearly square, but somewhat longer than they are wide. Of these, the smallest pass for a *dernier tournois*; the next size for a Venetian silver groat; others for one, two, three, and as far as ten *besants* of gold. The coinage of this paper money is authenticated with as much form and ceremony as if it were actually of pure gold or silver; for to each note a number of officers, specially appointed, not only subscribe their names, but affix their signets also; and when this has been regularly done by the whole of them, the principal officer, deputed by His Majesty, having dipped into vermillion the royal seal committed to his custody, stamps with it the piece of paper, so that the form of the seal tinged with the vermilion remains impressed upon it, by which it receives full authenticity as current money, and the act of counterfeiting it is punished as a capital offence. When thus coined in large quantities, this paper currency is circulated in every part of the Grand Khan's dominions; nor dares any person, at the peril of his life, refuse to accept it in payment. All his subjects receive it without hesitation, because, wherever their business may call them, they can dispose of it again in the purchase of merchandise they may have occasion for; such as pearls, jewels, gold, or silver. With it, in short, every article may be procured.[1]

Marco Polo was describing a monetary alchemy quite unknown to Europeans: the public issue of paper money, created from virtually nothing. The currency was not backed by gold or other metal, as some earlier societies had practised, including those making up the Mongol Empire. This currency, the *jiaochao*, was issued by the Great Khan and by him alone, guaranteed only by his authority and, by edict, to be used to settle payments between private parties wherever his rule extended.[2]

What Polo had discovered about money creation in medieval China applies equally to our system today. The government furnishes the economy with the money that private parties need for exchange, anywhere its authority is recognised. Recall from Chapter 8 that all production and exchange is based on credit, and in all but the simplest of economies there needs to be some generally accepted way of reflecting and settling the claims that private parties have on each other.

The most efficient solution, as the Great Khan discovered, comes about where the public authority, tasked with establishing and enforcing the laws of society, issues the money needed to facilitate such transactions. As with the role of banks, there is also much confusion about the state's role in money creation in the modern economy. The state licences banks and permits them to create money. But the state has an even more fundamental role: it designates what counts as money and manufactures it. Having clarity on this important feature of the economy is also key to understanding the rhythm of the cycle. This chapter explains how this process works and provides a simple framework to link it back to the cycle.

But how this confusion comes about in the first place is the subject of the next section.

Modern confusion: the government is not a household

After the 2010 election, the outgoing secretary to the UK's Treasury left the following pithy note to his successor, highlighting the parlous state of public finances in the aftermath of the financial crisis:

> Dear Chief Secretary, I'm afraid there is no money. Kind regards and good luck.
>
> Liam Byrne

The recession had slashed tax receipts by over £40bn at a time when welfare payments were skyrocketing. This led to a large deficit which meant, in Byrne's view, that the government had run out of money.[3] Similar claims were being made in the United States and across the European Union at the time.

A statement from Margaret Thatcher some years before clearly articulated the cause of the problem that the British government was now facing:

> The state has no source of money, other than the money people earn themselves. If the state wishes to spend more it can only do so

by borrowing your savings, or by taxing you more. And it's no good thinking that someone else will pay. That someone else is you.[4]

So deeply held was this belief that the incoming government set about administering large cuts to public expenditure while the country was in recession. The hope was that such cuts would restore public finances and put the economy on a sounder footing by bringing down the level of government debt.

Words that are used today about public spending reflect this belief: governments collect 'taxpayers' money'. If they spend more than they tax they are running a 'deficit' or, in the unlikely event they collect more, it is a 'surplus'. Government finance ministries that authorise spending are 'treasuries', implying that they store the nation's wealth until it is needed. If government runs up too large a deficit it is said to 'mortgage the country's future' because it will have to be paid back somewhere down the line by a future generation. (This is somewhat ironic given that a mortgage is a loan secured against property and it is the private, not the public, sector that has perfected the art.)

Beneath it all is the firm belief, an apparently self-evident one, that the government, like all of us, must earn money before it can spend; in this case, by gathering taxes. If it does not have the money, it must borrow and then pay it back at some future date. This is not sustainable, we think, so we have to keep a close eye on how much the government is borrowing. Public finance is an unbelievably arcane subject, but, like a good household, the government has finite resources and should live within them.

Just as the first major misunderstanding of money is that banks channel it between savers and borrowers (perhaps multiplying it as they do so), this is the second. It is one repeated endlessly by politicians and academics.

Money needs to be generally accepted

In Chapter 8, we saw that that money is in essence a social construct based on trust that supports the production cycle. The most essential component of money is the acceptance by all involved that it will settle a debt. This general acceptability is key. As the famous economist Hyman Minsky observed: "Anyone can create money... the problem lies in getting it accepted." Issuance of money by a trusted intermediary, such as a bank, is one way to achieve this acceptability. Yet, in modern society, who better than the sovereign – in the form of, or represented by, the government – to issue it?

The government (taking all national institutions together) has the power to legislate and to tax. It is tasked with providing public goods and services that create the marketplace where exchange takes place. And it has the power to require all parties to accept its money as payment.

To state it clearly: the government is not in any sense like a household. Charles I was right when he declared, moments before he was executed in 1649, that a subject, or ordinary citizen, is very different to a sovereign, at least in respect of money (though he was of course thinking much more broadly than this).

The privilege that the position of the sovereign accords the government is the power to determine what counts as money to settle the claims between private parties. If it so chooses it can issue its own tokens. This means that when the government spends its own tokens into the economy it issues them first. The administrative arrangements might vary from country to country, but typically the government will secure legislative approval to spend money on something, e.g., building roads. In most economies it will need to work with the private sector to ensure this happens.[5] When a party is due to receive this money, the government will instruct the central bank (its fiscal agent) to mark up the account of the recipient's bank with the appropriate amount of reserves. The latter will credit the recipient's account with the appropriate amount of money. This money is then available to be spent within the economy. As with a bank loan, the money is created from nothing.

Everyone is liable to pay taxes. At some point businesses and households will need to make a payment back to the government. Where does that money come from? It is the government's own issued currency that is used to pay the tax.

If the money had not been created by the government, it would not be available to be paid back. Money is not the same thing as the credit used in production (see Chapter 8), which is the lifeblood of a capitalist economy. Money represents the trust that is fundamental to exchange. Someone must supply the money so that exchange can take place, whether it is by mutual agreement, by a trusted intermediary or imposed by law. In the modern economy, the government supplies the money.

You might wonder, after reading Chapter 8: what about bank-created money – aren't banks also issuing money? But bank money is branded with the insignia of the state. Banks can only create money under licence. While it closely resembles state-issued money, it is not quite the same thing. All private money, created by banks, is paid back to them. If anything more than that is flowing back to the government, it has to have come from elsewhere. That elsewhere is the government. Any money paid in tax is ultimately state money – and this has first been supplied by the government.

Tax money that is 'returned' to the government is then effectively deleted. When money needs to be spent it is again created. Governments might maintain a fund that appears to have been drawn upon to spend, but this is simply to facilitate the tracking of receipts against expenditures.[6] It is an accounting tool rather than a financial arrangement. There is no functional relationship between what the government receives and what it spends.[7]

The issue of state money and the creation of bank money is depicted in Figure 15.

Figure 15: State money and bank money

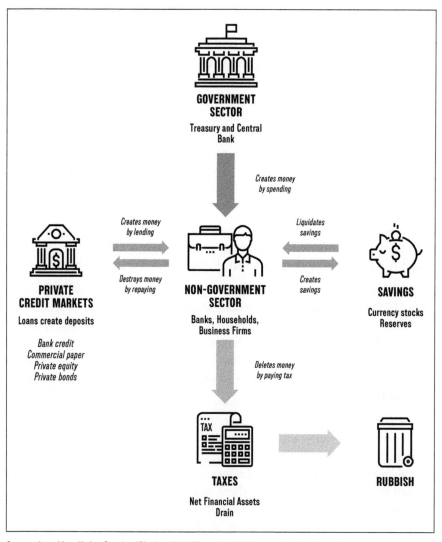

Source: adapted from 'Deficit Spending 101 – Part 3' by WIlliam Mitchell (billmitchell.org/blog/?p=381).

The flow of money from the sovereign into the economy is a vertical one. This is depicted with the downward arrows. This is different from a horizontal flow of money that takes place in private credit markets (essentially, banks) and the non-government, or private, sector. Horizontal money is created by banks and destroyed when borrowers repay loans. Over the long term, this does not add to the total amount of money in an economy because whatever is created by borrowing is destroyed by repayment.

On the other hand, vertical money issued by the currency sovereign remains in the economy until it is drawn out by taxes, and then it is effectively thrown away. As an economy grows, it needs more money to facilitate transactions. This growing need for money is met by the sovereign.

The ability to manufacture national currency and designate the unit of account in this way is known as 'monetary sovereignty'. It applies in varying degrees to the USA, UK, Japan, Canada and others. It does not, however, apply to the countries of the eurozone. In adopting the euro, these nations surrendered their monetary sovereignty to a higher power – the EU institutions, including the European Central Bank. This is why arguments about European bailouts became so vicious: member countries lacked a key tool to tackle the crisis when bank money supply contracted sharply. Monetary sovereignty also does not apply to countries operating a currency peg against another country, where they fix the exchange rate. A number of emerging countries are pegged to the dollar, for example, and are not monetary sovereigns. We will take up the issue of international trade shortly.

Liam Byrne could not have been more wrong. The British government had not run out of money. It just needed to create some more and spend. Doing so would have led the UK to a rather more robust recovery from the financial crisis, and perhaps the country would have avoided the worst of the political and social turbulence of the 2010s. It was no different in the United States. While the Obama administration stimulus in 2009 had a major bearing on the global recovery out of the prior economic cycle lows, politics took over the US budget from 2011, and cuts to public expenditure meant that it, too, experienced slow growth for a number of years. In Europe, the EU was not able to agree on how to recover from the crisis and condemned its southern periphery to many years of biting recession, which periodically threatened to erupt into a rather extreme form of governance.[8] Greater public spending would have created new money and boosted growth at a time when economies were flagging, people were out of jobs and businesses were struggling.

This is not to say that monetary sovereigns can supply money without limit. There are some very real constraints which we will come on to shortly. It is simply that none of these considerations are based upon a lack of funding – that is, a lack of money.

The erroneous thinking about public finance – that tax is required for governments to spend – is parallel to the error that many make about private bank finance – that deposits are needed for banks to lend. Government spending leads to tax just as bank loans lead to deposits.

Before examining a simple framework on how to think about public spending and its relationship to the cycle, we need to complete our description of public finances and consider why, if the government does not need to borrow or tax before spending, this rigmarole takes place at all.

The purpose of taxation and public borrowing in the modern economy

Though taxation and borrowing do not fund the government, they have specific functions.

Taxation is a tool of public policy. There are four main reasons why a government requires taxation.[9]

1. In relation to provisioning, rather than commanding production directly (as in a command-and-control economy), the government uses the private sector to provide what it needs.[10] By taxing in its own currency, the government creates the demand for that currency, which means it can be issued to get what it needs through the private sector. It creates its own purchasing power through the ability to require people to accept its currency as payment. Thus, there is a symbiotic relationship between the state and markets. They are co-dependent, with the demand from the state supporting the creation of private markets to serve it (and private parties).

2. Managing inflation: while governments are not financially constrained, they are constrained by the productive limits of the economy. Should it create too much money, beyond the capacity of the economy to absorb that money by increasing production and creating real assets, this will lead to inflation. Taxation is then a means to reduce the money supply by drawing money back out again.

3. Addressing the distribution of wealth across different groups in society, especially people at different income levels. As we saw from Chapter 5, there is a way to do this that solves the problem of unfair distribution of wealth – but it is not one that most countries deploy, or even consider.

4. Addressing harmful behaviours such as environmental pollution by imposing a financial penalty that reflects the harm that such activities create. Taxation represents this financial penalty.

Borrowing, on the other hand, is conducted for the following reasons.

1. Public spending without creating new money: government spending creates money, specifically when the banks of beneficiaries are marked up with an equivalent amount of reserves. This introduces new spending power into the economy. But perhaps this is not desirable. The creation of bank reserves leads to lower interest rates and may be below what the central bank considers good for the economy. We saw in Chapter 8 that interest rates are one tool that the central bank uses to adjust the amount of lending banks do (albeit it is an imperfect one). The bond market supports government spending without altering the quantity of bank reserves in the banking system. In this case, money parked in bank accounts will end up in the bond market instead, a type of asset swap.[11] The government can still spend, but the quantity of money within the economy has remained the same.

2. A saving vehicle for the private sector: bonds are effectively a vehicle for the private sector to park the money that the government has created in the first place. Money can be deposited in bank accounts, or it can be parked in investment vehicles such as government bonds. Seen like this, the government's deficit is a measure of the level of private sector savings (broadly defined to include investments).[12]

Many claim that greater public spending risks interest rates going up and creating 'unaffordable' debt. The risk is in fact the other way around. If too much government money is created, this will push interest rates down across the economy and may induce people to take on more debt than they ought to.

Commentators are preoccupied with public debt-to-GDP ratios, but in most cases this is not the right thing to focus on. As we saw in Chapter 8, it is private debt to GDP that is key. One wonders why more attention is not paid to that measure. It is almost as if it is deliberate: the greater the noise about public debt, the less focus there is on private debt and what it is mainly being used for: speculating in property and land.

This may sound controversial, but this is simply a description of how things work after the end of the Bretton Woods system in 1971 – at least for countries that operate under a floating-rate exchange system. It seems that most people still have not woken up to the new reality, even half a century later. But no less a figure than Alan Greenspan addressed this very point in a congressional hearing in 2005, when asked by Congressman Paul Ryan whether social security faced a funding crisis:

> I wouldn't say that the pay-as-you-go benefits are insecure in the sense that there is nothing to prevent the federal government from creating as much money as it wants and paying it to somebody.

In other words, the chairman of the Federal Reserve was saying that the government had no funding constraint.

I have suggested that there are some very important considerations that could cause a government to tax more or spend less. To understand what these are, let us begin with the important work carried out at Cambridge University in the 1970s, in order to develop a simple framework for how such issues should be viewed.

A simple framework to understand government money creation

The Economics Policy Group at Cambridge University began conducting an interesting programme of work in the 1970s. The programme focused on modelling the economy by tracing the flow of money between its different sectors. It was led by Wynne Godley, who would later be appointed as one of UK Chancellor Norman Lamont's 'Seven Wise Men', as his council of economic advisers became known.[13]

Godley's contribution was to model the economy in such a way that no transaction would remain unaccounted for.[14] He started from the premise that every outflow of money had an equal inflow somewhere else. Spending by one person was exactly matched by the earning of another. In some ways, this was the monetary equivalent of Newton's third law of motion: to every action there is an equal and opposite reaction. The flow models Godley created were elaborate, but essentially divided the economy into three mutually exclusive sectors:

1. a private domestic sector, consisting of households and businesses,

2. an external sector, through which a country would export and import goods and services to and from the rest of the world,

3. a government sector, where the state would spend money on public goods and services and tax money back out of the economy.

The Cambridge group – and succeeding analysts – essentially sought to understand the overall income to the economy as a function of what was going on in each sector, bearing in mind that every expenditure in one part of the economy had a matching income in another.

Using a set of simple accounting equations, the group was able to demonstrate that the total income generated by an economy – the gross national product – was the sum of the net contributions of the private domestic, external and government sectors. These equations were not part of some elaborate economic model that tried to explain what was going on; they were simply describing the flow of income. However, with this clarity, the implications are quite profound.

The equation suggests that the income to the private sector is positive when the contributions from the government sector or the external sector are, between them, positive. This means that for the private sector net income (or flow/balance) to be positive you need the trade balance to be positive or the government sector to be positive.

When we talk about the government sector being 'positive' this is when it is positively contributing spending to the economy (which other entities are taking as income). This means that the government is spending more than it taxes. In other words, government surpluses are not necessarily a good thing if you want the private sector to be growing and earning more money than before. This is a key consideration, because logically not every country can run a trade surplus. Every surplus is matched by a deficit elsewhere.

So what does a negative balance for the private sector mean?

If the private sector balance is negative, one of two things must happen. One is that the private sector spends less, which means that it will make a negative contribution to growth and will be in recession, which by definition is a contraction in the amount of money being earned or spent in the economy.

The other thing that can happen is that the private sector maintains the same level of expenditure and income but only by using up its savings (earned from previous times when it had a positive balance) or by borrowing more (which means it will have to use up future savings to pay off the debt). In other words, the net financial assets of the private sector go down.

So the fiscal surplus, at the wrong time, will lead directly to a private sector recession, or the private sector liquidating its savings or increasing its indebtedness.

The nature of the considerations that a country faces is set out in Table 5.

The main consideration under this framework is that the trade balance or fiscal deficit is a key determinant of the growth of the private sector. This is different to the rather facile public discussion about the size of deficits and the dangers inherent in government borrowing. As investors, we want the private sector to be acquiring net financial assets. This means we (should) want to see robust government spending, low taxation and/or a strong trade balance.

Table 5: The effect on private sector income of deficits and surpluses

		Government sector	
		Positive – budget deficit (government spends more than it taxes)	Negative – budget surplus (government taxes more than it spends)
External sector	Positive – trade surplus (exports are greater than imports)	Private sector growth/increases financial assets	Mixed: If government surplus is greater than trade balance, private sector recession/decreases financial assets If government surplus is less than trade balance, private sector growth/increases financial assets
	Negative – trade deficit (imports are greater than exports)	Mixed: If government deficit is greater than trade deficit, private sector growth/increases financial assets If government deficit is smaller than trade deficit, private sector recession/decreases financial assets	Private sector recession/decreases financial assets

We have seen this play out already. Think back to Chapter 1. The 'very good years' in the stock market take place when stock prices have fallen significantly, *and governments are providing liquidity into the system* – in other words, increasing the money supply. If you can identify these points in the cycle, there is an opportunity for large returns. This is also a reason why the Recession at the mid-cycle is brief; the government engages in stimulus at a time when the banking system is continuing to lend.

The proper limits of money creation

None of this is to say that the government can spend money without limit, just as banks cannot go on creating money indefinitely. The requirement to subject sovereigns to parliamentary authority and democratic oversight has been, in many countries, one of the people's hardest-fought victories. In addition, governments can spend on useless items and policies. This can do more harm than good, by distorting the operation of markets, favouring one set of groups over another, and creating a culture of dependency on government largesse rather than of private enterprise. The main considerations on when to stem the flow of public spending relate to inflation and international trade; and, most importantly, their effects on the land market.

1. Managing inflation

The constraint on a sovereign lies in the real economy and its full productive capacity. The amount of money created needs to match what is needed for an economy when operating at full capacity. Any more than this and there is inflation; less than this, and there will be idle factors of production (which means that people are involuntarily unemployed, and capital gets wasted).

Note also that when a national government spends to advance the public purpose on healthcare, education and infrastructure and the like, it is adding to an economy's productive base. This will not have any inflationary impact whatsoever. In fact, the effect is likely to be the opposite if it lowers the cost of living and doing business.

Inflation targeting by governments as a means of managing the economy is not a bad thing – but it has to be done through measures that also include (un)employment. Furthermore, the tools to be used to manage the economy through a business cycle should be primarily fiscal rather than monetary (i.e., public spending, rather than managing how much people borrow by adjusting interest rates).

One consideration that has appeared in recent years is the provision of a universal basic income to people on the basis that boosting spending will bring an economy nearer to full capacity. However, if done when there is little slack in the economy this leads to inflation.[15]

Globalisation and international trade

Public spending also has an effect on an economy's external trade position. Government deficits increase the supply of currency, which means it will typically depreciate against trading partner currencies. This will increase opportunities for export – the costs of domestic manufactured goods are cheaper abroad – but will make imports more expensive. The cost of what a country has to import, e.g., energy and food, will affect inflation measures and the standard of living, particularly for less advanced countries which are reliant on overseas supply of primary goods. The government would need to adjust its spending to take this into consideration.

The missing factor: land

The key consideration – missed by almost everyone – is what happens within the land market when the government spends money. What they fail to understand is that the primary reason for involuntary unemployment in an economy is that land is used unproductively, or held out of use.[16]

When the government runs deficits, they are often justified on the basis of investing in infrastructure. As we know from the example of the Jubilee Line, this will serve to push up land rents and therefore property prices (unless, of course, the increase is subject to higher land taxes).[17] The more this is done, the higher land prices will go. This will induce the distortionary speculative behaviour that accompanies the cycle.

Like bank credit, government money creation can be unsound. In these cases, government spending will not necessarily bring the economy to full capacity but will eventually result in inflation. Ultimately, higher rents squeeze out productive private enterprise. Under our system of land monopoly, however, governments (like private banks) are responsible for amplifying the boom.

———————— -·-■-·- ————————

In response to the mid-cycle Recession, governments are invariably in stimulus mode and enact large programmes of infrastructure spending. This swiftly returns the economy to growth and concludes the second Act of our drama.

Now that banks and government are both pumping newly minted money into the economy – a feature of the second half of every cycle – we are ready for Act III. Let us go back some 180 years to the United Kingdom of the 1840s and witness the next stage of the cycle: the Land Boom.

GOVERNMENTS CREATE MONEY; FOLLOW WHERE THEY INVEST

Key lessons

1. Governments are part of the cycle, not above it

Governments might give the impression that they sit above the economy and therefore manage it and the business cycle. This is not the case. Their survival depends on delivering growth and prosperity to the population, or at least the illusion of it. They act in ways that tend to push asset prices up and react strongly when prices are in danger of falling. When they invest in infrastructure, especially in good-quality projects, this will increase land prices and potentially start a boom. This leads to positive stories, stronger tax receipts and better poll ratings. As a result, more of this behaviour will follow. Invest in locations where this is taking place.

2. Governments create as much money as they can get away with

The power to create money is a key tool of public policy. Fashions will change in terms of how much money a government should be spending but make no mistake: they will spend as much as they can get away with. On the whole, this is bullish for growth and your investments.

3. Governments in stimulus mode push economic growth upwards (and vice versa)

We have seen how strong the reaction of markets is at the Start of the cycle when the government is in stimulus mode; this is because the government is pumping money into the economy to fill the gap left by the banking system after the prior crisis. Markets had fallen at the end of the last cycle, pricing in the lack of money and recessionary conditions; at the Start of the new one they adjust upwards as new money enters the economy. This is an excellent time to be an investor.[18] Similarly, when government reins back spending, particularly at the Summit of the cycle, this may precipitate the slowdown and make the system vulnerable to a crisis. As we have seen, banks may be slowing the pace of lending at the same time, putting further pressure on the money supply. This is the time for investors to be cautious.

ACT III
BOOM

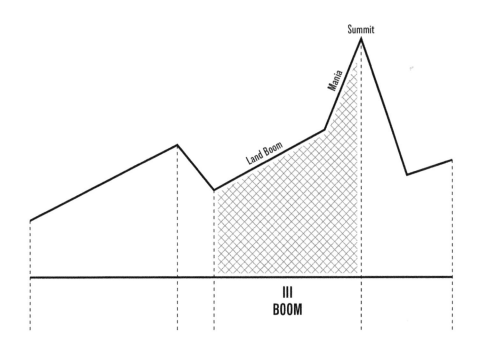

Summit

Mania

Land Boom

III
BOOM

In this Act, the second, larger, expansion takes place as economic growth is driven by a booming land and property market. It lasts on average six to seven years.

Chapter 10: The Land Boom sees higher growth and booming stock and property markets, driven by easy credit conditions. You should take advantage of the good times.

Chapter 11: The Long Cycle of Prosperity and War covers a longer-term commodity cycle connected to the property boom and to social and geopolitical tensions. Buy natural resources, infrastructure and some technology stocks.

Chapter 12: The Mania covers the final two years of the expansion, a period of rampant speculation when the cycle is pushed into overdrive. Do not follow the herd. It is time to rein back.

Chapter 13: The Great Delusion explains how financial theory misses the cycle and gets things wrong, particularly during the boom. This is how your financial adviser might (inadvertently) lead you astray.

Chapter 14: The Summit. The economy is booming and there is extreme emotion, but the warning signs are there for those who know what to look for. This is the time to exit and prepare for the crisis to come.

CHAPTER 10

THE LAND BOOM

The country is an asylum of railway lunatics.

William Wordsworth

One small journey, one giant boom

THE BIGGEST BOOM in history began with a short rail journey.

For the first time in her life, Queen Victoria boarded a train. It was just before noon on 13 June 1842 at Slough railway station, to the west of London. The train had a new steam engine, *Phlegethon* (named after the fiery river of the ancient Greek underworld), and seven carriages – including one bedecked with the royal insignia. The Queen arrived safely at her destination, Paddington station, 25 minutes later.

It was an unspectacular event, but it captured the public imagination about the new railway technology. The Queen said she was quite charmed by her new experience.[1] So were private investors, who began to pour capital into railway ventures. This was quite different to the early days. The opening of the first link – between Liverpool and Manchester – had been inauspicious: the MP for Liverpool had been accidentally killed by a moving steam engine in front of the prime minister.[2] Steam engines had been treated with some hostility. It was feared their fumes would pollute the countryside and affect rural livestock; and rural "landowners were also concerned that locomotives would shatter the tranquillity of their estates and injure land values."[3] How their views would change. For in the cycles of the middle decades of the 19th century, the land booms and busts, dominated by some of the most celebrated capitalists in history – Vanderbilt, Morgan, Cooke, Hudson, Strousberg – occurred on a scale never seen before, and perhaps since. The cause was the railroad.

Recovery from the mid-cycle recession

The British economy was in recession in 1839, the midpoint of that cycle. To engineer a recovery, the government increased spending to counter the effects of a drop in private consumption and reduced the cost of money. The policy worked, and the recession ended the following year. The stock market anticipated a return to growth and started gaining from late 1841, as company earnings began to recover.[4]

The improved economic conditions, and excitement generated by the Queen's journey, led to a new-found interest in railway investment. There had been a mini boom in the late 1830s, but this time it was on a much greater scale. To launch a new line, investors were required to provide just 5–10% capital up front while the venture sought the necessary parliamentary approval (at the risk that it might not be granted).[5] Once secured, the remainder would be called on demand to finance the building of the railway. The investors' returns would be paid out of the fares from operating a rail monopoly and associated property development. The low threshold for an initial investment also enabled a much broader investor participation.

New regulations inadvertently played their part in whetting investor appetite. Up to this point, routes had been haphazard, reflecting the whims of their sponsor and, in some cases, would duplicate that of a rival scheme, a situation that was hardly favourable to generating strong investment returns. The government wanted to build a more efficient network, and the 1844 Railway Act required proposals to be reviewed by a railway board. Services were required to carry at least one train per day at a cost of one penny per passenger mile. Lower fares increased passenger numbers and revenue, and the creation of a sensible network buttressed the monopoly position of incumbent lines. To prevent market abuse, the government retained the option to nationalise companies returning more than 10% in dividends to investors, in effect capping their profits. But this signalled that a 10% (monopoly-based) return was possible at a time when returns on alternative investments were much lower.[6] As ever, the stock market was ahead of events; the prices of the 20 largest railways stocks appreciated 20% in the second half of 1843, before the change in policy.

Easy credit

Aiding this boom were easy credit conditions, to which another government regulation also contributed. The 1844 Bank Charter Act removed the right of banks to issue their own notes, passing the function to the Bank of England, which, in order to keep inflation under control, was to limit the amount of money created by maintaining a ratio with gold reserves. This meant the Bank was required to supply money at commercial rates and consequently reduced its rate of interest from 4% to 2.5%. At a time when the economy was buoyant and investors bullish, this inadvertently added an additional flow of cheap money into the market and set off a spectacular boom.

Parliament was deluged with applications to build railway lines over the next couple of years, and by 1845 there were 1,238 separate schemes seeking capital. Company directors persuaded contacts in the railway press to write positive news stories about a new scheme's prospects to draw in investor interest. There were 16 separate railway periodicals which reported frequently on the upward movement of railway share prices, and acted as a cheerleader for the industry, publicly rebuking any sober-minded commentators who warned against the speculative frenzy that was starting to take hold.[7] This brought a cohort of new investors into the stock market. For the first time, shares in companies were denominated at low prices, as low as £1 (the average annual wage of an unskilled labourer was around £50). As only 5% of the investment was required up front, this drew in thousands of small investors. The share prices of railway stocks accelerated sharply, increasing by 100% on average over three years (see Figure 16). The price of some individual issues appreciated as much as ten times in just ten months.[8]

Figure 16: The market index for railway stocks, United Kingdom, 1843-1850

Source: Campbell, G. and Turner, J.D, '"*The Greatest Bubble in History*": Stock Prices during the British Railway Mania', *MPRA*, 2010 (available online: mpra.ub.uni-muenchen.de/21820/1/MPRA_paper_21820.pdf).

Land values boom

While the 'Railway Mania' can be clearly seen in the stock market, beneath it was the land market. After all, the bulk of the capital investment required to build a line went towards acquiring land, constructing stations, depots and turnpikes, and building out town centres: in other words, into real estate development.

The value of land along the rail route increased immediately upon parliamentary authorisation, and many MPs had a financial interest in the routes; as it was by and large the land of the aristocracy and gentry that was being purchased for such schemes. The 1845 Land Clauses Consolidation Act set out powers to acquire land, but ensured that said landowners were properly compensated by allowing them to demand an extra 10% *solatium*, or relief, on account of any distress felt at having to sell their land at market value (a value that, it should be noted, was greatly enhanced by the prospect of the railway being built).[9]

In the towns and cities now opened up by these railroads, land speculators rushed in and acquired all of the best sites prior to parliamentary authorisation. Thus most of the capital subscription being paid by investors went straight into the pockets of the landowners, in return for the future possibility of capturing the monopoly profits from revenue granted by a public licence. This was one rental flow being used to purchase another.

The seeds of the subsequent bust are always sown during the boom. In the desire to launch new schemes, the Railways Board found its recommendations were being ignored, even if companies were proposing duplicative routes. This rather undermined the idea of monopoly profits for investors, but in the good times these problems were overlooked. Parliamentarians themselves were often involved in some of these schemes and sold their votes in return for shares in the ventures they were authorising.

Good times and fraudulent schemes

Many of these schemes were fraudulent. One tactic was to introduce a flood of adverts into the papers outlining a new scheme and listing all of the company trustees, or committeemen, who were behind the proposal: these were supposedly upstanding members of their community, but in many cases they were anything but (*The Times* called them "the most notorious scamps"). They were incentivised to push share subscriptions and retained an allocation of shares for doing so (creating a shortage of available shares and bolstering the price even further). Often schemes were never intended to be built or were unlikely to be profitable enough to pay out the level of dividends anticipated at the outset.

During the good times, in the mad rush to make money, no one paid much heed to the possibility of fraud. The gains in the price of land were prodigious wherever the railways went in.[10] *The Economist* called it the greatest bubble in history.[11] So significant were the changes wrought by this new technology – and the possibility of land speculation – that they drove not one but two full cycles in the United Kingdom, Germany and France, and three in the United States.

The Land Boom analysed

The change in narrative at the end of the prior Recession stage sets the scene for the Land Boom. It begins when general conditions are difficult and, therefore, the subsequent boom is hard to foresee. As we have seen, the recovery out of the mid-cycle Recession is often unexpectedly quick, with measures to stimulate the economy proving to be effective (given that at this stage of the cycle, none of the problems relate to the land market).

The deeper the problems of the mid-cycle, the more effectively they erase the memory of the prior crisis. The feeling that we are moving into a new era is then really enhanced at the beginning of the Land Boom. This is due to a displacement event.

1. New conditions displace the old

The Land Boom often begins with a displacement event. This event does not cause the subsequent boom but is sufficiently large to change everyone's outlook.[12] The Queen's first train ride in 1842 built excitement in the new technology, on top of the easy money conditions of the early 1840s. The event may include a change in policy, such as a reduction in interest rates (this happens in most cycles), financial deregulation (e.g., 1980s Japan), large tax cuts (e.g., US, 2001), the ending of a war (1815 or 1921) or a pandemic and international crisis (1921 or 2021).[13]

2. The boom centres on a new technology

The Start of each 18-year cycle begins with use of a new technology to take the economy forward. While this brings the economy into a new cycle and drives the first half, it is in the Land Boom of the second half that the economy-wide effects become much more visible. Railways were built in the 1830s, but it was not until the 1840s that they reached a scale that enabled people to see their true impact: the building of new towns and areas, new leisure habits (e.g., weekend trips and tourism, coordinated timekeeping), new equipment and investment (e.g., rail carriages). Other examples: the canals in the 1820s, automobiles, telephones and electricity in the 1920s, personal computing in the 1980s and the internet in the 2000s (note that the 1990s may have seen the bubble in tech stocks, but it was not until the 2000s that the effect of the internet on the broader economy became apparent).

3. Infrastructure spending

Governments always support the Land Boom with a major increase in investment (either directly financing it or facilitating the private sector). The granting of licences to build railway schemes was one example. Other cycles saw roads built or adapted for automobiles (the 1920s); the interstate/motorway system and airports (the 1950s); fixed and mobile internet networks (the 2000s). Such investment increases the efficiency of the economy and boosts economic growth. Their effect is to extend the margin of production and push up land prices.[14]

4. The property boom spreads outwards to new areas

Increasing land values and infrastructure spending open up new places (new towns and unloved parts of cities). The story of the era creates new ideas for how money can be made. New businesses start. Seemingly authoritative forecasts of demand raise expectations. Businesses and people relocate. There is a shortage of commercial space. Higher property prices push people outwards in search of more affordable homes. As property and land prices rise with economic growth, this unlocks investment by inducing developers to build.[15] Property prices increase at a faster rate in outer regions than in central ones, reversing the pattern of the first half of the cycle. The Land Boom is broad-based. As the boom ripples out, construction and new lending for real estate go to more marginal developments; that is, into areas with smaller and less affluent populations.

As the economy is growing, investors focus more on commercial property, and in some cycles (such as the 1920s) this even leads the boom, especially in new areas.[16]

5. Easy credit

Following and fuelling the Land Boom are the banks. Having successfully survived the mid-cycle Recession, banks are ready to lend as the pace of economic activity picks up and building projects begin. Behind the scenes, they lobby for changes to regulations to enable greater credit creation. Politicians are happy to oblige because the banking systems appears to be in a sound position and because a profitable banking sector is good for the economy and generates large tax revenues. Besides, in this new era who really remembers the last crisis? With land prices rising and the economy growing they are able to lend more and do so more extensively. This increases their earnings. Bank lending also follows the boom outwards as central sites become mortgaged. New business comes from marginal sites and more marginal borrowers. More credit availability helps to push prices up even further.[17]

A sign that bank lending is pushing up house prices is when the ratio of private debt to GDP increases. In the 19th century, mortgage lending was not as significant as it is today, but nonetheless private debt was 50% of GDP by the mid-1840s. Rising private sector indebtedness is a feature of the Land Boom in every cycle.[18]

A period of increasing private debt also tends to mean that lending standards are loosening. During the Land Boom, things are roaring strongly for a time. The construction industry is a large part of any economy and is the one industry that needs a domestic base and so boosts employment and spending. In addition to this, other industries – especially those that are linked to the boom – are doing well. During the railroad era, these were steelmakers, builders of locomotives, train interiors, stations, depots and so on.

6. Government (corruption) fuels the boom

Whether it is well-intentioned regulations that have the opposite effect, or it is a blatant conflict of interest (or both), the authorities end up propagating the boom. Parliamentarians aided the 1840s railway boom by taking bribes in return for favourable votes. Nowadays, no government has any interest in slowing a booming economy, which is a vote winner. Indeed, politicians may themselves be significant beneficiaries of a Land Boom (witness British politicians fiddling with the parliamentary expenses system to take advantage of the booming London property market during the 2000s).[19]

7. The stock market boom

The stock market is a news discounting mechanism, anticipating future conditions. If the prevailing view – supported by seemingly authoritative forecasts of future demand – is of a continued growth in earnings, the stock market will quickly rise to meet this expectation. Investors' scepticism reduces as the boom continues. As markets reach and move into all-time highs and keep going, all investors are now in profit.

8. The global boom

During the boom times, surplus capital always goes in search of new opportunities. Many of the best ones are overseas, particularly in markets with a lot of untapped potential – in other words, emerging markets with a strong export base, young and educated populations and a rising middle class. British capital financed the booms in the United States during the 19th century, including the railway booms into the Summit of the cycle in 1854, 1872 and 1890, as well as the boom of the 1920s. Similarly, American capital helped to drive the booms in Latin America, East Asia and Europe in the post-Second World War period (though in the case of Europe, domestic banks played a very significant role too).

In the bullish conditions of the second half of the cycle, the US dollar typically depreciates against other currencies, further stimulating the global boom (see Figure 17).[20]

Figure 17: Change in the Dollar index in the Land Boom to Summit stages (percentage)

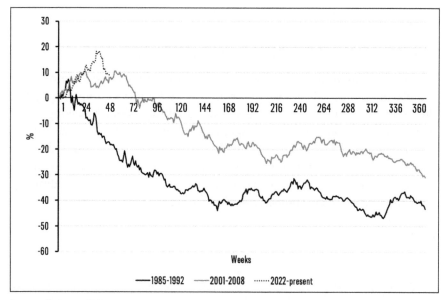

Source: author's own calculations.

9. Investor euphoria

The Land Boom is stoked by media interest because newspapers, magazines and platforms rely on advertising revenue. The railway boom of the 1840s was accompanied by a surge in interest in railway periodicals detailing new schemes and inviting subscriptions. Most investors ignored any of the warnings that things might be getting out of hand. Part of the problem is that warnings appear for years without anything seemingly negative occurring; these Cassandras lack the element of timing, because they do not see the link to the land market or understand the rhythm of the boom/bust economy.

The excitement of the new era – that 'this time it is different' – eventually turns to euphoria. This generates an emotional need to invest, to be part of the good times. At the beginning of the Land Boom, price rises are driven by general improvements in the economy. Investors put their capital in on the expectation of solid returns. But at some point, this flips to pursuing not income but capital gains. Buying something to sell later at a higher price is effectively paying today for tomorrow's growth in current earnings. One sign of this, in the housing market, is the divergence of the price of houses relative to their rents, as Figure 18 indicates.

Figure 18: Average increase in house prices relative to rents (percentage) into the Summit stage

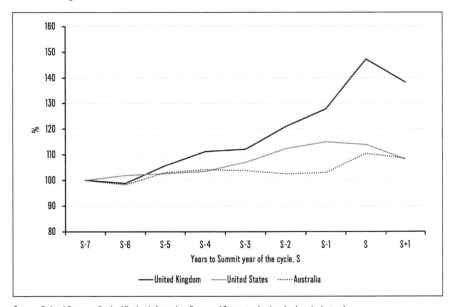

Source: Federal Reserve, Bank of England, Australian Bureau of Statistics (and author's calculations).

So the Land Boom goes on. Driven by new a growth industry, easy bank credit and positive investor sentiment, the economic expansion spreads outwards. In our era, this is taking place on a global scale.

As it does so, let us stop awhile in our cycle journey to take a look at the final feature – alongside bank credit and government investment – that determines how big the boom can get. To do so, we need to review a longer-term commodity cycle, one that takes place over a span of 55 to 60 years. It drives periods of both great technological innovation and disruption, at home and abroad. In the next chapter we examine the Long Cycle. To understand it, let us go back 100 years, to 1920s Russia, and learn of the man who discovered it – and why he was considered such a threat to the revolutionary regime of the day.

TAKE ADVANTAGE OF THE GOOD TIMES

Stage: the Land Boom

Approximate timing: years 9 to 12

Prevailing emotion: euphoria

Managing emotions

The confidence engendered by the feeling that this is a 'new era' builds over the course of the Land Boom. By its end, the prevailing emotion is one of euphoria. Asset prices are booming, business is strong, people are wealthy and they are spending. Now is the time to participate fully in the cycle. There will be many opportunities to generate strong investment returns.

Be mindful of your emotions. Recognise that there will be many tall tales of people getting rich quickly: these can have the effect of impairing your judgement. The many scams and cons, that prey on people's greed and fear of missing out, are particularly prevalent during the Land Boom (and Mania) stage of the cycle. Building wealth is a steady and patient exercise. Consult Part 16 of *The Handbook of Wealth Secrets* for rules to avoid getting swindled.

Managing investments

1. Continue to buy stocks

a. Having taking advantage of the likely 'very good year' in the stock market at the end of the Recession phase, build your stock portfolio. While tech stocks may lead the market out of the lows of the mid-cycle, they may underperform the broader market.[21]

b. Buy funds that are invested in emerging market stocks, especially those countries that are exporters, are in stimulus mode (from the mid-cycle Recession) and have comparatively low levels of tax and foreign debt.[22]

c. Buy funds that are invested in commodity-producing countries – they perform strongly as demand for raw materials increases during the construction boom.

d. Buy stocks in sectors that are most involved in the Land Boom. These include:

- Housebuilders: the Land Boom leads to a surge in building of new homes where people are moving to (see below).

- Commercial and residential Real Estate Investment Trusts (REITs): these funds provide dividends based on rental income from appreciating property assets.

- Banks: the creation of money against rising land prices boosts the earnings of banks (or financial institutions doing the bulk of the lending).

- Other stocks that benefit from rental income and licences (for example: internet, 5G, airports, intellectual property, network monopolies, franchises – see also Chapter 5 for a catalogue of sources of economic rent).

- Companies at the centre of the industry leading the Land Boom, as well as commodity, infrastructure and related stocks.[23]

2. Buy property in the locations where infrastructure is going in (and people and businesses are relocating to)

a. In the Land Boom, especially as it develops, the greatest activity may be in smaller (secondary and tertiary) cities or the outer areas of cities. Wherever you are looking to invest, ensure that the assumptions about future growth of the area and price appreciation projections are reasonable and robust. Remember that building becomes increasingly speculative over the course of the Land Boom.

b. Do careful due diligence on possible investments: ensure that there is sufficient margin of safety to withstand a downturn or rise in (for example, interest) costs. Do not buy property where the rental yield is lower than the rate of interest (no matter the prospects of possible future capital appreciation).

c. Residential property: as always, focus on what the main buyers in an area are looking for. Be wary about buying apartments, especially in new areas where there is a lot of real estate development planned or going on. These are likely to be the most over-supplied during a Land Boom when land prices are rising rapidly (apartments maximise the development on any given site and so are attractive to urban property developers).[24] This limits price growth for newer buildings (and owners of not-so-new stock will find themselves competing with newer stock if they wish to sell). If you do invest in apartments, make sure their features have some scarcity value, such as nice views or proximity to important local services.

d. Commercial property: invest in areas businesses are moving to.

e. Use leverage and have tenants pay off the debt; fix interest rates at a low level, as they tend to go up over the course of the Land Boom.

f. As the boom continues, sell those property assets you are looking to get rid of into a rising market.

Homeowners should know that the last really good time to invest in property with the prospect of several years of growth to come is at the opening of the Land Boom stage of the cycle.

3. Buy commodities and gold

a. The Land Boom increases the demand for raw materials. This means that your portfolio should have some exposure to commodity funds or to the companies that are extracting natural resources. Raw materials are mostly priced in dollars, which tend to depreciate during the second half of the cycle (see below), further boosting prices and drawing in capital.[25]

b. Gold and precious metals follow the general trend of commodities, though they may not lead. From a low a couple of years into the Land Boom, gold will start to rally towards the end of the cycle. This is a good time to buy gold.

4. Be long other currencies and short the US dollar

The dollar declines during the second half of the cycle (at least since the 1970s when currencies became free-floating). A depreciating dollar is a boost to global GDP. This pushes up the price of commodities and means that other currencies, especially those from the large commodity producers, appreciate in relative terms. The main counterpart to the dollar is the euro, which will therefore appreciate. Businesses that trade internationally should take this into account.

5. Buy alternative assets, such as collectibles

During the Land Boom, alternative assets such as art and fine wine can appreciate rapidly. By all means indulge in your passion for such, as well as things like non-fungible tokens and collectibles. But if the motive to buy them is solely for speculation, be mindful that acquiring assets with no earnings (and potentially significant storage or insurance costs) can be risky. They are often the focus of tremendous buyer interest and seller panic at various stages of the cycle.

CHAPTER 11

THE LONG CYCLE OF PROSPERITY AND WAR

Some time ago, when studying the dynamics of a capitalist society, I came across phenomena which were difficult to explain without admitting the existence of long and very deep cycles... both wars and social upheavals form part of the rhythmical process of the development of long cycles.

N. D. Kondratiev

THE SERGEANT MOTIONED to the guard: open the cell door.

The prisoner within was a sorry sight. He was so sick he could barely stand up, skin and bones only. One of the guards had to help him. Thankfully, he was too blind to see the guns pointed at him. He'd just returned from his trial. The authorities back west said he was a dissident. The sergeant shook his head: you couldn't survive as one of those these days, not with Stalin's thugs in charge. He didn't think the prisoner was guilty, but these bookish types had been rounded up in their thousands. The regime didn't want them causing trouble. Messing with people's minds, they called it. What could this guy do? He'd been no trouble, always polite. Just sad, especially these past few months. At first he had written to his wife and daughter often, but recently the sentence had broken him. You could tell. He'd become bitter. He'd lost hope. Not surprising, mind: time in Suzdal was hard, and he had been here six years. That would be enough for anyone.

The sergeant gave the order: fire. It was over quickly. Though forbidden, the sergeant said a little prayer for the dead man and then asked his guards to remove the body.

In these unfortunate circumstances one of the 20th-century's great economists, Nikolai D. Kondratiev, passed away. He was not guilty of any of the charges on which he was sentenced: being a member of the kulak party (no such party existed) and having bourgeois sympathies.[1] He was an unlikely threat to the regime. He was not a revolutionary seeking to overthrow it. Nor had he discovered some crime that the authorities wanted covered up. He was a keen student of history and an analyst – of commodity prices in particular. In the pages and pages of dry data he pored over he had discovered an underlying rhythm of history. But, inadvertently, he had unearthed a threat to the ideological foundations of the brutal Stalinist regime.

Why his discovery was a threat to the regime, and how it interacts with the 18-year cycle, is the subject of this chapter. This is important, because it describes many of the forces at play as the global economy moves through the 2020s.

The Long Cycle in commodity prices

In 1920, during the optimism of post-revolutionary Russia, 28-year-old Kondratiev had been asked by the Kerensky administration to head the newly-formed Institute of Conjuncture. Conjuncture is the study of the change in business conditions, in other words of economic cycles. By then an economist of some renown, he was highly regarded by Western scholars such as John Maynard Keynes, Irving Fisher and Wesley Mitchell.

One of Kondratiev's tasks was to identify the endpoint of Western capitalism. Marx had foretold that it would collapse, broken under the weight of its internal contradictions. The authorities needed to know when. Kondratiev embarked on an immense study, gathering as much data as he could on a wide range of things such as commodity and gold prices, interest rates and returns on capital investment, wages, foreign trade and the production of cast iron and lead. Even in our age this would have been a difficult undertaking. In his day, when none of this data was readily available and required painstaking statistical manipulations to ensure different data sets could be compared to one another, it was quite phenomenal.

On 6 February 1926, he presented the results of his investigations at the Institute of Economics in Moscow, to a meeting that included a number of distinguished Russian academics. There was, he claimed, a long-term rhythm in capitalist economies that could be identified through the movement of commodity prices. These went up for 25 to 30 years and down for a similar length of time, completing a cycle of 50 to 60 years.

Kondratiev identified that commodity prices had major inter-generational lows in 1789, 1849 and 1896 – approximately every 50 years – and peaked at similar intervals – in the years around 1814, 1873 and (just before he began his great study) 1920. He referred to this rhythm as the 'Long Cycle'.

This is depicted in Figure 19.

Figure 19: Commodity price indices, 1780-1925

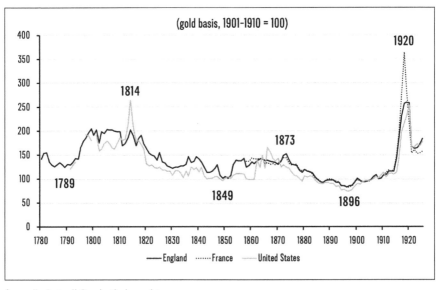

Source: Kondratiev, N. D. and author's own data.

This cycle in commodity prices, Kondratiev said, represented a rhythm of economic development. When the long-term price trend was rising, Western economies experienced expansion and great prosperity; when it was down, depression and difficulty. The next collapse was coming soon, he assured them. And it would be big.

But Kondratiev's brilliant research had failed in one critical way: he had not identified the *final* expiry date of the capitalist system. In fact, viewed from another perspective, his research was arguing that capitalism would survive. Since prices moved in cycles, low commodity prices would eventually give way to rising ones and, with them, the capitalist economy would regenerate and grow again. This was not at all in line with Marxist beliefs, so the authorities could not admit of this possibility. Following Stalin's consolidation of power, intellectual freedom in Russia had become severely restricted. The regime was hunting 'dissenters'. It was easy to paint Kondratiev's analysis, together with his strong views on how agriculture should be organised in a socialist society, as an endorsement of the market system and a rejection of the preferred programme of collectivisation.

Kondratiev was among the first of thousands of intellectuals to be arrested and imprisoned during the purges of the 1930s. Sentenced to eight years' solitary confinement in prison, he spent the first of those continuing his research, such as he could, though this became more difficult as his health deteriorated. After serving his full term, he was re-tried on 17 September 1938 and sentenced to death. The sentence was carried out that same day. He was just 46 years old.

In Russia, his work on cycles disappeared. Given his imprisonment and untimely death, Kondratiev could not complete his research and his conclusions remained tentative. But he influenced many Western scholars, such as Joseph Schumpeter, who developed a similar theory of economic and business cycles in the 1930s. Under the dominant Keynesian paradigm after the Second World War, however, the study of the business cycle all but disappeared – because it was thought the cycle had been eliminated. Paul Samuelson, the great post-war doyen of the economics profession, regarded the Long Cycle as 'science fiction'. The fallacy of this view was revealed in the real estate-led crisis of the mid-1970s. This reignited interest in the study of cycles, including the Long Cycle. Just as it had in the 1930s, Kondratiev's work proved its value: his thesis predicted that commodity prices would rise from a low in the mid-to-late-1950s, peak in the mid-1970s and then fall thereafter (Figure 20).[2]

Figure 20: Commodity price indices, 1946-1986

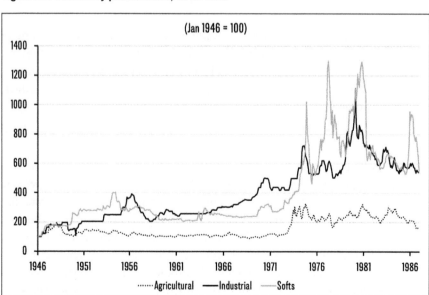

Source: author's own work.

What drove the cycle forward? Kondratiev argued it was the waves of technological investment which increased economic growth wherever they went in, leading to the creation of new industries. This in turn had a bearing on social relations because there would be winners and losers from the enormous disruption this caused, depending on whether people were able to take advantage of – or were undermined by – such innovation. It also greatly influenced the interactions between nations.

It was in effect a theory of history; and it unfolds as follows.

How the Long Cycle unfolds: technology and investment

The new cycle begins: a cluster of technology comes together

Kondratiev observed that the beginning of each Long Cycle brought about "significant changes in the main conditions of economic life" and these were to do with the mass adoption of new technology, either through multiple technologies coming together in a cluster, the discovery of new applications for existing technology or the costs of adoption falling dramatically (or all three).[3] For each succeeding Long Cycle there would be a lead, or primary, technology that would give rise to many new industries and influence the operating models of established ones.

Often these revolutionised the way goods were produced, the raw materials production required, and the way people communicated and moved – such that by the end of each cycle no industry was unaffected.

The first Long Cycle began with the Industrial Revolution, out of which came the factory system of production and the canals to transport goods. It peaked around 1815. The second, peaking in the late 1860s, was driven by heavy machinery, the telegraph and the railroad.[4] The third, which peaked in 1920, was the age of heavy industry and engineering, the telephone and the automobile. The fourth, peaking in the mid-1970s, was about automated production, mass consumption and the jet age. In the fifth – the present cycle – it is the internet, the mobile phone, high-speed wireless connectivity and the near-Earth economy. The dates for each cycle are presented in Table 6.

Table 6: Dates of the Long Cycles and key drivers (primary technologies, communications and transport)

	Start	Peak	End	Primary technologies, communication and transport
First	1789	1814	1849	Factory production and canals
Second	1849	1873	1896	Heavy machinery, railroads and telegraph
Third	1896	1920	1955	Heavy industry and machinery, automobiles and telephones
Fourth	1955	1975	2001	Automated production, commercial air travel
Fifth	2001	2027 (forecast)	2050s (forecast)	Internet and mobile phone, near-Earth economy

It was not that new technologies were invented only in the early days of each Long Cycle. In fact, they might have been around for a long time before. But early in each new cycle they found an application that led to their wide adoption. Often these moments coincided with the beginning of a new 18-year cycle, as we saw in Chapter 1.[5]

Capital investment is drawn in...

The key factor of each Long Cycle was where capital investment was flowing. In the prior downswing, the returns on investment are lower; capital is not invested to the same extent (it gets stuck in the financial system, going more into speculation than business investment). But new technology brings with it the promise of higher returns on investment; so as the new cycle begins, capital flows out of more established industries into newer ones. The rollout of new technology requires huge amounts of capital investment – to build canals, railroads, the electricity grid, highway systems, commercial airports, high-speed internet cables, servers and mobile masts.

During the upswing of each cycle there are periods of greater economic growth, while recessions tend to be shorter and sharper.

In our own era, the fifth Long Cycle, the spectacular earning power of technology companies is a reflection of this process in action. The recoveries out of the recessions of the present Long Cycle upswing – in 2008 and 2020 – have been comparatively swift, at least within the most innovative, technologically advanced sectors of the economy.

...leading to the re-ordering of all economic relationships...

Whole new spheres of human activity are created on the back of this new deployment of scarce capital. Ultimately, the Long Cycle sees a complete re-ordering of the economy, modes of communication and transport and interactions between groups of people – particularly between those stuck in the older industries and those riding the wave of the new ones.

Given the scale of the change, the first half of each cycle is highly disruptive. In the present Long Cycle, there is no industry that has been untouched by the internet and the smart phone.

...and causes greater social upheaval and revolution

The technological disruption on this economy-wide scale brings about the decline of old industries. This leads to social unrest because of the increasing gap in incomes between different groups of people. Further, new models of communication and transport enable previously marginalised groups to find a voice and challenge the dominant hierarchical structures. The result: mass social movements, cultural upheaval and even revolution.

Since 2001 there have been particularly powerful movements which challenged the status quo on such issues as same-sex marriage, race relations, sexual harassment and gender identity. The previous upswing of the Long Cycle, during the 1950s and 1960s, gave rise to the civil rights, feminist and environmental movements, as well as to the waves of decolonisation that led to the emergence of new nations. In the first two decades of the 20th century, the suffragette movement and the push for equal voting rights achieved significant victories.

Linked to this is a further aspect of the upswing of each Long Cycle – in international relations – which we will return to shortly.

Capital investment slows

As the upswing reaches its peak, the rollout of new technology slows down while changes to industries take effect. The opportunities for profitable investment reduce, leading to a lower rate of growth.

This means that boom periods in the downside of the Long Cycle tend to be somewhat attenuated and recessions are deeper and longer, especially in countries that are commodity exporters. In the last downswing of the Long Cycle, this was particularly true in Latin America and Africa – and even the economically advanced Australia suffered very significant recessions in the early 1980s and 1990s.

Financial speculation dominates real investment

Fewer investment opportunities leads to a build-up of capital in the financial system awaiting new productive outlets that will drive the next Long Cycle forward. With money stuck in the system, investment becomes more speculative. During the downswing, however, many innovations are developed, awaiting opportunities to be deployed. Eventually, such opportunities arise and give the impulse to the next cycle.

The process with which each Long Cycle unfolds involves higher growth rates and levels of investment, huge disruption and social tension, and competition to control and dominate new markets. Each 55 to 60-year Long Cycle spans (approximately) three real estate cycles, but they are linked, not just through the technology that moves them forward, but also, as we will consider, through economic rent.

Natural resources and the economic rent

The 55-to-60-year Long Cycle is related to the 18-year real estate cycle in a number of ways, but the most important, by far, is through the law of economic rent.

The first link is through commodity prices. We know that rent arises as a product of locational value (e.g., *The Big Issue* sellers), government-licensed scarcity (e.g., taxi medallions), enclosure of virtual land (e.g., internet platforms).[6] It also arises as a gift of nature, such as natural fertility of soil to grow crops – or the presence of natural resources such as oil and copper. When the prices of such commodities rise, as they do during the upswing of each Long Cycle, this leads to enormous rents for the companies and countries extracting them. These profits in turn are reinvested, leading to additional economic growth.

The second link is through the effects of technology and innovation. These increase productivity, which expands the number of sites in the economy where production might take place – in other words, the margin of production is extended. Lower costs translate, ultimately, into higher locational value and rents (and occasionally higher wages if there is a shortage of workers). This also increases the price of land – as we saw with the effects of the Jubilee Line extension.[7]

The final link is that the upswing of the Long Cycle coincides with the new countries actively participating in the international economy. This not only increases demand for products, but such countries become sources of cheap labour. Cheaper labour means lower production costs and higher rents. In turn, this high level of rents promotes additional economic activity to further exploit the resources of nature – more mining, drilling and extracting. This creates the means to build more and requires new markets for goods and services to sell into. As we know from the real estate cycle, higher rents lead to a bigger boom – which is what happens on the upside of the Long Cycle; because the level of capital investment – the benefits of which flow ultimately into the price of land – is greater.

We saw this in action during the last Long Cycle, which peaked in the mid-1970s. In the commodities boom of the 1960s and 1970s, the rents of oil-producing nations were deposited in Western banks, which used them to make loans to sovereign governments in the so-called 'third world' – many of which were themselves large commodity producers and, therefore, high-growth countries. This is why the upsides of the Long Cycles have been such prosperous periods in human history – because of a greater availability of finance to support economic development.[8] This also explains the greater incidence of social and economic upheaval. In addition to the disruption wrought on established industries by new ones, economic inequality, between those who own land and natural resources and those who do not, becomes greater and more visible.

The Long Cycle and war

Kondratiev also found that during the upswing of each Long Cycle world economic relationships became broader and more varied. This was in part because more established countries required raw materials to develop new industries and new markets to sell goods into. At the time of Kondratiev's research, this manifested itself as the involvement of new countries with young cultures: after 1850, the United States became more prominent internationally; after 1896, Argentina, Australia, Canada and New Zealand; in the 1960s, newly independent African countries.

The initiation of the present Long Cycle in 2001 coincided with China's accession to the World Trade Organization – which has been the economic story of our age – and with developments in India (information technology), Latin America and many countries in sub-Saharan Africa (agriculture and minerals).

There is, however, a darker side to the bullish conditions in the upswing of each Long Cycle. Kondratiev identified an increasing competition between the Great Powers for access to raw materials and for the ability to dictate the terms of world trade. Whatever their political leaders professed at the time, these countries competed in the hunt for resources and for markets to sell manufactured goods into.

This increasing competition between the Great Powers drew other countries to either side and led, eventually, to a major clash between both sides. Resource-rich nations provided the battlefields on which such rivalry took place. But the root cause of this was the appropriation of the economic rent. Examples from prior cycles include:

- The peak of the Long Cycle in the 1970s was at the height of the Cold War between the US and USSR and included the Vietnam War.

- In the cycle before that, into the peak in the 1910s, there was increasing tension between the European empires, the British and German in particular, eventually leading to the First World War.

- Before that, into the 1870s, the geopolitical competition was between the British Empire and Tsarist Russia as well as the American Civil War.

- In the cycle before that, into the late 1810s, it was Great Britain and France and the Napoleonic Wars that played out the first iteration of Great Power rivalry studied by Kondratiev.

It was the competition between powers that drove innovation and therefore great leaps in general prosperity. An example is the space race during the Cold War, particularly during the late 1950s and 1960s. This Great Power rivalry led to a whole host of technological developments that have widespread application today.[9]

The Roaring Twenties: prosperity and turbulence

The coincidence of the second half of the real estate cycle and the final years of the Long Cycle upswing happens once, or at most twice, in each century, around every 50 to 60 years. It is one of the reasons why the economic booms tend to be prolonged but also increasingly turbulent from a social perspective.

This means that the 2020s will see increasing tension, if not outright hostility, between the United States and China, the two Great Power rivals of the 21st century. The number of arenas in which the US and China might come into conflict is impressively large – the South China Sea; China's Belt and Road Initiative through and around the Eurasian land mass; the African continent, with its enormous stock of natural resources and growing middle classes to sell manufactured goods to. We are also seeing it in the attempts to control key trade nodes or routes, for example in the Middle East, the Panama Canal or, potentially, the Arctic. We are becoming increasingly aware of the competition in cyberspace or, indeed, in space itself.[10] To repeat the earlier point: whatever is claimed about the need for this strategic competition, the cause is always to attempt to control the economic rent.

Kondratiev said the following about the effect of war:

> Wars and revolutions cannot fail to have a very profound effect on the course of economic development. But wars and revolutions do not fall from the sky... They grow out of the soil of real, primarily economic, conditions... what circumstances lead to their occurrence in consistent clusters at specific periods coinciding with the periods of rising waves of long cycles, as noted above? It is much more plausible to suppose that wars themselves are created out of the soil of the increasing pace and intensity of economic life, accentuating the economic fight for markets and raw materials. But such an intensity of economic life is inherent in periods of increasing conjuncture [the upside of the Long Cycle].

The increasing intensity of economic life, as Kondratiev said, will eventually push the boom of the real estate cycle into overdrive. This will give a great boost, at least initially, to global prosperity; but increasing international tension will form a turbulent backdrop to investing in the 2020s. At the time of writing, this is becoming abundantly clear.

Once conflict takes hold, it ultimately destroys the boom which gave rise to it. Capital is sucked away from economic development and into armaments. In other words, money is diverted towards the war economy away from areas that are more productive and lead to greater general prosperity. Over time, this creates a shortage of money, setting off a chain reaction that ultimately results in a collapse.

Political leaders may initiate conflict abroad when economic conditions at home are difficult because war distracts people and shifts the blame for problems elsewhere. As citizens, we should remember this because the real estate crisis of the late 2020s will coincide with the peak and then fall in the Long Cycle. This makes those years a time of great geopolitical jeopardy. Great vigilance over, and scrutiny of, the actions of our political leaders is required.

This concludes the final chapter devoted to explaining how big the 18-year cycle can get. It also explains why the emotion of the remaining years of the present cycle will not be serene and calm, but big and bold, disruptive and turbulent, and even violent.

After this brief detour through the main rhythms of the Long Cycle, it is time to return to our 18-year cycle. While we have been away, the Land Boom has been bubbling along and is now reaching boiling point. Approximately 12 years in, we have arrived at the final, frenzied years of the boom: the Mania stage. To see how it unfolds we visit the country that, during the 1980s, experienced perhaps the most famous one of them all: Japan.

INVEST IN NATURAL RESOURCES AND INFRASTRUCTURE

Key lessons

The upswing of the Long Cycle involves great innovation and disruption in many areas: the final years of the present upswing are, as of 2023, coming up. Your investment portfolio should reflect this. Many of the themes of the Long Cycle are linked to those of the Land Boom – a booming industry (and related industries, including real estate), construction, infrastructure and commodities.

1. The emotion of the upswing will be significant

Remember, also, that the emotion of the era will be great, and this can make markets volatile. Investors will find it challenging to remain unflustered.

2. Invest in the Long Cycle

The following investments can be looked at:

a. Companies in sectors linked to the Long Cycle and Land Boom. These include infrastructure and construction companies.

b. Commodities: the boom in the economy and construction pushes up demand for commodities such as oil, copper, lumber, industrial metals and materials that support the rollout of infrastructure, e.g., lithium.

c. Companies mining or processing such commodities will have strong earnings. Speculative capital will also look for opportunities in other commodities that are trending up, such as agriculturals or soft commodities (e.g., wheat and coffee), if there is a poor harvest and other disruption to supply. These should be part of your portfolio.

d. Given the increase in international tensions, defence-related stocks should also have strong earnings.

CHAPTER 12

THE MANIA

The power behind the Japanese juggernaut is much greater than most Americans suspect, and the juggernaut cannot stop of its own volition, for Japan has created a kind of automatic wealth machine, perhaps the first since King Midas.

Clyde Prestowitz, an official in the Reagan administration, 1988

The greatest party on Earth

THE 1980S: A decade known for its discos and garish colours; for the pervasive influence of technology; for its hedonism and for the making and blowing of money in the most egregious and wasteful ways. Nowhere was this extravagance more apparent than in Japan.

The country was at the apex of a boom like no other, a bubble economy to rival anything seen during the Roaring Twenties or the Gilded Age. No one was making more money than the Japanese. Personal and corporate wealth skyrocketed. Youngsters, in search of fortune and experience, flocked to the neon-lit cities of Tokyo and Osaka. The world's celebrities gathered in posh Tokyo bars such as Lexington Queen. There was no party scene more vibrant than Japan's, showcasing a level of excess that could scarcely be believed in this traditional, conservative, frugal nation.

That this boom should happen in Japan was surprising, yet inevitable. It was surprising, given how far the nation had come after the devastation wrought on Hiroshima and Nagasaki. Its world-leading companies did what its armies could not: conquer the world. Not by force of arms but by the might of its economy, selling high-quality goods that transformed transportation, entertainment and culture across the globe.[1] In the three decades after the Second World War, its economy increased 50 times, enjoying double-digit growth almost every year throughout the 1950s and 1960s. By 1980, its national income had surpassed the UK's and was fast approaching that of the United States. Western scholars flocked to Japan to understand this economic miracle – how had it managed such rapid growth at full employment and low inflation? Business schools specialised in studying the seemingly superior management techniques of its corporate behemoths such as Sony, Panasonic, Mitsubishi, Toyota, Hitachi and Canon.

The boom was inevitable because the gains of such strong economic performance showed up in the land market. The Japanese economy was no stranger to the cycle. As in many other Asian countries, property was regarded as a symbol of status as well as a store of savings. That created an apparently inexhaustible demand for it, from both households and companies. Its economy displayed the common pattern: real estate speculation leading to a high point every 18 years or so, in 1890, 1909, 1926 and, post-war, in 1973. So it was again as the economy moved out of the crisis of the 1970s. By 1979, residential prices were back to all-time highs. They began to motor in the 1980s, and by the middle of the decade the Land Boom was underway (see Figure 21).

Figure 21: Japan residential property price index, 1955-1993

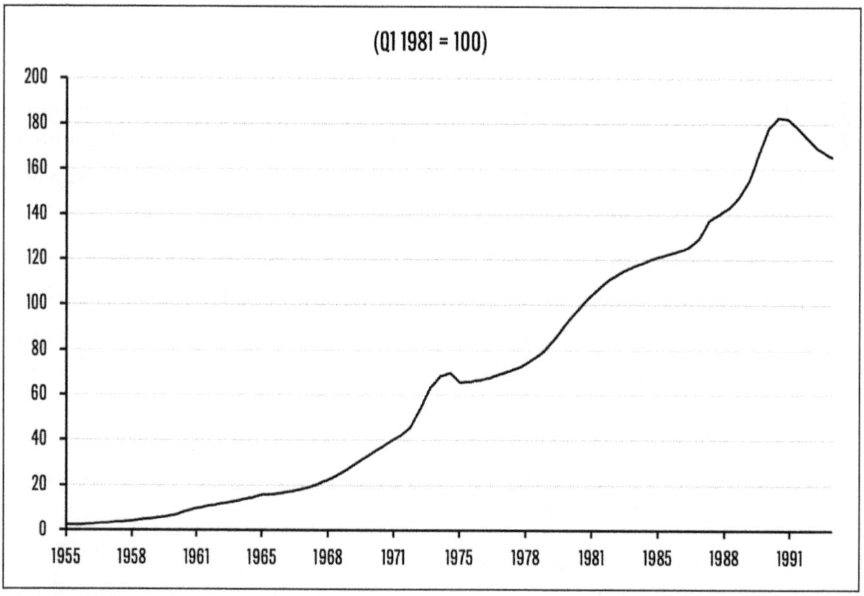

Source: Bank for International Settlements.

The Plaza Accord and the late 1980s Mania

The booming market turned into a Mania as the decade matured. This stage was ignited, as it always is, by a change in government policy. The Japanese miracle had been based on strong exports, assisted by its dollar peg. Through an agreement struck in 1985, known as the Plaza Accord, Western countries pressured Japan to allow the yen to appreciate in value. This was intended to reduce exports by raising the prices of goods traded overseas and making imports cheaper. Japan went along with this because in the crisis of the 1970s it had recognised its vulnerability to external shocks and wanted to rebalance its economy towards greater domestic consumption and investment.

The second change to policy was to reduce interest rates, a decision made by the Bank of Japan in an attempt to forestall a recession due to falling exports. A third change was the deregulation of the banking sector so that any reduction in growth from exports would be offset by increased domestic lending. Under these reforms, initiated in the early 1980s, bank loans would not be directed to areas prescribed by the state; they could go into anything.[2]

A final change was to focus investment on urban renewal. Japanese goods were known for their technical sophistication, but the quality of domestic real estate was shockingly poor for such a wealthy nation. 'Workaholics living in rabbit hutches' was the stereotype of Japan's labour force.[3] The government passed several laws and policies to encourage property development, creating a great renewal of the built environment as the grey office blocks and wooden houses of the post-war years were replaced by swish offices and stylish homes. Inheritance and corporate income taxes favoured unrealised capital gains in real estate, and a series of urban development plans directed local authorities to incentivise building on derelict land.[4]

The result was a Land Boom that swiftly turned into a Mania. There was an enormous surge in construction in all major Japanese cities, and by Japanese companies overseas. Large companies created glitzy corporate campuses in the suburbs for their employees, with leisure facilities such as tennis courts and golf courses. Building after building went up on an assumption that there were plenty of well-funded buyers looking for new premises. So great was the scale of activity that Japanese capital investment in the late 1980s, which was spent mainly on buildings, was annually equal to the size of the entire French economy.[5]

The bubble in lending

The surge in construction was fuelled by cheap, abundant credit. Banks secured all lending – even to businesses – against land collateral, rather than business prospects.[6] As real estate appreciated, companies could borrow higher amounts against their property holdings. This borrowing did not go into additional manufacturing capacity but into the booming stock and real estate markets.[7] Japan's model of capitalism was based on large corporate networks, or *keiretsu*, comprising manufacturers, suppliers, service companies, insurers, shipping companies and banks. Credit flowed from the banks to the other entities within each network. The members of a keiretsu owned each other's shares to bind them closely together and ensure they all enjoyed each other's successes. The banks were even permitted to hold shares of the companies they lent to, so their own balance sheets appeared increasingly healthy as the real estate market boomed from the appreciating value of both the land collateralising their loans and their shareholdings. This enabled even more lending which, in turn, led to higher share and property prices.[8]

It was a classic bubble. Loan volumes were increasing 13.8% per year and went mainly into commercial real estate (more than doubling from ¥75trn to ¥187trn) while business credit was directed towards riskier small businesses. Banks expanded their loans books as much as they could, chasing prospective clients and urging them to borrow. Their risk departments, which were supposed to restrain excessive lending, instead helped to overvalue collateral to ensure that lending practices appeared to be sound.[9] Even if they had been doing their job, new lenders – *jusen* – which were not subject to banking regulations, were flooding into the market to get a share of this immensely profitable activity. By 1990 such companies accounted for 15% of all private debt in Japan and 60% of their loans had gone into the property or constructions sectors. Such was the scale of the lending boom that, by the end of the decade, nine of the world's ten largest banks (measured by assets) were Japanese, and fully a third of all global lending was by Japanese companies.[10]

The boom that will never end

Japan's relentless rise begot the commonly held view that its success would be perpetual, that this was a new era and that this time things were different. This confidence fuelled even more speculation. Reflecting the increasingly manic real estate boom, there was an enormous stock market bubble. The keiretsu had enormous property holdings, the value of which was reflected in their share prices. The Nikkei opened in February 1985, the month of the Plaza Accord, at 11,947. It closed on 31 December 1989 at 38,916 – an increase of almost 330% in five years (see Figure 22).

Figure 22: The Japanese Nikkei 225 index, 1986-1990

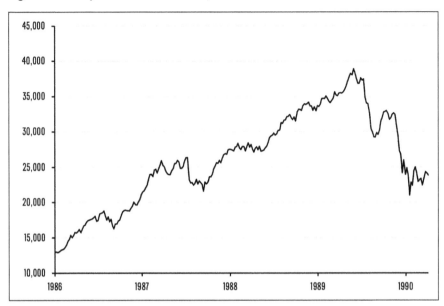

Source: Optuma.

The price-earnings (P/E) ratio of the index as a whole reached 60, an astronomical level.[11] Even the American Dow Jones in 1929, at the peak of possibly the greatest bubble in its history, only reached a high P/E ratio of 32.6.[12] No matter to investors in Japanese stocks. The P/E ratio of some companies reached 1,000, a price so exorbitant that investors in their stock would, on current earnings, have to wait a whole millennium to get their initial investment back. But who cared how expensive these shares were? To protect their portfolios, investment firms such as Nomura introduced products that guaranteed returns to favoured customers. No wonder the investment funds kept rolling in.

Nowhere was the Mania more apparent than in the property market. As it reached sky-high levels, Japanese lenders launched a new product: the interest-only mortgage, with the principal to be repaid at the end of the loan. When might that be? Well, lenders also introduced the 100-year mortgage, where the loan would be spread over not only the borrower's lifetime but that of their children and possibly grandchildren too, a unique bequest if ever there was one.

Everyone wanted a piece of the action. Professionals set up side-businesses to focus on real estate investment and soon found that this was easier and more lucrative than their normal jobs. Dr Kichinosuke Sasaki was the standout celebrity in this regard. A specialist in geriatric medicine, he invested in real estate on the side following the early 1970s downturn. By 1989 *Forbes* estimated

Sasaki was worth $3.5bn, the world's fifteenth billionaire.[13] Large corporates were involved too: in the late 1980s, the giant carmaker Nissan made more money from speculation in real estate than from manufacturing cars.[14] But there is no better evidence of Mania than the fact that even the *yakuza* – Japan's notorious gangsters – could not resist the allure of real estate speculation: "The [leader's] strategy was to modernise the yakuza and diversify its sources of income away from traditional areas like extortion and prostitution and into more legitimate fronts such as property…"[15]

Record prices... for everything

In the final manic years of the decade, real estate prices increased by a staggering 300%.[16] Such was the extent of the Mania that the value of land in upscale districts of Ginza fetched $2m per square metre. The land of the greater Tokyo area was estimated to be more valuable than the entire United States.[17] An enterprising Australian official arranged the sale of half of the land of its Tokyo embassy for A$640m. With the proceeds the Australian government was able to reduce its foreign debt by fully half.[18]

Taking advantage of the strong yen, and flush with borrowed money, Japan's companies went overseas and bought up the world. In 1987, three quarters of all net capital flows around the world were Japanese. Companies used the acquired land to establish factories in Scotland and north England, car plants in the American Midwest or hotels on Hawaii.[19] A particular fetish included buying Western trophy assets for ridiculous prices.[20] Mitsui purchased the Exxon Building in New York for $610m. Their offer was almost double the initial asking price, something that so shocked the seller that lawyers had to be consulted to ensure that such a high offer could be accepted. The Japanese had a particular affinity for Californian real estate assets, which created an impression on Hollywood. Films of the era expressed disquiet at the Japanese 'takeover' of America. In 1989's *Back to the Future II,* Marty McFly was fired in the future world of 2015 by his overbearing Japanese boss – which not only pointed to the uncompromising nature of Japanese management but also suggested the long-term future belonged to Japan.[21] The February 1987 cover of *Newsweek* magazine warned readers that "Your next boss may be Japanese".

Corporate Japan even muscled its way into the Cold War space race. In 1990 Japanese TV station TBS paid the USSR $14m to send an employee, Toyohiro Akiyama, to the space station Mir for a week of night-time reports. The launchpad was festooned with Minolta logos, while the Russian *Soyuz* booster was emblazoned with the branding of a credit card company, an electronics manufacturer and a sanitary napkin maker. Arriving at Mir, Akiyama was welcomed by Russian cosmonauts wearing TBS t-shirts. This was the first commercial spaceflight in history.[22]

Even more excessive was the number of golf courses sprouting up all over land-poor Japan. This led to a roaring trade in private golf memberships, which could be bought and sold on a formal exchange rather like stocks and were tracked daily by the Nikkei Golf Index.[23] At the height of the Mania, in 1990, this market was worth an estimated $200bn, an amount roughly the same as the entire economy of Switzerland. At auction, a van Gogh painting fetched $82.5m – $30m more than the previous record for an artwork.[24] A Japanese citizen was the winning bidder. Two days later he bought a Renoir for $78.1m. To demonstrate that the money meant nothing to him, he later declared that both paintings would be cremated with him when he died (presumably the art did not mean much to him either).

A 1987 law had provided tax breaks and cheap government loans to build leisure facilities in line with national plans. Local governments offered developers derelict land, which led to a boom in theme parks on the basis of wildly optimistic forecasts of demand. Soon after, property developers announced a plan to build the world's largest indoor park, the Seagaia Ocean Dome in Miyazaki. Housed in an enormous hangar, this attraction included a chlorinated 'ocean' which was six times larger than an Olympic pool and was kept hot at 28°C, a 200-variation wave machine and a fake rock lagoon that would erupt with 'lava'. The complex even came with the world's largest retractable roof, so on rainy days one could still sunbathe on its 12,000 square metres of beach (which had been created from crushing 600 tonnes of rock). The entire complex was located only a mile away from an actual beach.[25]

The Mania reached its zenith in May 1989, while in the background the US yield curve had inverted, meaning that the interest rate on a short-term, three-month bond was higher than the longer-term ten-year one. The Bank of Japan finally became concerned about the booming property market. It started raising short-term rates in an attempt to cool the market and slow down the rate of growth of real estate loans.

Was this a warning sign that there might be trouble ahead? To most, basking in the self-evident miracle of the Japanese economy, it hardly seemed so. The market is always right, isn't it?

The Mania analysed

Twelve years after the Start begins the Mania, lasting approximately two years before we reach the Summit. The boom of the second half of the cycle is typically based on a story that can be effectively summed up in four words: *this era is different.* The effect is always the same: to create the emotional need to invest. We are approaching the high point of the cycle, so there is plenty of money and bank credit looking for opportunities.

Those who spot the signs of the bubble early may have to wait an uncomfortably long time for the end to arrive. As we saw in 1980s Japan, this stage is the period of strongest growth in the stock and property markets. It draws in even sober, rational investors. They might recognise that things are overvalued, but they rarely have the choice – or the emotional stability – to sit it out. Even Ben Graham, the father of value investing (buying good quality stocks at a cheap price, or not at all), got carried away in the Mania of the late 1920s. Professional investors risk losing business and livelihoods by sitting back and holding cash: in a bull market this is not something they are allowed to do. The Mania has also been called the 'Winner's Curse', because it is the point in the cycle where the competition to acquire assets has pushed prices up to such levels that it is a curse to be the winning bidder for a piece of real estate – given what will soon happen.[26]

The Mania unfolds as follows.

1. The stage is ignited by a change in regulations – leading to a surge in land prices

The preceding stage – the Land Boom – was bullish enough, but often the governments inadvertently turn it into a Mania through a change in policy. The Bank of Japan lowered interest rates and encouraged lending. Tax breaks were offered for grandiose real estate developments. In the 1840s, the Bank Charter Act drew cheap money into the commercial money markets. In the late 1920s the US government lowered interest rates. In the early 2000s there were all three: looser regulations, tax cuts and the lowest interest rates in decades. The inevitable result was higher land prices.

The change in policy also has the effect of switching the flow of capital from productive investment to land speculation. Witness the number of businesses and professionals that turn to stock and property investment as it becomes more lucrative than their core activity. This results in an extreme surge in land prices.

2. The Mania is driven by new lenders

Rapidly rising land prices draw in bank credit. As land is collateral for bank lending, bank balance sheets are healthy, permitting more lending. The surge in private credit that began with the Land Boom reaches its highest level. Most additional borrowing goes to paying for ever-increasing land prices and not into production.[27]

Banks become fully loaned up within permitted regulations, or they bypass them altogether (in Japan this happened by inflating the appraised value of land). Further, regulations are designed to address the conditions that led to the last crisis. In a new era, there will be new practices or technology that regulators are unfamiliar with. Since banks seek to maximise profits, this invariably results in over-lending towards real estate. As the cycle progresses and land prices get higher, this goes increasingly to marginal projects.[28]

The increase in private debt comes primarily from new financing houses, such as the 1980s *jusen* in Japan, rather than banks. The newcomers are not bound by the same regulations. In the 2000s, a new financial technique called securitisation, memorably portrayed in Michael Lewis's *The Big Short*, enabled banks to quickly sell their loans on to a much larger range of finance providers. Look out for a surge in private debt provided by other financial institutions or shadow banks, offshore banks and personal credit providers. In the present cycle, there may also be crowdfunding and cryptocurrency-based financiers.

In the banking system, as all additional lending is in property (and not shorter-term commercial loans), the rate of turnover of bank loans decreases. The system reduces in terms of liquidity, which makes it more vulnerable to a shock.[29]

As things go over the top, the key driver is the confidence that people have in future growth. Lending by banks and credit institutions is based on inflated values. But this permits more lending, more purchases and more building.[30]

3. Construction surges

There is construction going on all over the place.[31] In the Land Boom, developers have focused more attention on outer areas where land is cheaper and will often develop sites in anticipation of demand. Outer, or more distant, areas have less real demand, so the profit margins are lower (and dependent on land prices increasing). Here, demand can reverse more quickly as businesses have lower surpluses and struggle to withstand higher costs. Smaller builders and even sub-contractors are drawn into developing sites, fuelling the construction boom.[32] This is where the seeds of the future crisis are sown, though this is only apparent to those who understand the law of economic rent.[33] Everywhere you look there are new houses and commercial premises springing up. Land subdivision goes to greater excess than any other variable in the cycle, with towns and cities spreading out over more and more land as the building boom progresses. The land market fails the most in this phase of the cycle. Rapidly rising land prices, inflated by credit and the speculative boom, send the wrong price signals and make many projects appear more profitable than they should. This creates an incentive to build more than a return-on-capital (building) investment justifies.[34] The returns to developers are illusory, because it is not their investment that is generating the return but the inflating price of land on which it sits. The result is extreme overbuilding, an enormous waste of capital that makes prices vulnerable to collapse once the Summit arrives.

The inflation in property prices is reinforced by experts who appraise the value of property on the basis of comparables. This means that the upward trend in prices is sustained. As land has no cost of production, there is no check on the value it can be appraised at. Even experts can suffer from a herd mentality during the Mania.

People begin paying for real estate under false assumptions of future capital growth, not based on present earnings. A growth in the flow of capital is needed to sustain the Mania. This makes the housing market much more vulnerable to even a minor change in conditions.[35]

4. The stock market surges, reflecting extreme valuations and the economic boom

With the economy awash with cheap money and business conditions buoyant, the stock market surges further into new highs. It is led by construction and banking stocks – the two sectors experiencing the largest boom. Surging stock prices also reflect the increase in assets valued on company balance sheets, much of which is related to property, and the fact investors are prepared to pay more in relation to company earnings.[36]

Prices are bid up to extreme levels as a flood of money enters the markets – because a new cohort of investors want a piece of the action.[37] Often this flows into a new vehicle for investing, reflecting a new fad.

The stock market is at all-time highs. Investors are in profit. They feel wealthy and spend more money. The savings rate goes down.[38] The economy, though booming, is getting more and more vulnerable to a shock.

5. Grand designs: the world's largest/tallest/longest/ deepest is announced

As this stage matures there will be an announcement that the world's tallest or longest structure will be built. In an era of large construction megaprojects, this one will stand out. The project is purely speculative and can only happen when land prices are high and credit is cheap, abundant and careless. Building taller or bigger ensures that the site pays, and such schemes can only begin when developers have access to plentiful credit. The same logic applies to any major scheme that breaks records for scale and ambition.[39]

In late 1980s Japan, the resort schemes were good signs of rampant speculation. Other cycles can furnish examples: the Empire State Building in New York (announced in 1929), the Sears Tower in Chicago (1970), the MesseTurm in Frankfurt (1988) and the Burj Khalifa (2004) were all started in the heady final years of their respective cycles and were, in their day, the tallest buildings in their continent or globally.[40] Figure 23 illustrates the link between real estate booms and the construction of tall buildings.[41]

Figure 23: Number of New York skyscrapers (buildings taller than 70m), 1890-2009

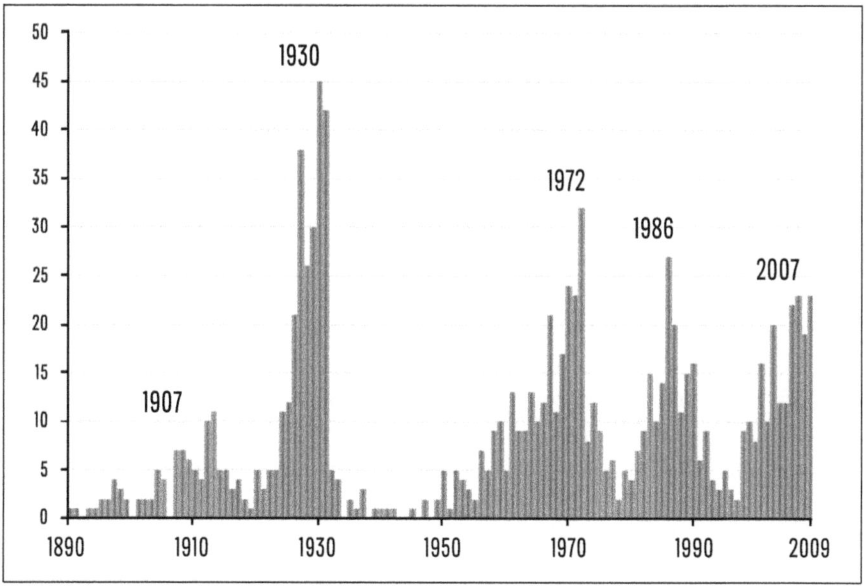

Source: bankingcrises.org (with author's annotation).

6. Inflation and interest rates rise

Eventually, more money chasing land prices higher (rather than leading to more production) can mean only one thing: inflation.[42] This begins to rise, but this signal is late for reasons set out in Chapters 8 and 9. Bond investors are sensitive to inflation, which erodes their capital value in real terms. So shorter-term bond yields start to rise, and borrowing becomes more expensive. This increases costs to businesses.

7. The yield curve inverts

Once the Mania has been going on for some time, the yield curve inverts.[43] Most investors will not notice the inversion because they are too busy speculating, and business looks good. Those who do see it think it no longer provides the signal it once did. The rest will be too distracted by the outrageous behaviour of the latest celebrity or some other frivolous news to pay attention.[44]

Even seasoned watchers may not understand the significance of what this portends: so close to the Summit, the inversion must be treated with utmost respect. The market is signalling that the financial crisis is close at hand; on average, there are just over 14 months between the inversion of the yield curve and the onset of recession.

8. Popular interest: your doctor, taxi driver or hairdresser; talk at dinner parties and extravagant behaviour

The Mania is aided everywhere by popular media. Everyone is (or wants to be) part of it. The talk of the town is about property investment (speculation). Newspapers are funded by advertisements, and they detail the latest property schemes. Magazines, advertising the latest luxury items (often promoted by the hottest new celebrity), have never been thicker. Popular TV shows show you how to flip properties for a gain. Taxi drivers and hairdressers discuss their property investments and consider giving up the day job. At parties, the talk will be of where the next hotspot is. Your real estate agent, flush with commissions from the booming real estate market, will be driving a flash car.

9. Excessive behaviour

The building of monumental structures is mirrored in the extravagant behaviour of newly minted (usually property) billionaires and business tycoons. A sure sign is the high prices that works of art (or other collectibles) fetch at auction, often record-breaking. The record amount paid by a Japanese buyer for the van

Gogh in 1990 lasted until 2004, when Picasso's *Garçon à la Pipe* fetched $104 million at auction, the first in a series of records that were broken in the run-up to the cycle's Summit in 2007.

———— ·-■-· ————

The game is now afoot. We are charging headlong towards the climax of the cycle. The economy is now at heights of prosperity never seen before.

As the great acceleration takes place, let us pause briefly. We previously looked at the factors (bank credit, government investment and the commodities boom) that determine how big the Land Boom can get. But with everything so euphoric this close to the top, we are in danger of getting carried away by the great delusion that is taking hold of the crowd: that the good times are here to stay. How can we maintain our emotional balance and avoid putting our hard-earned savings into a patently overheating economy?

Staying safe is the subject of the next two explanatory chapters. In the first, we will consider why, at extreme points of the 18-year cycle, your financial adviser might inadvertently lead you astray.

DO NOT FOLLOW THE HERD; IT IS TIME TO REIN BACK

Stage: the Mania

Approximate timing: years 12 and 13

Prevailing emotion: greed

Managing emotions

The Land Boom evolves into the Mania when greed dominates people's thinking. This emotion overrides any regard for the fundamental value of an investment; all that matters is extrapolation of what has happened in recent years – high growth – into the indefinite future. Investors jump in, confident that the price tomorrow will be substantially more than the price today. Behavioural economists have analysed the emotional patterns that possess the crowd during such heady times. The normal price anchoring that restrains investors when prices start to rise is suddenly moored to much higher values; and herd instinct leads people to follow the crowd.[45]

Any case study covering the Mania cannot fail to point out its high emotional temperature. The key component of investor greed is the fear of missing out on what appears to be limitless, easily attainable and imminent riches. This causes otherwise sensible investors to chase assets at ridiculously inflated prices.

Managing investments

The key investment goal now is to ensure your capital is well-placed and secure by the end of the Mania. You should have plenty of cash (or liquid assets) available, and all the assets you want to dispose of have been sold at high prices. Whether you dip in and out of the market is up to you, but you need to be nimble and be prepared (and able) to exit quickly.

If you invest, do so on the basis of fundamentals and not the promise of paying today for gains that may (or may well not) appear tomorrow. If this means not purchasing some assets, even if they appear to be a good investment or a 'sure thing', so be it.

1. Continue to hold stocks most closely linked to overheating real estate markets and investment mania, then get ready to sell

a. During the Mania, as with the Land Boom, the stock market sectors that do best are linked to the real estate market and the industries at the centre of the investment boom. If you are invested in these sectors, ensure you hold the shares of companies with solid earnings rather than those only in possession of assets that are appreciating in value. Be very wary of companies that are highly leveraged. Finally, bear in mind that the prices of companies with low current, but high perceived future, earnings are likely to be the most speculated in; this may look good on paper right now, but they are most vulnerable in a crisis. As the Mania matures, you should not commit more capital into the stock market but use it to build up reserves.

b. Note that real estate stocks tend to top out before the broader market.[46]

c. It is not necessary to sell all your stocks before the Mania ends. But you should enact a similar plan to the one at the mid-cycle Recession stage to protect profits through a hedging instrument or by rotating your capital into large, strong companies with solid earnings in your portfolio.

2. Be selective with property investing

a. The property market will be hot, as we have reached the final years of the property boom, the culmination of an expansion that began 12 to 14 years before. Do not buy or add to your portfolio at this stage, particularly as it continues.

b. Property developers must ensure that all stock is sold before the end of the Mania (or that they are able to hold some for a long time after that). New schemes should not be initiated during this stage.

c. Commercial property investors must ensure their tenants are strong businesses (and will be capable of withstanding the economic crisis that will soon arrive).

3. Buy commodities, including gold and silver

The price of gold and silver should increase. This is partly because of the general strength of commodities, linked to the real estate and Long Cycles, and partly because of concerns about inflation and the amount of leverage within the economy. You should buy or add these to your portfolio.

4. Do not purchase any more alternative assets such as collectibles

If you have bought alternative assets for speculation, do not purchase any more, even if there is much excitement around them. In fact, as this stage goes on, get ready to sell them.[47]

5. Business owners: time to exit or reduce risk

a. Times are good for business owners. Revenues and profits are up and growth prospects for future years are solid. There will be a strong desire to invest in extra capacity and premises and to hire staff. This must be done prudently. While it seems that the good times will go on forever, businesses must have plans flexible enough to be able to reverse course in case the positive forecasts are wrong. They should also develop contingency plans on what to do during a difficult period that may entail a significant reduction in customers and revenue.

b. In the easy credit conditions of this stage, there will be many banks willing to lend, but businesses should resist further borrowing and instead look to pay down debt. What liabilities remain should be manageable, even if there is a significant economic recession.

c. Surpluses should not be fully reinvested or paid out as additional dividends but should be used to increase cash reserves.

d. There will be increasing temptation to shift the focus of the business to speculative investments, especially in real estate, which appear to offer better returns on invested capital. Businesses should remain focused on their core activities, which offer better long-term prospects and have less downside risk in a crisis.

e. Now is a good time to critically review the business and dispose of assets or parts of the business that are no longer relevant to the future, are not as profitable, or do not generate cashflow. This is also a good time to review costs and, if possible, reduce them (or have plans to do so in the event of a downturn).

f. If owners have a plan to sell their business in the not-so-distant future, they should bring forward their plans and effect a sale now. This is the best time to agree a high price (and have sufficient time to execute a good deal).

6. Do not borrow more; reduce borrowing if possible

a. You should ideally begin to reduce your borrowings. This is the stage of the cycle when banks will be pushing loans out to customers. Their siren song must be resisted. This is particularly true of any loans that can be called in at the discretion of the lender.

Review covenants within loan agreements very carefully, such as kicker rates that adjust upwards when money is tight (the adjustable-rate mortgages resetting to higher rates in 2006 precipitated the credit crisis in the US).

b. Any loans should be easily serviceable from earnings (even if there is some disruption to such earnings). Make sure that any borrowing does not need to be rolled over in the next four to five years.

c. Borrowing to speculate is extremely risky as the Mania develops and should be avoided altogether.

7. Build a pool of safe, liquid assets

This is the stage when investors and business owners should be building a repository of safe, liquid assets, ideally inflation-protected, that can be deployed if needed; including high-quality bonds with inflation-proofed returns. These will provide some returns now, but their real value lies in their optionality, i.e., their ability to be sold in order to acquire cheap assets in the years after the Crash.

8. Dispose of weaker assets and realise profits

The Mania is the time to look at your investments and decide what to keep and what to sell. Lower-quality assets should be sold, such as property in less favourable locations or assets where earnings are volatile or low. Now is the best time, because when credit is abundant and the economy expanding you are likely to find someone willing to pay a good price for them.

CHAPTER 13

THE GREAT DELUSION

In an efficient market, at any point in time, the actual price of a security will be a good estimate of its intrinsic value.

Eugene Fama

DR ALAN GREENSPAN was the longest-serving chairman in the history of the Federal Reserve. His time in office coincided with one of the longest periods of economic expansion in American history, when growth seemed relentless and perpetual. Much of this robust performance was attributed to his sure hand on the economic tiller. None of his predecessors were as fêted. *Time* magazine ranked him higher than even President Clinton in its 1998 list of influential people. He was known in the financial press as the 'Maestro' to whose tune markets danced. In the heady post-Cold War period, it was an article of faith for many that markets possessed a god-like wisdom; and to these faithful, Dr Greenspan was the high priest.

The unshakeable belief was that the market was always right: that all you needed to know was the quoted price to make a decision about what to buy and sell, how to run your business and where to invest your savings. Regulation, tax and other government interventions should be minimised so prices could signal the truth to the economy. For the period after the cyclical downturn in the early 1990s, this seemed right. Not even the events of 9/11 stopped it for long. By 2004 Greenspan's deputy, Ben Bernanke, claimed that the economic volatility (in other words, the business cycle) had been eliminated.[1] So when the Maestro retired in February 2006, his stock had never been higher.[2]

Greenspan's faith in markets – one shared by everyone, whether they knew it or not – was not based on whimsy but on decades of research and practice. Ironically enough, this research came out of the real estate-led crisis of the 1930s.

Taming the financial Wild West

We saw in the Prologue how the unstoppable bull market of the Roaring Twenties sucked a new generation of investors into the stock market. At the time, there was very little guidance on what they should do to be successful. The study of finance – of explaining the prices of securities and how these related to the underlying value of enterprises – did not exist. By today's standards, investing in that era was a bit like travelling through a financial Wild West: there was very little by way of law and order, i.e., financial regulation. There were few funds where professional managers could pool money to invest on behalf of the public. Beyond the pricing of individual stocks, there was no indexing to inform one of how the market in general was performing. Publicly traded companies were not required to make financial disclosures or present independently audited financial statements. There were no protections for investors who might inadvertently fall foul of salespeople touting financial snake oil. Investing in the stock market took place in both a regulatory and an intellectual vacuum.

In the real estate-led crisis between 1929 and 1932, the American stock market lost 90% of its value. It was a financial calamity for most investors, particularly those who had been suckered into the market during the Mania two years before the Summit. But one benefit of the crisis was the emergence of a much more systematic (and empirical) study of financial markets.[3] The goal was to develop a system that could help investors avoid the speculative fever of the late 1920s and the despair of the early 1930s. Noble in its intent, it has had a rather different consequence, as we shall see.

The birth of the stock portfolio

The study of finance coincided with a broader interest among economists in quantifying human behaviour. It was not until the 1930s that data for even basic metrics, such as national income (or GDP) were gathered.[4] Before that, politicians had no idea about the level of growth in the economy. During the Depression, the US economy had contracted by a quarter, but those running the country had no idea of the extent of the damage caused by the crisis. No wonder they were slow to react.

In relation to the study of finance, this quantification manifested itself in an attempt to measure financial risk, a key piece of information required to make sober investment decisions (as opposed to casino-like speculation). But it was not at all obvious what financial risk was and how it could be measured.

In the 1950s Harry Markowitz, a young academic in Chicago, came up with a solution while writing his doctoral thesis: the risk of a stock was the fluctuation or 'volatility' of its price around an average. Stocks were being continually repriced by market traders, and some prices moved a lot, others less so. Larger price movements meant more risk, because if one had to sell a stock a more volatile price meant a higher probability of selling at a loss. Mathematically, this volatility could be measured by a stock's standard deviation.[5] Here was the first insight: investors buying more volatile stocks needed to be compensated with higher returns; financial risk and reward needed to be in balance.

Secondly, Markowitz pointed out that while the risk of individual stocks was important, investors rarely owned one stock; they should really be concerned about the risk of their overall portfolio. It was not the risk of any individual stock that mattered but the way it moved in relation to other stocks in the portfolio. He was able to prove mathematically that the overall risk of a portfolio could be reduced by having a series of stocks that did not move in sync with one another. In this way, if the price of one stock was down, another would not be, at least not to the same extent – reducing the overall variability in returns (or risk). This led to the second insight that has become the cornerstone of investment theory: diversification.

Other scholars, including William Sharpe, improved upon the mathematics of Markowitz's theory. It was not the covariance of stocks against one another but against the underlying market that was key: in statistical terms, this was its 'beta'.[6] Out of their work emerged a body of knowledge that holds sway today: modern portfolio theory. For the individual investor, it sets out an internally coherent and logical framework for investing.

They were able to show that there were *optimum* portfolios which, because of the covariances between the stocks within them, maximised return for a given level of risk, or minimised the risk for a given level of return. This was known as optimising one's 'risk-adjusted return'. These portfolios were on an 'efficient frontier' in the sense that they should not be beaten in terms of the balance between return and risk. To get to this frontier, you needed to be well-diversified.[7]

These insights meant that one needed only a small amount of hard, objective data to calculate an expected return from a stock. This gave people the ability to calibrate their ideal risk-return ratio and gave rise to the Capital Asset Pricing Model (CAPM) which holds sway in much of the finance industry to this day.[8] In fact, it is hard to overstate the influence of the model in the economy – it plays a role in supporting retirements, budgeting in charities and universities, compensating management in listed companies, regulating entire industries (e.g., public utilities) and even working out energy bills.[9]

The market is always right

For the model to function, the price of a security must convey the right insight about risk at all times. As Markowitz and Sharpe were completing their work, there was another branch of enquiry that set out to prove this very point.

The erratic movement of stock prices had long been of interest to researchers, many of whom had a background in physics. To them, fluctuations in stock prices resembled a phenomenon studied by Robert Brown, a 19th-century English botanist: the patternless, seemingly random, motion of pollen grains. Their movement had come to be known as 'Brownian motion' and could be used to model the movement of stock prices. During the 1950s and 1960s much serious economics research examined the idea and pondered why this might be. Paul Samuelson, who is sometimes referred to as the father of modern economics, described it as follows:

> The market quotation… already contains in itself all that can be known about the future and in that sense has discounted future contingencies as much as is humanly possible… we would expect people in the market place, in pursuit of avid and intelligent self-interest, to take account of those elements of future events that in a probability sense may be discerned to be casting their shadows before them.[10]

Samuelson argued that markets would price in expectations of what was going to happen. As these expectations changed, so did the price. Eugene Fama, another Chicago academic, took up this insight and extended it. He argued this movement was consistent with an 'efficient' market; that is, a market that was constantly absorbing, at every moment, new information about the intrinsic value of a stock. To an outsider, the motion might appear random; but market participants were receiving new information all the time and making buying and selling decisions accordingly. This also meant that market price had to be right because it was the only thing that reflected all current information. This claim came to be known as the 'efficient market hypothesis'.

Applied to investing, this meant the price was indeed the most important piece of information and that no investor had an advantage in the marketplace. The market cannot be timed. The best thing would be to own a portfolio that mimicked the market itself – this meant being well-diversified – and then hold for the long term.

The mathematical rigour and precision, as well as the faith in the market information transmission mechanism, were highly influential and successful. It also coincided, in the 1970s, with the view put forward by influential scholars, such as Milton Friedman, that markets were self-correcting and did not need managing.

This body of work was successful in bringing systematisation to what was, prior to the 1930s, a chaotic universe. It served the finance industry very well because it was able to draw in huge volumes of investor capital – which today amounts to trillions of dollars worldwide.[11]

The more unrealistic the assumptions, the better the theory

These models relied on a series of assumptions. Investors are constantly making decisions based on new information – but these need to be the right decisions, and to be right they need to be clear-eyed about their goals and how to achieve them. *Homo economicus*, it is assumed, is a rational being. He or she must also have full access to information. Another assumption is that there cannot be any other factors that influence buying or selling decisions – the models ignored costs such as taxes and transaction fees.

These are big assumptions to make. Are investors really rational about what they want? Do they know how to make decisions to achieve their goals? Are not other costs significant factors in decision-making? It turns out there are many reasons to question the validity of the assumptions these models make.[12]

More importantly, the entire theory has divorced the business of investing money from understanding the underlying companies that investors are buying shares in. All investors are told to care about is the price, which ought to reflect key information about the company fully. This is a high standard to meet given the myriad factors that go into making a company successful, including its ability to generate earnings, the quality of its management and its business strategy, the strength of its competitors and so on. There is also an inherent paradox: if prices are properly efficient – such that no one should care about the company, only its share price – who is doing the work to ensure that the market price is right in the first place? Economists refer to this process as price discovery, whereby the collective action of many buyers and sellers, through their interactions, move prices to their 'right' level (reflecting available public and private information).[13]

This has also contributed to a casino-like attitude to the market, ironically repeating the mistakes of investors in the 1920s. Because the price of a security

THE SECRET WEALTH ADVANTAGE

is a critical variable for investors, it has led to the poor design of management incentives – managers are rewarded with stock options that might result in practices to manipulate the share price (even if it is to the detriment of the company's health), for example borrowing too much or buying back shares to boost their price.

The consequences of these assumptions are hugely significant for our economies. These fit the dominant ideology of the time – to leave the market alone and remove government intervention. If markets were efficient at pricing in information and allocating resources to those who could best use them, then the worst thing to do would be to interfere with them. The then-Soviet Union provided a clear cautionary (if rather extreme) example of what could go wrong if governments sought to control markets. In this scenario the role of government was to ensure that information was available to everyone and leave the market to its own devices.

Do unrealistic assumptions undermine these theories? Not at all, in the eyes of their devotees, as Sharpe wrote some years later – citing no less an authority than Milton Friedman, whom he was quoting:

> The proper test of the theory is not the realism of its assumptions but the acceptability of its implications.[14]

If markets were truly efficient, then the entire hedge fund industry would be wiped out because there would be no strategies that could exploit the market for any but the briefest period. There would be no possibility of gaining an 'edge' in the market. But hedge funds do exist, and some make a huge amount of money for their investors.[15]

Perhaps the final word on this subject should be given to the man who started this revolution 50 years ago, Harry Markowitz:

> The CAPM is a thing of beauty. Thanks to one or another counterfactual assumptions, it achieves clean and simple conclusions... Now, 40 years later, in the face of empirical problems with the implications of the model, we should be cognisant of the consequences of varying its convenient but unrealistic assumptions... My own conclusion is that it is time to move on.[16]

Four decades on he was having doubts about his own modern portfolio theory and recognised that it needed to incorporate a much broader range of factors to be useful in the real world. But this has not stopped the influence of these theories, at the very highest level.

Greenspan's flaw

Let us return to our hero, Alan Greenspan. A product of the Markowitz-Fama generation of economists, Greenspan believed that markets would respond to price signals and self-correct if they went too far in any one direction. To allow them to do their job without interference, he helped to unwind regulations that had been put in place after the Great Depression to temper banks' risk-taking.

Greenspan's tenure in charge of the Federal Reserve lasted 18 years and, ironically, was bookended by the highs in the land market in two successive cycles. Not that this long span of experience helped him identify the cause of the economic cycle and therefore how to navigate it. He presided over not one, but two, stock market bubbles and a housing bubble. Worse, his faith in the self-regulating nature of markets meant he did not intervene to forestall them, particularly the Land Boom of the 2000s, because excesses would be corrected by themselves. In fact, he saw what proved to be the damaging practice of securitisation as market innovation at its best, allocating risks to market participants who wanted to bear them.[17]

Such instruments followed the model. They were traded in large, liquid markets where people could observe prices, which reflected available information. They were well diversified in terms of their underlying assets (mainly property). But in 2002 billionaire investor Warren Buffett labelled them 'weapons of financial mass destruction' for spreading the risks throughout the economy – and these risks were related to the property market.[18] Such vehicles were the point at which modern portfolio theory came up against the law of economic rent. There was only ever going to be one outcome: boom and bust.[19]

Greenspan's fall was great. As financial markets crashed in late 2007 and 2008, his reputation plummeted with them. In October 2008, a month after Lehman Brothers had collapsed, and just two weeks before the Queen visited the LSE to ask why no one had seen the crisis coming, Greenspan was hauled in front of the US Congress.

Prior visits to the US legislature had been occasions for lawmakers to celebrate his economic prowess. Not so now. There was a bitter reckoning, and Greenspan was subjected to the harshest examination of his career. In a series of exchanges that resembled an interrogation, irate legislators time and again questioned his abilities and his blind faith in his ideology. Why had he supported financial deregulation? How could he have been so wrong? Had he changed his mind?

In the end, our tragic hero was forced to confront his hubris, his worldview now shattered:

THE SECRET WEALTH ADVANTAGE

The whole intellectual edifice collapsed in the summer of last year... I
still do not fully understand why it happened,

he admitted, his ignorance revealed to the world.

> ... I discovered a flaw in the model that I perceived is the critical
> functioning structure that defines how the world works. I had been
> going for 40 years with considerable evidence that it was working
> exceptionally well...

> ... I don't know how significant or permanent [the flaw] is. But I have
> been very distressed by that fact.

The flaw he had found, though he was incapable of articulating it as such,
was that when linked to the land cycle financial markets are incapable of self-
regulating. The land market does not allocate land efficiently, and banks do
not allocate credit appropriately; they create improper incentives, as Professor
Garicano pointed out.[20] This creates an economic vulnerability that stock
markets, blindly following the land and credit markets, cannot see in advance.
In fact, they amplify the boom and bust. In the case of financial innovations
such as securitisation, they ensure that everyone in the economy is directly
exposed to the downturn.[21]

Nothing has changed

Given the admission that went against this market ideology, it is surprising that
nothing has changed since the crisis, at least not for average investors. When
you go to your financial planner, the process you are taken through reflects the
principles of modern portfolio theory to a large degree. You are asked about
your goals and your financial situation; you are asked about your tolerance for
risk. The planner enters this information into a programme, and it spits out
a series of financial products that match your profile – the right mix of risky
assets such as equities and lower-risk ones such as bonds. It ensures you are well
diversified in assets that have seemingly low correlation to one another. There
is no point doing anything else, you will be advised, because you cannot have
an advantage in the market.

Within the parameters of prevailing practice, it is a sound process. And it
works, for a time, because during the expansionary years of the cycle markets
go up steadily. The question is what happens as the cycle matures, when you
are in the midst of the Mania? The intellectual framework underpinning the
approach, and the investment rules it provides, leads most to continue happily
shopping for expensive assets in the knowledge that, though high, the market
price is right.

The point at which you need this process the most is precisely when it lets you down. Even if the market did reflect all available information, market prices would still be flawed because knowledge of land, economic rent and the economic incentives these create – particularly to create as much credit as possible against high land prices – has been deliberately expunged from our collective consciousness. At extremes, the market is not capable of identifying when and where the risks in the system are.[22] It gives investors an illusion of control they do not possess.

———— ·■·— ————

Let us now return to our cycle journey. By now, the Mania has been going two years, longer than even the doomsayers can believe (and some may even have come around to accepting it as a new standard of economic activity). You now know why investors continue to jump enthusiastically into the market. Delusion is everywhere. We are now fast approaching the top of the cycle, the Summit.

THE MARKET CAN BE TIMED

Key lessons

A significant amount of your wealth – particularly towards the end of the cycle – will be tied to the stock market. Therefore, you need to understand the limitations of the industry's standard approach to investing. This is not to say that it is all wrong. It is always important to consider what your investment goals are, your time horizons and how risky you want your investments to be. These are important questions. But the following *Wealth Secrets* must be used to inform your decisions.

1. Always know where you are in the 18-year cycle

As the stock market is heavily influenced by what is going on in the economy and as companies themselves react to the dynamics of the cycle, it will dictate how well your investments will do.[23]

2. Markets can be timed

a. The biggest falls in markets take place at the extreme points of the cycle, especially at the mid-cycle Peak and end-cycle Summit. Of the 25 falls of 25% or more in the US market since 1900, 23 have occurred in the aftermath of the Peak or Summit stages.

b. Very good years in the stock market generally coincide with key cycle points, typically the Start and the Land Boom.[24]

c. The great bull markets coincide with the Start/Expansion and Land Boom/Mania stages.

d. Do not invest more money at the end of the Expansion or Mania stages of the cycle, approximately 6–7 and 13–14 years after the Start respectively.

3. Use knowledge of the cycle to assist where to invest and whom to follow

a. Use knowledge of dynamics within the cycle to identify strong stocks to invest in.[25]

b. There are many superb commentators on markets, producing wonderful charts and analysis; but unless their knowledge of markets is based on the law of economic rent their insights are only ever going to be partial. If you follow them, do so selectively.

CHAPTER 14

THE SUMMIT

Nobody rings a bell at the top of the market.

Wall Street proverb

T**HE CHAIRMAN OF** the board called the meeting to order.

The next item on the agenda: *the 2026 financial year results and staff compensation.*

Sunny vistas and skyscrapers

The CEO presented the paper. "It has been a fantastic year," he said proudly. "Our business is strong and will only get stronger in the coming year. This is the third year of record profit growth, and we are in a position yet again to increase our dividend to shareholders. The changes we made to the staff bonus scheme are proving their worth – the more they go out there and find the deals, the more money we make. So I recommend we increase this year's bonus pool, and in 12 months' time I will report to you another record-breaking year."

Board members around the table applauded. The company's share price had never been higher: in the last three years it had doubled. Their share options were now worth a lot of money. They quickly waved the CEO's proposal through.

One of the board's non-executive members gazed out of the window in contentment. It was quite a view from the hundredth floor of the building. In the distance he could see the sunlight sparkling off the deep-blue water of the bay and the glimmer of hundreds of yachts moored in the marina. On the other side, he observed that the new Royal Tower was rising rapidly. It was the centrepiece of the country's economic renaissance. It was truly going to be a landmark, and the world's tallest. But what made it so unique was its internal floorspace, efficiently maximised using the revolutionary 'verizontal' lift system that moved people not just up and down but also across the vast building. The skyscraper would be a small city in its own right. When completed it would have hundreds of residences, a couple of hotels, several restaurants, offices and a mall. It would even have the world's first virtual theme park and nature reserve. The board member had shuddered when he found out how high the cost of renting space in the Tower was going to be. Thankfully, because of the boom, there were plenty of companies willing to pay that much (otherwise the project would not have been viable).

The new hyperloop station – the Grand Central (modelled on the famous New York landmark) – directly served the Tower. The board member still could not believe how quickly those train pods moved, almost 300 miles per hour, faster than any high-speed train. It was part of what was being called 'the Loop', the line that connected all the main hubs in the region. It had halved journey times. There was now a lot of construction around each station as developers built offices, retail and leisure venues to cater to the demands of local business. The commercial property boom was now even bigger than the residential one that started a few years back and which, thankfully, was cooling off a bit (prices were high and had not dropped; but they had stopped going up now).

It had been an inspired choice to appoint this young CEO. The board member didn't mind admitting that he had been sceptical at first. He had thought the CEO too young and lacking in experience, too keen to expand the business aggressively and corral the board into following him. The results of the last couple of years had allayed his doubts. The CEO was clearly a person of this era, which was new in so many ways. He was the best of his generation of business leaders: young, ambitious, tech-savvy, environmentally and socially conscious. He had a massive presence on social media. People listened to him. Most importantly, the shareholders loved him. *So do I. I am a follower now*, the board member thought.

The largest deal ever

The next item on the agenda was important. The CEO introduced this one too. He wanted the company to acquire a smart city operator, the world's first carbon-negative one. As the CEO described it, the board member nodded along; but truth be told he did not fully understand how it worked: how its proprietary technology helped to optimise energy usage, generate and store clean electricity, capture carbon from the atmosphere, earn carbon credits and all the rest.

The deal would not be cheap, at least not in relation to the target company's current earnings. It owned valuable intellectual property, a large portfolio of carbon emissions reduction certificates and a significant real estate portfolio, both physical and virtual. Yes, it owned real estate assets in several of the larger metaverses which had become quite valuable spaces for all manner of city-related activities – meeting places for businesses, large retail shopfronts for big brands, virtual discos and leisure facilities. The operator's business was starting to generate rents from letting out its virtual space. Only last month, one of its sites had broken new records, for hosting the largest sale of designer virtual handbags ever. A young, attractive Hollywood star had hosted the event. Its rental income was payable in cryptocurrency; in fact, these crypto-assets would soon be collateralised and form the capital base for a virtual bank (which was a new form of organisation called a DAO, or a decentralised autonomous organisation). The board member's head started to spin; but he just about understood that this bank would be creating new business by extending credit to those wanting to acquire their own plots of virtual land. This had become quite lucrative in the 'metaverse land bubble' of the last two and a half years. Overall, the CEO said, there was huge potential with this acquisition, and the target's strong balance sheet justified the high acquisition price.

This would be the largest deal in the company's history. To conclude it they would have to borrow heavily. Finance was available from a consortium of eager Chinese lenders who required fewer covenants than their domestic counterparts, albeit that the loans were short term and would require refinancing once the deal was done. While interest rates had been rising, partly because central banks across the world were attempting to temper the global boom, the margins on these loans were reasonable. The deal therefore stacked up.

The mention of Chinese banks caused the board member to pay close attention. He asked if any credence should be paid to the rumours of troubles in the Chinese banking system. Clear information was hard to come by; the authorities had got to the whistle-blower quickly, but before he was hushed, he had claimed (and said he could prove) that the volume of Chinese property lending had been understated and in some cases was hidden in off-balance sheet vehicles to bypass regulations. Some of the board member's friends in Asia were following this development carefully and had started selling assets and moving to cash.

The CEO was not worried. He assured the board that according to his contacts in the Party the Chinese authorities were on top of the situation. There had been some fraud, but it was small in scale and had only involved deals in faraway areas, tertiary cities in China – nowhere big enough to worry about. The authorities were adamant that they would not hesitate to intervene if needed. Remember how they had handled the fallout from Evergrande back in

2021 and had bailed out the property sector in 2022? The Chinese system was much more robust than the Western one; China would never have a 'Lehman moment' as American had in 2008.

Besides, the Chinese market was largely closed off from the rest of the world, so it was no problem. And yes, he acknowledged, the deal was expensive. The valuations of companies were high everywhere. There was a huge amount of bank lending going on and many interested buyers. He pointed out that there may be speculative fever in some areas – someone had just paid a record amount for a digital artwork at auction, and the papers had reported that a classic painting by one of the Masters had been sold for almost half a billion dollars – but they were buying a real company with valuable assets. The acquisition price also reflected the high value of carbon credits the company generated, and now that the world was serious about delivering a net-zero carbon future, carbon market sales was a lucrative source of revenue. Several trades bodies had provided authoritative forecasts on the continued demand for such credits and their prices. This had been confirmed by the serious droughts that had occurred last year. Wiping out a proportion of the global food crop, they had sent the price of agricultural commodities surging upward. The world needed to do more to combat dangerous climate change. Property prices – for real and virtual real estate – were also high. This was reflected in the valuation of the target's assets.

'Prices will not fall'

In any case, after a couple of boom years the CEO was hopeful that things were starting to calm down and banks were not quite so willing to lend money as before. Central banks seemed to have successfully cooled the market, and the risk of recession had reduced now that the yield curve was back in positive territory. The fact that their deal remained bankable was a positive sign. The excessive levels of consumer spending – much of it done by borrowing – were becoming more moderate, which meant that the speculative fever was reducing. Things would be on a more sustainable footing from now on. This meant the price of commodities, such as industrial metals, gold and copper, would also come down, and inflation would reduce.

"In summary," he said, "I recommend the acquisition wholeheartedly. It is safely generating a strong flow of income in terms of carbon credits and rents. We are not overleveraged, at least not compared to some of our competitors. Our lenders are secure. Yes, we may have reached a point where the boom years will moderate a bit. And the property market as a whole is in a good state now that central banks are taking action.

"Prices may flatten, but they will not fall," he declared.

The Summit analysed

And so we come, 14 years after the Start, to the Summit of the cycle. The promise of the new era, that (to most people's minds) began out of the mid-cycle Recession and which was propagated by the Land Boom and Mania, has now been realised. The world is very different to the one in which we started our cycle journey. There will be no announcement that we have arrived at the top, but after several years of booming construction, ample bank lending and consumer extravagance you will be able to identify it if you are paying close attention.

1. The grand declaration

A young, media-savvy entrepreneur declares that property and asset prices are never going down. His followers, who hang on his every word, will follow his lead and keep on buying. Business is good at the Summit, and companies are hiring. With markets at all-time highs, everyone is in profit so what the entrepreneur says seems true. People are feeling rich and, on paper, they are. They spend money. According to many metrics – such as growth, jobs, bank lending and tax receipts – the economy is in good health.

Government leaders are lauded for their management of the economy. This is a new era, one of the 'great moderation' (2004), or one where poverty has been eliminated (1928). Political leaders are surrounded by yes-men advisers, none of whom will challenge the views of the boss. Experts and business leaders make statements to reinforce this view.[1]

Even those who have previously been sceptical of how explosive the boom has been have now accepted the view that things will keep going up (though later they will tell you they had seen the top coming all along). With things going so well, who wants to ask questions? Those who answered the Queen in 2009 admitted as much.

Meanwhile, the world's tallest or largest building, announced during the Mania, is under construction. It will be opening in a year or two. Elsewhere, art auction sales continue to break records, and other news suggests some investor and consumer behaviour has become absurd.

2. High costs are squeezing businesses and households; spending reduces

Underneath the surface, all is not well. High rents, property prices, inflation and interest rates on bank loans – which began during the Land Boom and Mania – now really begin to squeeze businesses and households.[2] Even though the economy is booming, and there is a lot of activity, business investment is going down. Consumer spending mysteriously begins to reduce.[3] Bank credit, plentiful over the last few years, is increasingly tied up in illiquid assets, especially property. By this point some banks will be fully loaned up; some, having expanded too quickly in the boom, rely on short-term funding from money markets to keep up lending growth; others will increase interest on deposits to attract new customers. The flow of new lending slows as rates rise.[4]

3. The property market slows

In the land market, prices have now peaked. But signals in the property market are a bit mixed: commercial property is still doing well and is the sector where most construction is taking place. This is where the lending is now going. Commodity prices are therefore still strong.

In the housing sector, sellers are still asking for high prices, but buyers are not willing to meet them, leading to a fall in sales volumes, the first sign that the cycle approaches its Summit. House prices stop rising (in some areas they may even be falling now, especially in peripheral areas where there has been the most overbuilding). To the discerning mind, those authoritative forecasts of population growth and demand for housing (always very sensitive to their underlying assumptions) no longer look quite so robust. To most others these events are taking place far away and are not connected to what is going on at the centre of the economy.

When prices have lost the link to fundamentals, and are based on the prospect of continued growth, they cannot moderate at permanently high levels: once they stop rising, they have to fall. Housebuilding is now slowing and the recession will soon arrive.[5] A good indicator of a slowing property market is that, while the stock market as a whole continues to move up, the stocks of housebuilders are starting to fall – because their investors no longer foresee a continued rise in profits (Figure 24).

Figure 24: Select housebuilder stocks versus the broader market, 2003-2008

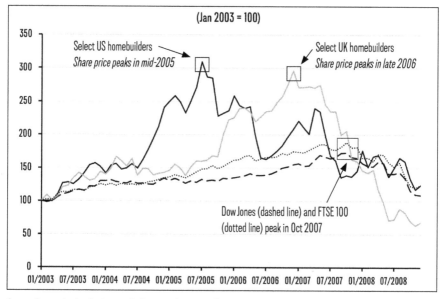

Source: Optuma (and author's own calculations and annotation).

4. Central banks try to rein in lending and engineer a 'soft landing'

As inflation has been rising, central bankers can see that the economy is in danger of overheating and are forced to act. Interest rates are raised (they may have started during the Mania), but this will not moderate the boom. They may turn to other measures to bring inflation and runaway bank lending under control and to cool the economy. But there can be no 'soft landing' because land prices have now peaked. Rising interest rates will eventually cause them to fall.[6]

5. Investment and lending flows slow down

The first sign of trouble may be trivial enough and come from left-field. It may be seemingly inconsequential or irrelevant: a piece of bad news such as a case of fraud, an accident or a weather event. Usually, it takes place in a peripheral location and may not garner much attention. But it leads to some economic losses, and some investors – particularly the older, more experienced ones – begin, quietly, to sell assets. This may cause markets to dip because by now there is no spare money on the side to buy what some are selling – everyone is now fully invested.[7] Those who have borrowed to speculate (for example the callable capital that drove the Railway Boom of the 1840s) must hope that nothing now comes along that requires all that money to be paid up.

The turn is disguised by other economic events which take place simultaneously, since activity is frenetic at the Summit. The public, encouraged by those in authority, is distracted by other issues, because no one wants to point out any real problems. If details emerge, governments do what they can to ensure that they remain hidden, as Julian Assange, the founder of WikiLeaks, discovered in 2007 when he exposed the problem-lending by Icelandic banks. He has been on the run ever since.

At the Summit, let's pause and look back at how far we have come. What a journey it has been! We have ridden the great waves of innovation and prosperity. We have lived through a boom the likes of which, we are told, the world has never seen before.

The third Act of our cycle story is now over. As we are at the Summit, most see only broad, sunny vistas ahead. But those of us who understand the cycle can see the storm clouds gathering on the horizon. We are now entering the fourth and final Act, the Crisis. The Crash is imminent.

THE LAST MOMENT TO SELL

Stage: the Summit

Approximate timing: year 14

Prevailing emotion: delusion

Managing emotion

The moment of greatest celebration is also the moment of maximum danger, the emotional point where delusion is everywhere. You will see the same excessive behaviour as at the mid-cycle Peak, but now of a far greater variety and scale. Investors will have become used to high prices, and the upward momentum of markets seems to them unstoppable. They are prepared to pay high prices today in the belief that they can sell at higher tomorrow. There are many vehicles to indulge in the pastime of speculation. It will be difficult to resist its pull at the Summit.

Managing investments

The gift of knowledge of the cycle is greatest at this stage (as it is at the Start) because you understand what all this emotion really portends, and you now have foresight of what will happen next. Use this knowledge well. Your preparation for this stage began during the Mania. You should have already been building reserves; avoided buying at high prices; selling (or preparing to sell) into a hot market; not indulging in reckless borrowing (especially for speculation), but rather paying down debt. You must not buy or invest at this stage, nor borrow any more. It is the time to protect your investments. If you hold assets now then sell quickly, or prepare to hold them for a few years.

1. Stock portfolio: sell, hedge and get ready to short-sell

a. Now is the last moment to sell your stocks, if you have not done so already, especially in sectors most closely linked to the Land Boom and Mania (especially real estate stocks), and move largely into cash in preparation for the Crash. Or you can deploy a hedging or defensive strategy.[8] Do not invest in any more stocks.

b. Begin to identify weak companies to short-sell in the subsequent Crash. The best candidates will be in the banking sector, will be the most highly indebted and will have expanded quickest during the boom (borrowing to do so).

2. Secure your property investments

a. Unless you can do it quickly, it is probably too late to sell property.[9] If that is the case, you should expect to wait until the Start or Expansion stages of the next cycle, some four or so years away. However, if you purchased good-quality, well-located real estate during the Land Boom (or even earlier) then prices should be comparatively robust during the crisis. These assets should be held. Your portfolio should be able to withstand falls in value, because they will not last forever.

b. You should ensure that you have good tenants in place and can comfortably cover interest payments to the bank with a margin of safety. You may need to be prepared to reduce rents should the downturn be particularly severe. For most investors, having lower rental income but secure, paying tenants is better than having no tenants at all.

c. This is a time of great danger for property developers, as the property (especially housing) market slows down and other developers are trying to sell stock at the same time, causing prices to fall sharply. Speed is of the essence if you still hold stock.

d. By now you should have reduced your borrowings to the extent it is feasible. You should not be in a position where you need to refinance or roll over bank loans during the difficult times to come, when bank lending might be severely curtailed. If you have too much debt, or you risk having to refinance it in a year or two, sell assets now to bring your borrowing level down.

3. Prepare to take advantage of the flight to quality

In the Crash there will be a flight to quality assets, including government bonds and gold.

a. At the Summit buy government bonds, which will have high yields and low prices. When the crisis arrives their price will go up, so you will have capital appreciation as well as a higher level of (secure) income.

b. Having been short the US dollar, investors should now sell other currencies and buy the dollar at low prices. Investors can also buy other 'safe haven' currencies such as the Japanese yen and Swiss franc.

4. Continue to hold commodities, gold and silver

a. Continue to hold commodities bought during the Land Boom and Mania stages of the cycle. These will tend to peak after the stock market.

b. If you have not already, put some of your investment portfolio into gold and silver, which will rise in line with other commodities and then be further boosted during the crisis.

5. Sell fine art, wine and other collectibles immediately

a. Sell those collectible items and alternative investments that are being held as investments. In the Crash, such assets are sold, but as they do not generate income, they are unlikely to have many buyers. Assets that have no earnings will lose the most value.

b. Bear in mind that rising interest rates can be very damaging for such assets, so these investments may peak before the broader market.

6. Businesses must prepare for the crisis

a. By now business owners should be prepared, having ensured debt levels are low (and remain serviceable), costs are under control, operations lean and that they have a significant cash reserve. This is the same preparation as at the mid-cycle Peak and Recession, but in readiness for a much deeper and prolonged downturn.[10]

b. Businesses should not be at risk of banks calling in loans or of needing to refinance for at least two (or possibly four) years after the Summit. Ensure no part of your business might potentially breach loan covenants or other terms that might give the bank an excuse to investigate. The goal is to maintain as much capacity as possible for the Start of the new cycle.

ACT IV
CRISIS

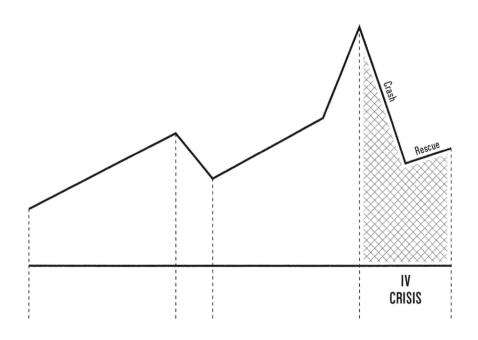

In this Act, the economy crashes, authorities desperately intervene to arrest the collapse in asset prices and restore the banking system. It lasts on average four years.

Chapter 15: The Crash; the stock market collapses. The property market slumps and brings the banking system down with it. There are widespread business failures. But despite the difficulties, you have prepared well. Therefore be steadfast, do not panic, and ride out the storm.

Chapter 16: Of Conmen and Fraudsters shows you how to resist the charms of the conman and protect your investments. Attempts to defraud you are an inevitable feature of the cycle.

Chapter 17: The Rescue is the last stage of the cycle. Authorities finally stop the Crash and enact measures to rescue the banking system and property market. Be patient and get set. Now is the time to prepare to buy as bargains appear.

Chapter 18: The Global Cycle covers key lessons from the cycle and new themes for the remainder of the present one. But remember, the more things change, the more they stay the same. Learn the lessons of this book well so that in any cycle, present or future, you will know what to do.

CHAPTER 15

THE CRASH

Once the defaults mount, and they typically begin to mount on the periphery, every market participant will necessarily seek to protect itself by calling in claims against others and rebalancing assets that have lost value. If all do so at the same time the system will self-destruct.

Katharina Pistor, *The Code of Capital*

S OME OF THE older heads on the street are worried. "Something is not right," they claim.

But their younger colleagues are not listening. The year has started out much like any other: calm. Sure, a trading firm out east has run into difficulties, and the director of an investment bank has been found to have embezzled funds (the authorities shut it down quickly). But these things happen from time to time: what is there to be worried about?

Their older colleagues still shake their heads. "Something is not right," they insist. "You've earned your millions in fees, but you have overdone the property loans. What about our traditional clients – the merchants and shipping houses? They have exemplary credit, but they are being charged higher interest rates. What's going on, if times are as good as you claim? Be careful," they warn, "Money is getting scarce. The authorities are looking at what we are up to and will do something about the high rates of interest. We've seen this before. There's trouble brewing."

The youngsters scoff. "You old men: you're always stuck in the past. The world is different now. It is more connected, trade is strong. New cities are springing up with all the latest amenities and housing. There's business to be done. Stop worrying, and let's go out and make money."

Some weeks pass. No one pays heed to the rumours that some loans are not in good shape. A few of them, though, concern large investments projects in the European periphery: they might be in trouble. There is only a passing mention here and there, but many banks have interests in that part of the world. If they default in large numbers, in the tight money conditions, there might be a problem. But no one is really discussing this openly, and on the face of it everything is fine. "Relax," they tell themselves. "Things will settle down soon enough."

More time passes. A bank approaches the money markets for an injection of funds. People are surprised: why would it need money? It is in good health, surely. The rumours about problem loans can no longer be ignored. Now everyone is wary, and no one steps forward to help out. The bank's depositors panic and rush to take out their savings. Fear is in the air. Interest rates are rising. As they increase, a number of loans are classed as 'non-performing' because borrowers are struggling to keep up with repayments. This only adds to the sense of panic.

At the same time, aggrieved customers are taking lenders to court because banks have ignored regulations on the charging of interest. The rates have suddenly shot up, leading to a wave of delinquencies. In prior years, there was lax bank supervision and the regulators failed to enforce the rules or had been bamboozled by ingenious schemes, such as offshore vehicles. In an attempt to contain the problem, the authorities belatedly enforce the regulations that they had wilfully ignored in years gone by.

Now real estate prices have started to fall, also under pressure from high interest rates. The government now attempts to lower rates. It also issues credit guidance, requiring lenders to set aside a proportion of their capital to prop up the falling market. The authorities inform the banks: you have 18 months to meet these new regulations. Normally, these measures should work; but in the panic the attempt to ensure an orderly sell-off in the property market has precisely the opposite effect. Though banks are given enough time to meet the new rules, in the precarious market conditions, with funding scarce, banks call in their loans at once, and in full. The panic now breaks out everywhere.

Businesses suddenly find their previously friendly bank managers at their door demanding immediate repayment of loans. In desperation they are forced to sell their assets. But everyone is facing the same problem: no one has any money and there are few buyers. The few who are safe are waiting until prices have hit rock bottom. Asset prices collapse. Businesses that were the most highly leveraged prior to the Summit face the greatest difficulties. Shipping, mining and construction companies cannot access any finance for their operations, no matter how sound the venture. Borrowers default on their loans. The entire banking system is compromised and on the brink of collapse. What had started with profligate lending for real estate has now spread so far that the commerce of the entire world is grinding to a halt.

The Crash analysed

This account might have been a description of the great panics of 1847 or 1929 or 2008, or indeed of any of those that take place at the end of every real estate cycle. But it is not. It covered the events that took place some 2,000 years earlier, in Rome of AD 33.

For all the differences of the ancient Roman world to our own, in a critical way it was exactly the same: dominated by land speculation and bank credit. The panic of AD 33 precipitated the largest financial crisis of the ancient world. The episode highlights the universal nature of the law of economic rent and the forces that lead from boom into bust. Like our own world, land and property were bought and sold in private markets; huge programmes of infrastructure investment created the features of Roman civic life; ownership of urban real estate was concentrated in the hands of a small number of wealthy landlords. It, too, had a sophisticated financial system, offering a wide range of banking and financial services and an array of products for investors to put their money into. Bouts of land speculation fuelled by bank credit erupted in episodic financial crises. The era might be different, but the Crashes unfolded as follows.

1. Pre-conditions to the Crash

In the couple of years prior to the Crash, capital had been pulled into the land market. This was due to the Roman elite purchasing auctioned property that had been confiscated from Sejanus and his followers. Once the second most powerful man in the Empire, he had fallen out of favour with the emperor Tiberius and was executed in AD 31.

This caused, noted the historian Tacitus, a 'dearth of money': higher interest rates would have been the result.[1] Before the Summit of the cycle there are always tight money conditions. Higher rates then undermined regulations which capped the rate of interest on loans. Unsurprisingly, borrowers complained to the relevant authorities – the praetor's court – that rules were being broken. Belatedly, the legislation was enforced by edict of the emperor.[2] One thing would clearly have happened: high interest rates eventually stopped activity in the real estate market, causing property prices to fall and defaults to increase. The other aspect of banking regulations at the time was that a proportion of lenders' capital had to go into real estate. This would have been instituted to prop up property prices: another feature of a maturing cycle.[3]

THE SECRET WEALTH ADVANTAGE

On the eve of the crisis, all of the elements come together to create a perfect storm: a slowing property market (when everyone is fully invested), rising or high interest rates, borrowers under pressure, a lack of liquidity and tightening regulations. As we saw from the prior chapter, the land or property market is the first to peak. But there is often a lull in activity – the calm before the storm.[4] Most are going about their business, seemingly blissfully unaware of what is about to happen. But seasoned investors will know that something is not right. In this context, otherwise trivial events will concern them: the loss of richly-laden ships in a Red Sea storm caused problems for their backers; fraudulent activities of bank directors in a financing house in the east; and at the other end of the Roman world, there were rebellions in the province of Gaul. It was there, and to the other peripheral regions of the empire, rather than in Rome or the Italian hinterlands, that much investment had flowed.[5]

These are the pre-conditions to the Crash which is about to unfold. All it needs is a trigger event.

2. The trigger event

At the Summit of the cycle, the system is in a critical state. While the Crash may not take place for another year or two, the system is vulnerable and the crisis will break out at its weakest point, the one most susceptible to the risk posed by rising interest rates. This will expose the people who are most highly-leveraged, either because they have to roll over loans at higher rates or because the interest on loans adjusts upwards. Either way, the debts are no longer affordable.[6] It may not take a very significant event to initiate the Crash.[7] Just as a trivial problem, seemingly unrelated to the boom, might be the first sign of the Summit, the Crash begins after a trigger event.[8] This event reveals the system for what it is: mired in debt, under stress. All regulatory safeguards have been circumvented. Panic ensues. This event invariably involves a financial house – a bank, a shadow bank, an investment fund – failing in some way.

In AD 33, the critical state was reached when available money was tied up in illiquid property loans and banks could no longer absorb losses from shipping ventures and loans in Gaul. The trigger event was the failure of banks on the Via Sacra to lend to each other following the reports given by two banks that were exposed to trading problems and fraud by a third.[9] In 1845, during the Railway Mania, it came to light that many railway schemes were fictitious, and many of those in operation could not offer anything like the flow of dividends that they had originally claimed. Similarly, in 1929 the failure of the Hatry business empire in London caused British investors to pull out of their investments in Wall Street. In February 2007, HSBC's announcement of losses within its subprime portfolio had the same effect: bond yields for non-government debt suddenly rose, indicating worry.

As a result, other banks lost trust in each other's solvency, or financial health.[10] This is when the full impact of the earlier troubles really starts to bite, because banks without liquidity cannot support the economy (a bank whose assets were illiquid would need help from other banks to absorb losses from a shipping concern, for example). This led to a general worry within the financial system. Similarly, in March 2008, Bear Stearns had to suspend subscriptions and redemptions to hedge funds that owned debt instruments linked to the US housing market.[11]

The rush for liquidity is now not far behind.

3. The rush for liquidity

After the trigger event, people want to sell their assets and get out before it is too late.[12] Those who face margin calls as prices fall will be forced to liquidate what they *can* sell, which means high-quality assets. The price of these falls also. As the quote at the start of the chapter points out, when everyone does so at once the system self-destructs because there is no liquidity (a function of excessive property lending). People cannot buy what is being sold. The inability to sell causes everyone to suddenly revalue their assets downwards. The fall in price becomes precipitous as it enters a vicious spiral. Selling begets more selling. Anyone who does have cash will only buy when prices have hit rock bottom.[13]

4. The bank failures

The initial attempt to contain problems by reducing interest rates will not work if the price of real estate and the value of other collateral is still falling and bank loan write-offs are increasing. After a land boom fuelled on bank credit, no one knows how far prices will fall. It becomes clear by degrees how exposed everyone is to a falling property market.

Owing to a lack of liquidity, there may be a run on banks as depositors withdraw their money. The bank may not be able to meet demand for payment. They are forced to close or secure emergency funds. The first banks to fail are those that have lent to the most marginal and speculative property schemes during the Land Boom and Mania stages.

During the Great Depression, the bank failures came in waves as panic spread to different parts of the banking system, beginning with those banks exposed to defaulting farmers and the collapsing Florida real estate market. Then there was a short period of calm as the market tried to work out if the problems had been contained, followed by the recognition that they had not, setting off the next wave of failures in Chicago and then Detroit. Finally, the largest wave induces a general, economy-wide panic.

Nowadays, central banks are quicker to intervene, making lending windows available to those entities deemed to be at risk. During the summer of 2007, the Federal Reserve and other central banks opened up lending windows to commercial banks to quell the panic that manifested itself in the run on Northern Rock in September. This settled things down for a time, until investment banks reported not having enough liquidity, setting off another panic in early 2008. The lending windows had to be extended. During that summer concerns extended to other specialist financing entities such as the monoline insurers, and then, in July, to Fannie Mae and Freddie Mac. After the collapse of Lehman Brothers in October, the panic became general.

5. Business failures and economic depression

As the banking system freezes, banks stop lending, withdraw working capital and credit facilities and call in loans from otherwise viable businesses, something my family's business experienced in 2009. Businesses, especially small ones, fail. Business profits are also very pro-cyclical and evaporate in the Crash and downturn. This is because, in the short term at least, major costs are fixed or cannot be easily reduced (rent, wages, interest and taxes). Businesses operating at the margin collapse entirely. As businesses employ around two-thirds of the working population, unemployment rises sharply.[14]

Construction is a major domestic industry in any economy (after a Land Boom it may comprise up to 20% of the economy) and it is the first to collapse as the property market freezes. As a significant employer, especially of low-skilled labour, its slowdown leads to a large number of job losses. The average rise in unemployment following a crisis is almost 10%.[15]

Businesses that are most heavily reliant on external finance from banks are the first to fail. These tend to be the ones that have borrowed most heavily in the boom, taking on too much debt that cannot be serviced or rolled over. Even companies that are reliant on internal finance, though in a stronger position to wait out the storm, have to cut back because profits drop sharply.

An economy starved of credit cannot function and contracts below its long-term trend, i.e., it is in an economic depression.

6. The market crash

Stock markets are generally falling before the problems really come to light. At the end of the cycle, stock markets quickly price in the dire economic conditions to come.

These trigger events often incite a panicky sell-off, as they did in October 1929 and October 2007. Since the problems then appear to have been contained, markets often make it back halfway as investors buy back at what they regard as low prices (on the basis that the problems are not systemic). This lower top is the prelude to a more significant fall, or series of falls (see Figure 1 in the Prologue, p.16). However, the full-blown market crash tends to follow bank failures. The average decline has been 46%.[16]

Each new wave of bank and business failures induces another significant fall in stock prices. The shares of companies that are most exposed to the falling property market – real estate companies, housebuilders, banks and other financing companies – decline the most.

The market only finds a low when it is confident that the government has adequately backstopped the banking system and there is enough liquidity in the system for businesses to start to recover. There is an old Japanese rice trader's saying which sums this up appropriately: "It is not safe to buy until a market has halved and the would-be buyer takes 80% of that figure and then a 20% discount."

7. Property market collapse

In the aftermath of the crisis, the average fall in property (house) prices is approximately 35% in real terms. The length of the decline is six years, longer than the bear market in equities. But these average falls mask the much greater fall of property and land prices in outer locations.[17]

The Crash typically takes two years from the Summit to the lowest low point of the cycle. As it takes place, adding to the deep distress of the investing public is the revelation of the great cons and frauds perpetrated in the prior boom. In every cycle these succeed in luring away the hard-earned savings of a large number of people. It is possible, indeed likely, that either you or someone you know has been affected. This is the other way in which your investing can be led astray, resulting in great harm to your financial health.

In the next chapter, we leave the cycle briefly to look at how we can stay safe.

STAY CALM AND WAIT FOR THE LOW

Stage: the Crash

Approximate timing: years 15 and 16

Prevailing emotion: panic, fear

Managing emotion

This is when fear is extreme. You must remain calm. Do not panic. You will have prepared for this. Your profits are protected. Your assets are high quality, and you are not overleveraged. Be confident and steadfast. Things will eventually turn around.

Managing investments

Your success in this phase of the cycle will largely depend on how well you have prepared in the prior stages and how well you manage your emotion. If you survive this stage, you will be very well positioned for the future. Therefore, preserving your capital is key. The value of most assets will fall; you must not be a forced seller in a falling market.

1. Wait for the lows

If you have prepared well your expenses will be manageable, your debt is serviceable, your investment portfolio is robust and you will have spare cash.[18] You must not be dependent on rolling over loans, because obtaining new loans will be difficult – if not impossible – to do during the Crash. This applies in particular to businesses. The cash reserve is key: it helps alleviate a fall in income or revenue, and if you are required to reduce your borrowings it can plug the gap. Survival is key and is the main aim.

2. Short-sell weak stocks

If you wish to take advantage of the violent moves in the markets:

a. Short-sell the stock market if you can, using a tracker fund, which rises in value as the market falls. There are now a number of funds to help investors take advantage of falling prices.

b. Short-sell real estate and banking stocks. These fall the hardest in this phase given the problems that they run into in a falling property market. Note that the bear market will not go on forever. So do not wait too long to take profits shorting the market.

c. Do not buy dips in the market, particularly in the rally after the first panic. If the US market has not fallen by 50% it is unlikely to be the end of the Crash. Be patient and wait for the bailout to stabilise the system in the next stage of the cycle.

3. Manage your property portfolio

Continue to manage your property portfolio to generate rental income. At some point during the recession, rental income from property in good locations will rise; because people begin moving in search of jobs, and there are more renters than buyers. You should be on the lookout for this.[19]

4. Continue to hold safe assets

You should continue to hold your government bonds and safe haven currencies, which appreciate during panics.

5. Continue to hold gold but sell commodities

a. Continue to hold gold and silver; these appreciate when there are fears for the health of the financial system and deflation threatens (which can occur as a result of a recession with high levels of debt overhang).

b. It is time to sell commodities. Commodities have peaked after the US stock market in all but one cycle since 1800. As the economy moves into recession the prices of commodities should fall, so do not hold for too long.

CHAPTER 16

OF CONMEN AND FRAUDSTERS

It's only after the tide goes out that you see who has been swimming naked.

Warren Buffett

The prospect of getting rich, quickly

O NCE UPON A time, an investor was contacted by someone he knew about an exclusive opportunity. It was a crypto coin mining scheme, and he was given details of a mining technology that would be used to generate coins. His acquaintance was an expert on cryptocurrency and had a large public following on social media. The investor was pleased to be asked: on the face of it, it looked to be a highly profitable scheme.

The investor was pressed to make a decision quickly: exclusive opportunities that earn fabulous returns are not available forever, he was told. But being financially savvy (at least by his own estimation), he knew he had to do some due diligence about what the scheme actually entailed. He had questions about three things in particular. First, he had never invested with this person before and wondered if his acquaintance might just take his money and run. Second, he did not really understand the scheme. There was no prospectus, nor anything in writing that might explain, simply, what the investment involved. And third, he wondered why he, and not someone else, had been approached with this potentially lucrative opportunity.

'You can trust my expertise'

He was the first to admit that cryptocurrency was not an area he knew much about, especially in relation to mining. But he knew that in the past 12 months many people had made a lot of money in the space and he wanted to be one of them. The expert talked vaguely about "other income streams" and he was known from his public profile to have some success in forecasting the movements of cryptocurrencies. In the absence of more information (answers to further questions were a little vague), the investor assumed that these additional returns must be based on trading the coins that had been mined. He also trusted in his acquaintance's expertise and assumed that a person with such a following would be risking too much of his reputation to be doing anything nefarious. Besides, the investor was a busy man and would not know how to conduct further research himself. His main calculation was:

1. It promises large rewards and will pay out on a specific day in the not-too-distant future.

2. I am only going to invest a small amount which I can afford to lose if the scheme does not work.

3. Even the profit share arrangement seems reasonable (the expert, who is my account manager for this scheme, is entitled on the pay-out date to a commission of 10% of the profits).

So he took the decision to invest. The reality was that he had already become emotionally tied to it when he was first contacted and heard about the potential return on offer. By the time of the formal decision, it would have actually taken quite a lot for him to walk away.

Once the decision was made, he was invited to open an account with an online platform and then provided details, via the messenger function of the app they were chatting on, of a crypto wallet he could transfer some of his bitcoins into to buy into the scheme. This initial outlay was immediately credited to his account online. At least his first concern – that the money invested would simply disappear – had been swiftly allayed.

Adding to the investment

Once the coins were deposited, the account manager got back onto the chat to inform the investor that the scheme he had invested in had different tiers. The tier he had accessed was a good one, certainly, but it was not the best. With a higher investment he could more than double expected profits. He was gently pressed to consider it: the expert wanted what was best for him. At this point the investor had some doubts; not least because if he went ahead he would be putting in an amount that was more than he could really afford to lose. But his account manager was persuasive – he wanted the investor to succeed and should trust him. The investor thought: *he is an acquaintance and I know him through some of my friends; that's why he wants to help me. The investment horizon is short, and I've already committed to this investment. I can see the initial funds in my account – so let's go for it.*

He decided to go ahead, and within a few days he was thankful he did because the scheme started generating mining profits almost straight away. This assuaged his second concern somewhat, that the scheme could not deliver what the manager had promised. Within a few days it had earned enough profit to return his entire initial investment and it was accruing continually. Interestingly, though, the profits credited to his account were only in round numbers. And while the expert had claimed there was some risk involved, the investment returns only went in one direction: up.

When questioned about it his account manager merely said he was very good at what he was doing. The manager was friendly, checked in with the investor every day, and discussed how well things were going. But he did not provide any further detail about why the scheme was doing so well. As the profits were by now quite high, the investor did not feel like questioning him and did not want to jeopardise the good relationship they had by seeming not to trust him. He felt a bit vulnerable because, while there was profit in his account, he knew his funds had been deposited with the manager's company, and not an independent party who controlled the money at arm's length. It was far more pleasant to think of benefits that would soon be his: *perhaps I will build a much larger stock portfolio. I can add to my property portfolio and effectively cover my current income passively. Perhaps in a few years I will have enough money to proverbially 'live happily ever after'.*

About a week before the scheme ended, the manager asked if in the final few days he wanted to deposit an additional amount to take advantage of a new mining opportunity that had just come up. It was a small amount, but the investor refused. He was still a bit suspicious that so much profit could accrue so quickly with seemingly no risk. His concerns about what the scheme was involved in had never been fully put to rest. In his mind, while holding to his rosy dreams of how he could invest the profits, he made a decision that he would withdraw profits in the amount of his initial investment at the earliest available opportunity. That way, should anything go wrong, at least he would not have a loss to his initial capital. If the remainder compounded quickly he would have a profit; if not, so be it.

On the day the investment was due to pay out the manager contacted him to congratulate him on the large profit he had made and was about to take hold of. Now was the time to withdraw! Per the initial agreement (albeit not one that had been formally signed) he had to share 10% of the profits, a common feature of many crypto-based trading schemes. The investor was happy to do so. It even seemed a little unfair that the manager's profit share was only 10% when the scheme had proven to be so lucrative.

You can't get your money out until...

There was a catch: it was payable as a commission up front, before the full profit could be withdrawn. Ten percent of the much larger profit by far exceeded the initial investment. The investor's initial fears about the scheme now returned. He angrily confronted the manager, refusing to pay the commission. But after much discussion he was persuaded to focus on how much profit he would have within minutes of this being sorted out. The expert offered, as a favour, to cover half the commission as a personal loan. The expert made it clear he was doing the investor a favour and was now placing his trust in him to actually return this loan. The investor was somewhat mollified by this, so decided to transfer half the commission.

The investor waited for the funds to arrive. But soon he was informed that there was a glitch. The account manager told him there were some problems with the payment process. By now, it was clear that something had gone badly wrong. So the investor reached out to a mutual friend to find out whether she knew if the expert was involved in any scams. Up to now, he had been embarrassed to ask for help because, despite the profits that had been made, he knew that if he were to explain it to someone else they might be alarmed at the way he had got involved. But his friend was sympathetic. As an investor and entrepreneur herself, she knew how many people find themselves in difficult situations like this.

His friend did a bit of digging around. She agreed that the delay to the payment was strange. Perhaps it was a Ponzi scheme where their mutual friend had got in over his head and was struggling to return money to prior investors, having to delay paying out later ones as a result. Or maybe he had violated some regulations and was being investigated. Maybe those large profits were not available right away after all. It was a puzzle alright.

The truth was far simpler. The account manager was not his acquaintance at all. It was a professional scammer who had faked their mutual friend's profile and used it to run a fraudulent investment scheme taking money off his followers on social media.

The platform and the account was fake. There were no profits. All the transferred bitcoins had been stolen. As they were untraceable, they were never coming back.

An attempt to defraud you is inevitable

It seems obvious now what was going on in the example above. It was clearly a scam and should have raised red flags almost every step of the way. The investor considered himself financially astute and should never have been duped. In the section that follows we will go over some things that he could have done to avoid the trap in the first place. The things he missed are common to many such frauds.

Some warning signs are clearer in hindsight. At the time, the prospect of fast profits, particularly in an area where other people were making a lot of money, is powerfully alluring and causes one's judgement to go awry. I know this directly, because the naïve investor of the story was me.

The memory is bitter, even now. Any significant loss of money is traumatic: it is made worse by having to come to terms with one's rank stupidity. In order to tell my own story, I must suppress the significant embarrassment this episode causes me still – because scammers rely on the self-imposed silence of victims to prevent lessons being learned that might keep others safe.

There are many different types of frauds and cons. Some, like this one, make you a paper profit and then ask for an advance fee to unlock a much larger one. Others, like Ponzi schemes, promise unrealistic profits over a long time and target newer individuals to pay off the initial investors. Still others, like corporate fraud, are more general, based on misleading public statements about levels of earnings, inventories and business assets (or liabilities), and aim to boost the value (or share price) of a company. But all frauds rely on misrepresentation (ranging from overly optimistic forecasts to blatant lying) and are built and sustained by various confidence tricks.

Most investors put money into something that could go badly wrong. It is part of the business of investing. But the next part of *The Handbook of Wealth Secrets* contains rules that increases your chances of staying safe (while recognising that it may not be possible to follow all of these in every case).[1,2]

As the world collapses in the Crash, frauds perpetrated during the Land Boom and Mania are revealed in ever more gruesome detail. For the two years or so of the economic depression the news is dark indeed. This is the point of maximum fear. But there is light at the end of tunnel: the authorities have been scrambling to turn the economy around. Regardless of whether the crisis takes place in AD 33 or 2008, governments put in place similar measures to deal with the problems in the banking system. This is the Rescue stage of our 18-year journey, and it is thither we now go.

PROTECT YOURSELF AGAINST THE CONMEN

Stage: all stages up to the Summit, but especially Land Boom and Mania

Approximate timing: years 1 to 14, especially years 10 to 14

Prevailing emotion: excitement, fear of missing out

Most of the wealth secrets in the *Handbook* are about making money by investing at the right time. Some are about taking measures to protect one's investments at difficult points in the 18-year cycle. But the secrets in this section are about protecting oneself from people who would do you wrong. This can happen at any point in the cycle but is most likely at points when you are most gullible. This will be when there is a general feeling that times are changing, bolstered by a new investment story, and signs that other people are making lots of money – most often during the Land Boom and Mania. This is why the stories of bubbles are invariably accompanied by the tall tales of the great tricksters of the past – Ponzi, Krueger, Milken, Trump, Maxwell, Madoff and the rest.[3]

As with most of the wealth secrets in this *Handbook*, the key is to manage your emotions and investments carefully.

Managing emotions

1. Resist FOMO (fear of missing out)

Frauds can happen at any time, but as the preceding chapters made clear, we are particularly prone to falling for them during the Land Boom and Mania.

Emotions run high during these phases. Everyone is making money. Some of your friends are telling you how wealthy they are getting. The newspapers are telling you about the latest millionaire (or billionaire). You will see lots of building going on. New businesses are opening and are busy. People you know are buying nicer homes, expensive furniture and fast cars. Emotionally, you will be more open to an approach by someone who presents you with a scheme for making lots of money.

Make sure you are investing for the right reasons – a sound opportunity that you understand – not because everyone else is doing better than you and you do not want to be left behind.

2. Have realistic expectations

Understand your market history, and be wary of schemes promising abnormal returns. This can be easier said than done when people are making absurd profits by investing in such assets as cryptocurrencies. What seems too good to be true generally is. Just remember that hardly anyone makes above market returns consistently for more than a few years, and market returns over a long period are not much more than 11% per year. [4] Critically examine the track record of an investment manager or opportunity. A genuine track record will have good years and bad years. There are few real-world investments that do not run into difficulties at some point. You will know this better than most now that you understand the dynamics of the 18-year cycle. Be prepared to dig in and ask for explanations of why some years are good and others bad, though bear in mind that newer funds may not have a track record. This is not necessarily a problem. But you should check that the manager understands there will be downturns in the market and can explain how they will handle them.

Remember, the higher the return the higher the risk. If they are promising unreasonably high returns for a low level of risk – as many of them do (a 'sure thing') – this should be a warning sign.

Managing investments

1. Understand what you are investing in

Interrogate any proposal rigorously: where does the money go, and into what? How does it make money? Ask as many questions as you want. If the manager resists answering, this is a warning sign. Two tricks they will use to resist your questions: claiming you do not trust them and saying that you run the risk of missing out if you do not decide quickly.

Any professional manager of good standing should be able to give a clear, simple account of what their strategy is. Fancy terms, financial jargon, technical language and investment gobbledygook are all deployed to lull investors into thinking that there is something highly sophisticated behind it all that they need to be part of.

Ask yourself the simple question: does what I am being told make sense? Never invest in anything you do not understand. Making money from investing is a steady, patient exercise that yields huge rewards over the long term. If you follow the ideas in this book, you will get there. This should give you confidence that you do not need to chase short-term windfall profits. Have the discipline to walk away. The only sure way to avoid getting conned by a dodgy scheme is not to invest in it.

Avoiding scams is not fundamentally a question of how intelligent you are. In some ways being smart can be a liability: you are likely to avoid asking simplistic questions because you do not want to seem ignorant. I made this mistake.

2. Ask advice or consult friends

You are not alone in this. Solicit the advice of other people. Even if you do not have any friends who are experienced in finance, find someone who likes to question things and then explain the opportunity to them. If you have trouble convincing them, you likely do not understand it well enough or have made some unreasonable assumptions.

3. Calibrate your risk

If you decide to invest in something, make sure it is affordable – i.e., losing the money invested would not ruin you financially. Do not borrow money to invest in such schemes. Do not go all-in. The only times you should do either of those things are for schemes that you directly own and/or control.

4. Separate the decision-maker and the custodian

This may not always be possible, but one way to increase the chance of your money remaining safe is to ensure those who decide on how your money is used are separate from those who have custody of your money. The scammer is often caught pilfering money from investors, or misusing it to make up for bad years. This is how Ponzi schemes work. But they cannot do so (easily) if the custodian is a different entity.

Ideally, the custodian should be a large organisation that offers real-time and continuous access to information about your investment portfolio. As my own experience demonstrates, it is not hard to fake a platform that shows returns coming in (though in hindsight the round numbers clearly meant things were being faked).

5. Ensure that the investments are held in your name

Your money should not be co-mingled with others'. It should be held in your name, and it should be clear what returns your money is earning. You should have access to your money if you need it, and ideally you should have the option of withdrawing it.

6. Trust conditionally

Don't trust what your investment manager says unconditionally. Ensure your trust is earned, based upon a proven track record for managing money. Critically, do not allow your trust to be based on irrelevant factors. Your manager may hobnob with important people, be trusted within your faith or professional network, be regarded as a pillar of the community or have a large public profile on social media. They may be generous with donations to charity or have a well-known name. These things are all well and good, but not relevant to your decision to invest with them.

Regard origin stories with scepticism, particularly the rags-to-riches tale, often implying that honest labour and street smarts have got them so far. Reliance on names or brands emblazoned everywhere is often a warning sign. Be suspicious of the outward trappings of success – pretty or handsome partners, expensive cars and the rest.[5]

7. Do not rush

"Here is exclusive access to a time-limited opportunity." A key sales tactic is to lull you into thinking that you can only invest through them and that you need to do so quickly to avoid missing out. Creating a sense of exclusivity and urgency is designed to make you decide quickly without having time to question or think about it. This is a bad sign. No genuine opportunity will be so urgent that you cannot take a few days to examine it thoroughly. If you miss out because you are taking your time to look into something, so be it.

8. Middlemen can be inefficient, costly and increase the risk of fraud

The more distance between you and the investment decision-maker, the more inefficient things become. Going through middlemen can be problematic because you may not be able to get quick answers to your questions. It is also inefficient, because every link in the chain will want fees. This reduces returns and increases the possibility of fraud taking place.

9. Manage the risk of accounting fraud

A common issue for business owners is accounting fraud, by which their own bookkeepers cook the books to siphon money into their own pockets. The justification for such deceit is often that they are not paid well and are helping themselves to what they are owed. Whether this is fair or not, it should underscore the importance of hiring good-quality professional staff and paying them properly. It will save you money and problems in the long run. It is also harder to hide fraud if accounts receivable and accounts payable are handled by different people (though this may be difficult to do in small businesses) because this would require collusion between two people, which is difficult to sustain over an extended period. If you separate out the accounting/audit function as well, having three parties involved diminishes the risk even more significantly.

10. Keep asking questions

When you invest, you do so with more than your money. You also invest with your emotions, and this can impair your judgement. The conman will toy with them, appealing to your greed and to your hopes by showing how much money you are making. This leads to the peculiar situation that for a time both the embezzler and the victim are feeling wealthy.[6]

The euphoria from an investment going well creates a second problem: you will not walk away from it, and you will do less to rock the boat with intrusive questions – especially if the manager is also the custodian of your money. You desire to maintain a good relationship with the schemer, and they will inevitably play on this by deploying the 'trust me' argument or getting angry if you show any signs of doubt.

11. Do not invest more in the same scheme

Once you are invested in a fraudulent scheme you will be asked, somewhere along the line, to put in more. Frauds continue in one of two ways. Either new investors come in to pay out the old, or existing investors are asked for more money. They depend on a continuous flow of money, and it is much easier to get it out of someone who has paid in before. Being asked for more capital is a major red flag, unless this expectation was clearly established at the outset (e.g., successive funding rounds) and you understand what the additional money is being used for.[7]

The rationale you will be given for putting in more money is that it will compound the gains you have made on paper (they will generally not admit that they have lost your money). They will claim that they are looking out for you and want you to benefit even more. Usually, the additional amounts will be smaller than the initial investment. This will be easier for you to agree to. Otherwise, it will be small in relation to the outsized gain you will be promised, particularly if this gain will come in the near future. Sometimes there will be pressure to put more in rather than sticking with what you have – and an implication that not putting more in would jeopardise your initial investment.

Remember that profits only exist on paper (or cyberspace) until they are paid out to you. Paper profits can be falsified extremely easily, as I found to my detriment.

12. When the fraud becomes apparent, get ready to walk away

Once you discover the fraud, getting your money out is all but impossible. Use any legal routes available to you, but do not expect the process to be easy.

This may seem obvious, but do not put any more money in. There may be occasions when you are not quite sure that you are being defrauded, but you have suspicions. There is pressure to put more money in to see the investment to a successful conclusion. Do not.

This will just lead to higher losses when the con is no longer sustainable. Better to take a smaller hit sooner than a larger one later.

13. Forgive yourself

When you realise the losses, the end is bitter. You will rail against the world, and you will be highly critical of yourself. The final rule is once again about emotional management: be kind to yourself. There were probably many warning signs that you should have paid attention to but missed or wilfully ignored. They become only too apparent in hindsight. You will regret what you did and what you did not do. You will be angry because the lost money could have bought you so many things.

Ultimately, however, our entire world runs on trust; and we would not want it to be any other way. Fraud is inevitable and, in the age of social media (where the cost to devise schemes and then draw in millions of people is extremely low), widespread. Acknowledge and own up to your mistake. You will not be the last person to be conned, just as you were not the first. But you must also forgive yourself. This is the only way you will be able to move on. The money may not be coming back, but do not allow your sense of self-worth to be lost too. Otherwise, the fraudster will have deprived you of something of far greater value than money.

CHAPTER 17

THE RESCUE

If we don't do this [bank rescue] we may not have an economy on Monday.

Ben Bernanke, chairman of the Federal Reserve, 18 September 2008 (a Thursday)

T HE YEAR 1973 changed the course of modern economic history, but not for the reasons most people think. This was the year when, in retaliation for Western support of Israel in the Yom Kippur War, Arab nations cut the exports of oil and sent the price up by 30%. This shock to the system, so the official story goes, hastened the financial crisis of 1973–74. The subsequent recession introduced a new type of crisis: *stagflation;* that is, economic stagnation, combined with high levels of inflation. 1973 also reshaped international politics, leading to the formal creation of the oil cartel, OPEC, to control oil prices and led to far more significant American involvement in the Middle East.

The real story

Needless to say, having learned about the cycle, you and I know better.

The crisis took place 14 years after the low in land prices in the late 1950s. The intervening period had seen much post-war investment, an economic boom, a construction boom and, particularly in the early 1970s, two years of sharply accelerating land prices. On top of this, the American government was printing money to pay for its war in Vietnam; and the commodity boom, coinciding with the upswing of the Long Cycle, meant that money was flowing around the international system. The boom was taking place in multiple countries at once.

In that era, while government credit control measures restricted how much lending the major banks could do, capital still found its way into the real estate market, for example through a new financial vehicle, the real estate investment trust (REIT). The assets of these REITs had doubled in 1969 and doubled again in 1970 and 1971, a sure sign of the Mania stage of the cycle. Then restrictions were eased on the banking sector, further adding to the flow of capital.[1]

In the UK, credit restrictions on the main banks led to 'secondary' or fringe banks stepping into the gap. The boom was fierce. In between 1971 and 1973, the price of a building plot went up 300%, and average house prices doubled. In Japan, the post-war miracle economy, the government encouraged construction; and companies were only too happy to take the bank credit on offer. Urban land appreciated by 50% in two years. Similar gains were seen in Australia, Europe and elsewhere.[2]

Central banks had tried to slow the boom, but it was too late. The American stock market peaked in January 1973 and then started falling. This was many months before the oil shock. Economies went into recession, and then into crisis as lending collapsed: the usual outcome after the Summit.[3] War and geopolitics added fuel to an already combustible situation that was about to burst into flames, but this was not the cause of the downturn. Official blame has also been placed on the wage demands of the trade unions, which exacerbated the rising inflation that always accompanies the cycle to its Summit. It is far easier to blame foreigners and workers than the real culprits: speculators in the land market.

So why did this crisis change the course of history? It is because of how governments responded in order to rescue the system.

Rescuing the system from crisis

The economic collapse started later that year. In the UK, fringe banks struggled to refinance short-term loans in the money markets after London and County Securities found itself struggling to raise funds. This was the usual dearth of money that happens when investors are wary, manifesting itself as problems in the interbank market. All banks faced the same problems. The Bank of England coordinated a response with the London clearing banks to furnish the markets with liquidity, and that settled things down.

That only worked for a while, because by now the property market was tanking. What the Bank of England had identified as a liquidity problem (banks being unable to access short-term funding) became one of solvency, which damaged the health of their balance sheets. Domestic turmoil – strikes, a tough budget and by now high oil prices – contributed to the problems, but the real cause was the falling real estate market. And this was not just in London: a wave of bank failures crossed the world, such as that of the Franklin National Bank in the US, the Israeli-British bank in Tel Aviv, the Bankhaus Herstatt in Germany, and the Signor Sindona empire in Italy. As ever, fraud and malpractice were revealed by these collapses. The crashing stock markets reflected the problems in the banking system. REITs led the way down, losing over 80% of their value.

The Rescue began with central banks, including the Bank of England, massively increasing the support available to the banking systems (not just the fringe banks). Governments played their part in arresting the slide in property prices. Interest rates, which had been put up to 16% in March 1975 to combat inflation, were cut to 5% by June to save the economy. The Wilson government increased infrastructure spending, which boosted land prices. In the US, the Tax Reform Act of 1976 created a series of tax reliefs for investors to stop selling and extended tax cuts. The French removed rent controls. Australia spurred demand for land by entering the market as a buyer.

The result was a very rapid recovery in property prices all over the world. In fact, so speedy was the response that 1975 ended up being a 'very good year' for stock markets.[4]

A new template is created

This was the reason why 1973 changed the course of modern history. Until this era, governments had been slow to respond to financial crises; now they signalled a willingness to act quickly and comprehensively. It set the template and the expectation for the speed and breadth of the government response to slumps in the property market at the end of the cycle. Banks are now rarely allowed to fail, even those that have overdone their property lending. Such lifeboat operations may have boosted bank balance sheets but prevented the marketplace allowing property prices to correct to levels at which they became affordable again, at least until the next Land Boom (as seen in Figure 25). In the words of Harrison,[5]

> In previous structural recessions, land values collapsed heavily. This facilitated the subsequent recovery, by readjusting the distribution of income among the factors of production. Rental payments were reduced to a level consistent with the true economic surplus of the economy, and there was little point in speculating in the selling price of land unless one were willing to tie up funds for 10 to 15 years. As a result, investors were attracted by the increased yields accruing to capital: this led to fresh investment, new jobs, and the engine of economic growth restarted itself... This time, however, something unique happened. Following the 1973/74 collapse at the end of the previous cycle, land values recovered rapidly, reaching their 1973 speculative peaks within five years and

during a period of ongoing recession. So the shake-out which is the usual prelude to fresh economic growth was stopped dead in its tracks.

So, a new mode of rescue came into vogue and lives with us today, even as property becomes ever more unaffordable to the average wage earner.

Figure 25: Real house prices, United States and United Kingdom, 1970-1989

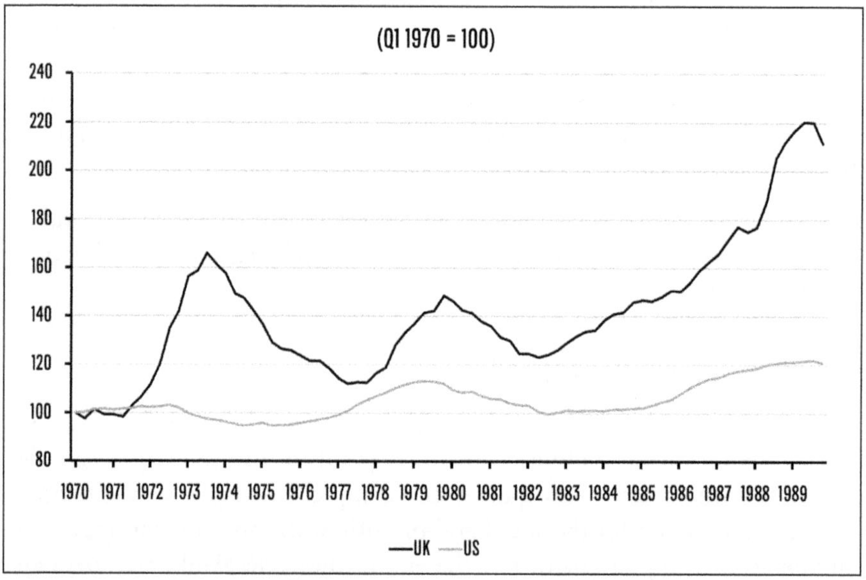

Source: Federal Reserve, Bank of England, Nationwide.

The crisis also ended the post-war economic consensus based on the ideas of John Maynard Keynes; that is, economic management by an activist state, with high levels of tax and regulation. The new policy was based on the teachings of Milton Friedman: small government, low tax, limited regulation and market forces operating in all areas of the economy and society. The UK tasted a sample of this, having to go cap in hand to the IMF for a sovereign loan. The price of the bailout was to severely cut back public spending, notably for social welfare. This was yet another example of the banks being saved but the people ruined.[6]

This new economic doctrine would drive the next two real estate cycles. The irony, of course, is that in rescuing the banking system and large financial houses, government spending (outside of war) has never been higher.

The Rescue analysed

The Crash ends at the point when government intervention stops the extreme selling. As we saw from the last chapter, this takes time. The government itself may take a while to recognise the trouble because it has confidence in regulations.[7]

Government officials might also be concerned about sending the right message to the financial system: you should sort your own houses out. They do not want to create moral hazard, i.e., if the government will ride to the rescue whenever there is a problem then banks will take more risks.[8] In reality, as they do not understand the importance of land to the economy, they do not recognise the systemic nature of the crisis.

Concerns about moral hazard disappear soon enough. As the crisis continues, minds focus on how quick and broad the rescue should be. Usually, the government needs a few attempts before the intervention works. Successive measures attempt to contain the current problem, e.g., saving a troubled institution or supplying lines of credit to a group of financing houses. This helps for a while, until the problem emerges somewhere else, at a larger scale; and thereafter spreads like wildfire throughout the financial system, indiscriminately damaging all institutions.

1. Reduction of borrowing costs

Governments lower interest rates, almost as the first response to problems. The memory of the successful response to the mid-cycle Recession will support this view (as we know, it worked then because there were no problems in the real estate market).

This is never going to be enough. No one wants to borrow in a crisis, particularly with demand collapsing. Banks do not want to lend. As the real estate market falls, they have large loan losses to write off or write down. The fall in the collateral value against which their loans are secured needs to be stopped first, and banks need to free up their capital before they can resume lending operations. This means they have to be allowed to write off losses, or their bad assets need to be taken off their books.

And so the government turns to arresting the precipitous fall in the market.

2. Addressing a market rout

In trying to stop the market panic and collapse (and so protect the balance sheets of the banking system) governments introduce measures that inject money into banks and other financing companies. They need to ensure a liquidity crisis does not turn into one of solvency. The questions they have to answer are: to whom should emergency funding be supplied, in what amounts, on what terms and secured against what collateral? The longer they delay in making these decisions, the greater the subsequent rescue will have to be.

Other measures to quell the panic include preventing sales (e.g., closing exchanges), stopping withdrawals (bank holidays) and limiting price movements (stock market circuit breakers). In prior cycles, confidence tricks were also tried to give an appearance of soundness and induce a sense of calm.[9]

This forestalls a disorderly sell-off that would lead to a deeper collapse. Both of these measures buy time to design a proper, and more systematic, rescue operation (it is hard to design anything when the panic is in the air, so the panic must be stopped first).

3. Rescuing the financial system and stopping a banking collapse

Once the panic is over the focus turns to designing the rescue package. The measures vary from cycle to cycle: organising the sale of a bank, taking bad loans out of banks, nationalising a failing bank or requiring shareholders to increase their capital. Examples include the Bank of England's rescue of secondary banks in 1973 and Congress's bailout of the Savings and Loans banks in 1990. The names given to such programmes reflects this: 'reconstruction' and 'recovery', 'lifeboat operations'. In the most recent crisis, governments opted for something much murkier – 'quantitative easing' – but the objective was the same: assist with the recovery and recapitalisation of the banking system.

This ensures that, once complete, the banks will be able to extend credit to the economy again. They can only do this once their balance sheets have been restored. Loan books damaged by underwater mortgages can be quietly offloaded when the time is right. In general, governments have become exceedingly efficient at intervening.[10]

4. Rescuing the property market

Property prices are sensitive to interest rates. The reduction in interest rates, together with supply of liquidity, might help to stop them sliding further – at least in the best locations. This eases pressure on bank balance sheets and enables an orderly rescue to take place. As short-term interest rates fall, this has a stimulative effect on the economy as well as on bank profits (or recovery of losses) to go along with regulatory forbearance. The prices of bank stocks may remain low, however, especially if they are not permitted to issue dividends.[11]

Other measures that governments enact to support property prices and get them rising again include mortgage relief, shared equity schemes, tax breaks, building affordable homes, stamp duty holidays and first time buyer grants. All are designed to enable a new cohort of buyers to re-enter the market at higher levels. No one ever looks to the real cause – the private capture of economic rent that has induced the boom and then the bust in the first place. Of all the complex measures enacted during the Rescue stage of the cycle, no one ever seriously proposes the one thing that would deal with it comprehensively: a properly designed land value tax.

Meanwhile, with the market in dire straits, the world's tallest building opens. It began construction during the heady days of the Mania, when it seemed there would be no end to the boom years. Now, no tenants can be found to pay its high rents. It sits empty, a monument to the extreme folly and hubris of those earlier years that the rescue work is now trying to resolve.

Once the Rescue is underway, the government will act to reflate the economy through stimulus. It will design new banking regulations, which it claims will prevent the next crisis. With this, we move forward: back to the Start of the new, age-old cycle.

———— · ■ · ————

The Rescue typically takes two years, completing a full cycle of 18 years. The true cause of the crisis is never diagnosed and never resolved. All that has been done has been to preserve the system for another round of boom and bust. As countries continue to develop and prosper, the cycle will grow broader and greater than even before. It is to this issue, and prospects for the remainder of the present cycle and beyond, that we turn in the final chapter, thus completing our journey.

BE PATIENT AND GET SET

Stage: the Rescue

Approximate timing: years 17 and 18

Prevailing emotion: despair

Managing emotion

The panicked emotion of the Crash subsides, to be replaced by the dull acceptance of despair. Things are bad, and it seems they will never get better. The news is grim, the economy is moribund, job losses are mounting by the day and businesses are closing down. But in every crisis there is opportunity, and if you know how the cycle works (which you do now), you can find it.

You must tune out the noise. Ignore the emotion and use this time, while measures are being taken to rescue the system, to prepare for what will soon be the best time to buy in the coming two decades.

Managing investments

As with the Crash, the preparation that you began during the boom will continue to prove its value.[12] The end of the Rescue blurs into the Start of the next cycle, and so the actions in Part 1 of the *Handbook* apply here (and vice versa).

1. Buy stocks

The stock market lows may arrive before the end of the Rescue (the stock market often prices in the recovery before it begins).

Look for higher lows on negative news. This is a good time to buy (see *The Handbook of Wealth Secrets*, Part 1.1). Short positions should have been closed and profits taken.

2. (Prepare to) buy property

Though the property market is likely to continue falling during this stage, being prepared when the market does show signs of life is important because the greatest bargains are not on the market for long. Build contacts with agents and search for areas you would like to buy in at the Start of the new cycle.

a. Rising rents are a sign of life in a location. However, be prudent in what you buy. You may well need to buy largely with cash as banks may not be lending.

b. The Start of every cycle will involve new areas becoming favoured where, at least initially, cheap property can be found. Identify areas that have high yields (which means cheap property in relation to the rents they can be let out for) but where investment is going in. Often these will be adjacent to more favourable areas.[13] Look out for interest from large developers and the return of building activity.

c. Banks may offer wealthy clients (and businesses) the chance to buy property from customers who have run into financial difficulty. Well-located property with decent tenants will be fabulous investments over the course of the next cycle. Buy if you have the resources to do so.

3. Prepare to sell gold and other safety assets

As it becomes clear that the system has been rescued, it is time to realise gains on investments that were bought to take advantage of the Crash, such as gold and other safe-haven assets. This will provide a pool of cash for investment at the Start of the new cycle.

4. Businesses that have survived should be prepared to take on distressed assets

Those businesses that have survived to this point and are in good shape should now get ready to expand, potentially by finding companies to acquire at favourable valuations.

CHAPTER 18

THE GLOBAL CYCLE

Plus ça change, plus c'est la même chose[1]

Jean-Baptiste Alphonse Karr

SO THERE WE have it. In this final chapter we reach the end of our 18-year journey through the cycle. As of writing, the present cycle is very much on track. The Land Boom is building, and it promises to be big, despite all of the worries of the moment: the war in Ukraine, inflation and the cost of living crisis, the widespread concern about imminent recession, the high levels of public debt, the lockdowns in China and various other events taking place right now, that people are only too ready to label 'crises'.

You will see the boom develop in the coming years. While you now have the knowledge and guidance to take full advantage of the cycle, it is important to recognise that it can never repeat exactly. It is a well-worn cliché that history never repeats but it rhymes. This applies to the cycle too, otherwise it would be obvious to everyone. Each iteration throws up new things that make the look and feel of it (but not its rhythm) different. Hidden beneath the surface (events) are the deeper forces at work, and they never change. Events themselves also transpire to make the cycle repeat on time.

Let us briefly consider some of the new plot lines that will be woven into this edition of our cycle story (while acknowledging that this is not an exhaustive list).

New twists to an old story

Is China leading the cycle?

Over the past century, the United States has led the world into and out of each cycle, arriving to the Summit and exiting the Rescue stages before other economies. This has been tremendously advantageous to investors elsewhere, because by monitoring what was going on in the US it was possible to obtain at least a few months' advance notice of problems in their own countries.

American leadership of the cycle was based on it being by far the world's largest economy, its biggest property market, its main creditor and, since 1945, the owner of its reserve currency. In the coming decades, some of these elements may no longer hold true. The breathtaking speed of China's development has thus far been the economic story of the 21st century.

It seems inevitable that the Chinese economy will one day be the largest in the world. Indeed, by some measures it already is. China is also now the world's largest real estate market. Does it have a real estate cycle? On the one hand, Chinese investors and property developers have as much (if not more) interest in speculation, and get into just as much trouble as those in other countries.[2] On the other hand, the Chinese government can intervene in the economy to a far greater extent than its Western counterparts, and recent events have reinforced this impression (e.g., reining in technology and educational companies, supporting property developers). Perhaps it will be able to dampen the speculative excesses of the Land Boom and Mania. Perhaps it can even manage the cycle. Time will tell. But we should note that in the past other governments have claimed to have eliminated the cycle, and history has proven them wrong time and again. The risk is that the more people assume the Chinese authorities are all-powerful, the more they will act accordingly. The crisis of confidence arising from the hint that this assumption no longer holds true will be significant indeed.[3]

China is also now the world's creditor nation, supplying finance to many other countries. Even though there are restrictions, China is a huge source of cross-border finance. In the coming years, the current flow of money outside China might become a deluge as it loosens its capital controls. This could amount to the equivalent of trillions of dollars. Chinese savers will invest in foreign financial markets as part of a diversification strategy, and banks will follow Chinese firms abroad. Chinese capital appears to have an affinity for real estate, and this will have predictable results. In addition, this will boost easy money conditions in other countries and defy attempts to manage them. As we get to the Summit of the cycle any slowdown in the flow of capital (for example, if the Chinese authorities decide to restrict lending) could trigger the next Crash.

It is interesting that the Chinese economy appeared to recover most quickly from the global financial crisis. Perhaps this was the first sign it will lead the real estate cycle in the future. But the passing of global economic leadership does not happen quickly. In the final decades of the 19th century, the United States overtook the United Kingdom as the world's foremost economic power; London, however, remained the dominant financial centre right up until the outbreak of war in 1939.

Will the US dollar continue to dominate global finance?

Increasing challenge to American hegemony has led to many forecasting the demise of the dollar's role in the international financial system.[4] It is true that we are now in a multipolar world and, as we approach the final years of the upswing of the Long Cycle, in an era of Great Power conflict. Both factors will affect the dollar. For the time being, for all the expectation and hype, the reality is that countries still need dollars; a lot of them. Half of all international trade is settled in dollars, regardless of whether American firms are involved. Commodities are still, for the most part, priced in dollars; and there are deep pools of dollars held overseas. This means that if you want to sell your dollars for something else or need to obtain dollars it is easy. In a crisis, people want dollars; and markets fall when there is a shortage of them.

The Federal Reserve's policy remains critical to the development of the cycle. Since 1971 (when currencies started floating against one another), looser monetary conditions in the US have fuelled the Land Booms and weakened the dollar in the second half of the cycles. A weaker dollar acts as a boost to global trade (and GDP) and, ultimately, drives up property prices.

Will technology change the cycle?

The pace of technological change leads to a common view that the cycle is accelerating. It is true that banking and finance, communications, doing business, trade and transportation are quicker than ever before. But this is a classic sign of the upswing of the Long Cycle. In other similar eras the effect of innovation has arguably been even greater. Think back to the middle of the 19th century, for example: before the railroad, it took at least three weeks to cross the United States. Afterwards, it took just three days. The telegraph enabled long-distance communication in a matter of minutes as opposed to days.[5] As great as the impact of any epochal technology has been, it has not so far made the cycle shorter – and is unlikely to do so this time around.

What technology *will* do is vastly increase the value of location and economic rent, and multiply the avenues to speculate in it. This will increase the net income that can potentially be generated on each site in an economy, through reducing costs or increasing output (or both). It also extends the margin, bringing newer sites into the market.[6] While technology might alter where businesses and people choose to locate, they will still need to be located *somewhere*, and wherever that is it will increase demand for the only fixed factor of production: land. As people move in and the economy grows, this generates a boom in a new area.

Technology could have other effects. Buying a house might one day be as easy as buying a share – settled in a matter of days. Or it might permit the widespread ownership of fractions of a property or other assets (which could eventually be traded on an exchange). A robo-adviser (an AI algorithm) might take charge of your portfolio, scouring the planet for the best possible investments, given your risk profile and goals, and execute your strategy in seconds. Unless such programmes discover the cycle (bearing in mind the old adage about models: *garbage in, garbage out*) it is a fair bet that they will end up making them boom and bust bigger than ever.

Higher prices for real estate allow more money creation by banks. Every era sees new advances in the pace and ease with which banks create loans for real estate: in the current era mobile banking has all but eliminated the need for bank branches. The blockchain – with its secure, distributed ledgers – promises to revolutionise banking again. The technology may support a new (possibly global) digital currency that efficiently bypasses intermediaries and makes the payment for goods and services anywhere frictionless and virtually costless. Such money will eventually flow into the real estate market. This will drive up prices, especially if banks – or institutions like them – are permitted to create credit against them.

The world is addicted to chasing the rent and creating new vehicles to do this. Recent years have seen SPACs (special purpose acquisition companies) raise money to acquire assets and Natural Asset Companies (NACs) that aim to securitise the value of the environment. Similarly, there is a major push out into space by private companies that control locations, orbital pathways and even bits of celestial bodies for mining. This rent-seeking will be aided by legislation, even though it is expressly forbidden by the only governing international treaty on the matter (the Outer Space Treaty). This is the means by which humanity will take the cycle into the farther reaches of our solar system.

The boom and bust will be global

There has been a demonstrable increase in the correlation of house prices in major cities and countries around the world. The easier credit conditions become, the more house prices move together.[7]

This is due to the fact that the economic growth in countries and regions are increasingly aligned. Indeed, most economies emerged from the last crisis at roughly the same time; even more so from the mid-cycle Recession of 2020. As they grow together, land and real estate prices rise at the same time. Lending, construction and the demand for raw materials will all boom concurrently. Large international banks look especially in the faster growing regions of the world for business opportunities; they are outside the direct supervision of local authorities. Credit becomes abundant, with domestic and foreign banks competing for business. New forms of finance become available. New investors are drawn in, looking for strong returns. All countries are rolling out huge programmes of investment. This increases the amount of capital deployed at home, further boosting economic growth and land prices. Very large investors – such as pension funds and high-net-worth individuals – cross borders to find the best investments, and international trade and finance linkages deepen even further. International capital flows end up in the real estate market in many countries. The Land Boom is global.

Economies arrive at the Summit together, and they crash together too. Here is the additional difficulty. On many measures any given economy might look healthy. It takes a problem elsewhere in the world to transmit quickly around the financial system. It might involve an investment vehicle that most thought did not present a risk. It might be in a different sector, such as commodities. If, for example, problem loans rise after a fall in the price of a commodity against which some lending has been secured, this will make others wary if capital is also becoming scarce. Because houses in major cities are increasingly treated like financial assets, housing markets are more exposed to global financial conditions than ever before; and once housing turns down, the problems in the banking system become widespread.

Global boom then turns to global bust, and regulators are left wondering what they missed and how this disaster happened on their watch.

———— - ▪ ◼ ▪ - ————

Our journey is now complete. It has been quite the expedition. You have come to know the various contours of the cycle, its peaks and troughs; you will have felt its beat, slow and unsteady at first, with some pauses along the way; then the change in pace, the rise in intensity, the violent crescendo to a climax; and finally, the capitulation. You will have come to understand why land is key to the cycle, as fundamental to the economy as gravity is to the physical universe. You will have seen how deliberate, wilful blindness of this is inculcated into our leaders: you can have confidence that the cycle *will* repeat.

You have seen how the modern economy amplifies the cycle, principally through bank credit and government investment, significantly raising the stakes during each boom. You know that when times are good a legion of actors come together to lead you astray, through their confidence that things are going well or through their confidence tricks that make you believe you can get rich quickly. When the crisis eventually arrives, you have seen how rapidly the euphoria of the boom turns to panic: the fear humans face at the edge of economic ruin is an ancient trait. And you understand how the cycle ends, when the authorities make a series of desperate interventions to rescue the economy. In those dark and difficult times people have to confront, again, the age-old question: why did no one see it coming?

But you will have. I hope that this book helps you to see the order in chaos. As you travel through the remainder of the present cycle or through the booms and panics of the future, in the years up to and beyond 2026, 2045, 2063, 2082 or 2099, you will know what to do.

This is your Secret Wealth Advantage.

THE MORE THINGS CHANGE, THE MORE THEY STAY THE SAME

A financially integrated world means spectacular booms and crushing busts in the coming years. Here are the final *Wealth Secrets* to ensure you are ready for them. These are in part a recapitulation of what we have learned before and some final instructions to help you navigate the cycles of the future.

Key lessons

1. Remember the law: the economy is driven by the law of economic rent

The economy's hidden order is the law of economic rent. Land takes the gains of progress, given its unique characteristics. While urban land is the most important source of rent in the modern economy, there are others: natural resources (such as commodities); the global commons (such as the atmosphere and outer space); other gifts of nature (the electro-magnetic spectrum); government-enforced licences; and the virtual space of the internet.[8] No one else focuses on this, so they will continuously struggle to forecast the direction of the economy.

2. Do not blindly follow smart people: they cannot see the cycle

You know that experts cannot see the cycle: they have been trained not to. Their diagnoses of the problems of the modern economy will be off the mark. But as we have seen, it could get much worse. This is a problem that affects us all: governments everywhere are captured by those seeking the right to take the rent for themselves. Over time, policies tend to increase the likelihood of the cycle repeating. When things are going over the top, who will point this out? Political leaders are surrounded by yes men and women; independent media is reliant on advertising revenue from wealthy (especially banking and property) interests; and the public, fully in profit, is not really interested in hearing that the good times will not last.[9]

3. Be confident that the cycle will repeat

If no one has any knowledge or interest in pointing out what is *really* happening, then the cycle is free to continue. Young business leaders become prominent towards the Summit stage and make decisions as if the property market could never slump. Indeed, in their experience it cannot, because they came of age after the last crisis.

The only thing that has interrupted the cycle's rhythm has been a major war. The only thing that could eliminate it is tax policy where the economic rent is returned to the public to fund further development (and the tax on other things is abolished). Absent either of these, the cycle will reliably repeat, and repeat on time.

4. Understand how money is created and where it goes

All money is created out of nothing, largely by private banks. Most of this is unproductive. This pushes up land prices even further, increases inflation and amplifies the boom. It also makes banks vulnerable when property prices fall and ultimately they need to be bailed out, at enormous cost to the taxpayer.

Money is also created by governments when they spend. Governments that issue their own currency can do so in unlimited quantities if they so wish. When it is used for productive investments that improve an economy, it is not inflationary. When it is not, it causes inflation. The second half of every cycle involves large-scale public investments and banks pushing loans into the economy. When you get a call from your bank begging you to borrow money, you will know where we are in the cycle (and your answer should be no).[10]

5. Know that things can go much further that you think

With each passing cycle the numbers get bigger. They have to. Land absorbs the gains of progress and, as our economies are highly sophisticated, these gains are greater than ever. This means higher prices for land, more debt secured against it and stronger company valuations. It follows that the cost of rescuing the system must get higher with each passing cycle because it is ultimately linked to the scale of property lending in the prior boom.

Do not be surprised to hear of various economic data reaching 'record' levels. Do not think that something different is happening that has never happened before. It has. This is the cycle repeating.

It generally means that the boom will go on longer and more broadly than you think is possible. By the Summit everyone has to be loaned up, and the entire economy has to be squeezed by high rents and rising interest costs. It is only then that a slowdown in the flow of capital precipitates the first dangerous fall in asset prices, followed by an outright Crash.

6. Watch carefully: the system will crack at its weakest point

It is entirely possible that when the next cycle Summit arrives, a financial regulator or central banker, surveying many of the most important indicators of the economy, might conclude that things look rather healthy. Bank leverage may be within regulatory limits; bank credit to GDP ratios may be at reasonable levels; house prices in relation to median earnings may be stable (even though both will inevitably be rising).

Given that we have a global cycle, the trigger event that leads to the system cracking and the subsequent Crash may originate from elsewhere. This will be at the system's weakest point. In the 2000s securitised lending exposed the entire financial system to excessive property lending in marginal locations. In the 1980s the largest problems were in Japan, with its seemingly unstoppable economic power and particular mode of corporate capitalism. In the 1920s it was the huge glut of commercial building on top of the sorry state of agricultural loans.

Predicting where the weak point will be and how the system will break is difficult. It is unlikely to be in the same place and via the same route as in previous cycles. But it will have the same fundamental cause: land speculation. Houses built on sand will eventually fall.

7. Manage your emotions and stick to the plan

In the preceding parts of *The Handbook of Wealth Secrets* you have been given an indication of the prevailing emotions at each stage of the cycle and some guidance on what you should be doing to tune out the noise and make decisions. Follow it. Be confident when others are fearful and prudent when others are euphoric.

You know when these times are likely to be. Remember that building wealth is a long-term process, whether you are an investor or building a business. If you can navigate the cycle, buy and sell at the right times, and avoid getting carried away or conned, you will be successful.

APPENDIX 1

DATES OF REAL ESTATE CYCLES

Countries affected	Start	Summit	Crisis year(s)	End
21st century				
Global	2011–12	*2026*	*2027–28*	*2030*
italics indicated forecasts as of the time of writing (2023)				
20th century				
Since WW2				
Advanced capitalist countries	1992	2006–07	2008	2011–12
	1975	1989–90	1991	1992
	1955 (approx.)	1972–73	1973	1975
Before WW2				
United States	1933	*Interrupted by WW2*		
United Kingdom	1923	*Interrupted by WW2*		
United States *also Australia, Austria, Denmark, Finland, France, Germany, Japan, Switzerland*	1911	1926–27	1930–31	1933
United Kingdom *also Norway*	1902	*Interrupted by WW1*		

Countries affected	Start	Summit	Crisis year(s)	End
19th century				
United States *also Australia, Canada, Germany, Italy, Japan, Sweden*	1894	1907	1907	1911
United Kingdom *also Germany, Netherlands, Norway*	1884	1899-1900	1900-02	1902
United States *also Argentina, Australia, Italy, Japan*	1877	1890-92	1893	1894
United Kingdom	1867	1880	1880-84	1884
United States *also Canada, Sweden*	1858	1872	1873-76	1877
United Kingdom	1848	1864	1865-67	1867
United States *also Canada, Denmark*	1839	1854-56	1857	1858
United Kingdom	1832	1845-46	1847	1848
United States	1822	1836	1837	1839
United Kingdom	1812	1825-26	1828-31	1832
United States	1800 (approx.)	1818	1819	1822
18th century				
	1781	1792		1798
	1762	1776		1781
Great Britain	1744	1753		1762
	1727	1736		1744
	1711 (approx.)	1724		1727

Note on sources:

Some sources do not refer to the real estate cycle but were nonetheless useful for obtaining dates for parts of the cycle, especially crises. Occasionally dates cited might differ depending on the datasets being analysed, or for different countries. In such cases, the author made the final determination of the date based on weight of evidence or other historical insights from the cycle in question.

Since World War 2 the United States has begun and ended each cycle first. Prior to that there was an alternating rhythm between the United States and United Kingdom, with other countries following them. There was only a continuous dataset for these two countries. Lack of data for other countries does not mean the cycle was not present. The list in the tables above covers mainly wealthier countries which had more established banking systems and land markets over the time period.

Main sources used:

Anderson (2008), Dalio (2020), Dimsdale and Hotson (2014), Harrison (1983), Harrison (2010), Hoyt (1933), Quinn and Turner (2020) Reinhart and Rogoff (2009), Vague (2019), Werner (2020)

ACKNOWLEDGEMENTS

Any author who brings forth a work knows it is invariably the product of a thousand influences, all in their own way vital to the final creation. While I have the space to acknowledge only a few by name, my gratitude to all who have helped me over the years is deep and enduring.

Particular thanks go to the following:

To my friend and business partner, Phillip J. Anderson, whose book, *The Secret Life of Real Estate and Banking*, profoundly altered the way I look at the world. I will be delighted if my own book has even half the impact on others that his has had on me. In the years since we first met, over a decade ago, Phil and I have collaborated on many projects and have built our Property Sharemarket Economics (PSE) business together to help subscribers 'remember the future'. Having worked closely with him, I can say without fear of contradiction that, as an interpreter of economic events and market action and how they fit into the economic cycle, Phil has no equal.

To our PSE colleagues: Agung, Alan, Ama, Anna, Cathy, Darren, Glorya, Irfan, Kuki, Maya, Melda, Tio and Tricia, for their great efforts in helping us to build a service of value to our subscribers; and also to the readers of my work over the years, for their ongoing interest, excellent questions and, above all, their desire to learn new things.

To the staff at Harriman House for their assistance in the unique challenge of making the ideas in a book proposal a published reality; in particular, to Craig Pearce, for sage advice about structuring and writing a book of this nature, and to Nick Fletcher, for precise queries and patient edits which did much to shape and sharpen both my own thinking and the final manuscript.

To the many friends and acquaintances who have helped me along the way with advice, encouragement, accountability and sustenance (it really was a team effort):

Christine Al Khalil, Lucy Allen, Steffi Baker, Izolda Biro, Tim Bonnici, Jonathan Brown, AdaPia d'Errico, Rob Dix, Sally Fazakerley, James Fletcher, Rowena Ganguli, Rafaelle Gelein, Jaya Govindan, Mish Grubisa, Fred Guetin, Ben Hulme-Cross, Kuki Hundal, Andrea Iro, Alison Jones, Suzi Keller, Alan Longbon, Elodie Loppe, Perry Marshall, Melina Mandelbaum, Nikki Mawhood, Kate McQuaid, Julia Mills, Julia Monosova, Alice Munro, Maureen Murphy, Sara Nasralla, Jeremy Naylor, Nick O'Connor, Andy Pancholi, Priscilla Parish, Jason Pizzino, Tim Price, Mandeep Rai, Shelley Revill, Susanna Robinson, Paul Rodriguez, Randeesh Sandhu, Lewis Schiff, Boaz Shoshan, Emily Smyth, Cathy Stacey, Anastasia Taylor-Lind, Jessica Templeton, John Tippett, Wilson Wang, Caroline Ward, Nigel Wilcockson, Steven Wilkinson, Jennifer Dawn Williams, Alex Winston, James Young, Jean-Pierre Zigrand.

And finally, to my family, without whom neither this nor much of anything else would be possible: my parents, Nalini and Girish; my sister and brother-in-law, Archana and Rana Chatterjee; my dog Izzy, whose daily demand for walks, food and attention was an enduring reminder that there is more to life than the selfish routine of the writer; and my nephew and niece, Syon and Keya. At its heart, this book is for them and their generation, written in the hope that it helps them to understand more precisely the system they are growing up in, to navigate what may be stormy seas in the decades to come, to take advantage of the opportunities that life affords them, and, perhaps, to shape their world for the better.

It is therefore to them, and all who come hereafter, that this book is dedicated.

London,
1 March 2023

BIBLIOGRAPHY

Adams, M. (2015), *Land: A New Paradigm for a Thriving World*, North Atlantic Books.

Alt, M. (2020), *Pure Invention: How Japan Made the Modern World*, Constable.

Anderson, P. J. (2008), *The Secret Life of Real Estate and Banking: How it Moves and Why*, Shepheard Walwyn.

Barker, C. A. (1991), *Henry George*, Robert Schallenbach Foundation.

Belton, C. (2020), *Putin's People: How the KGB Took Back Russia and Then Took on the West*, William Collins.

Calverley, J. P. (2009), *When Bubbles Burst: Surviving the Financial Fallout*, Nicholas Brealey.

Campbell, R. M. (2010), *Timing the Real Estate Market*, 4th edition (self published).

Christophers, B. (2020), *Rentier Capitalism: Who Owns the Economy, and Who Pays for it?*, Verso.

Dalio, R. (2020), *Principles for Navigating Big Debt Crises*, Bridgewater.

Dimsdale, N, and Hotson, A. (2014), *British Financial Crises since 1825*, Oxford University Press.

Donovan, T. (2019), *It's All A Game: A Short History of Board Games*, Atlantic.

Doucet, L.A. (2022), *Land is a Big Deal: Why rent is too high, wages too low and what we can do about it*, Shack Simple Press.

Fisher, K. (2009), *How to Smell a Rat: The Five Signs of Financial Fraud*, with Lara Hoffmans, Wiley.

Fridson, M. (1998), *It was a Very Good Year Extraordinary Moments in Stock Market History*, John Wiley & Sons.

Gaffney, M. (2009), *After the Crash: Designing a Depression-Free Economy*, Wiley-Blackwell (edited with an introduction by Clifford W. Cobb).

Galbraith, W. K. (2009), *The Great Crash, 1929*, Mariner Books.

Gann, W. D. (1923), *The Truth of the Stock Tape*, Lambert Gann.

Gann, W. D. (1949), *45 Years in Wall Street*, Lambert Gann.

George, H. (1905), *Progress and Poverty: An Inquiry into the Cause of Industrial Depressions and of Increase of Want with Increase of Wealth – The Remedy*, Kegan Paul, Trench, Trubner.

George, H. (2004), *The Science of Political Economy* (Abridged edition), Robert Schalkenbach Foundation.

Graeber, D. (2014), *Debt: the First 5,000 Years*, Melville House.

Gustafson, T. (1999), *Capitalism Russian-Style*, Cambridge University Press.

Harrison, F. (1983), *The Power in the Land*, Shepheard Walwyn.

Harrison, F. and Gaffney, M. (1994), *The Corruption of Economics*, Shepheard Walwyn.

Harrison, F. (2006), *Ricardo's Law: House Prices and the Great Tax Clawback Scam*, Shepheard Walwyn.

Harrison, F. (2010), *Boom Bust: House Prices, Banking and the Depression of 2010*, 2nd updated edition, Shepheard Walwyn.

Hodgkinson, B. (2008), *A New Model of the Economy*, Shepheard Walwyn.

Hoyt, H. (1933), *One Hundred Years of Land Values in Chicago*, University of Chicago Press.

Hudson, M. Miller, G. J. and Feder, K. (1994), *A Philosophy for a Fair Society*, Shepheard Walwyn.

Kelton, S. (2020), *The Deficit Myth*, John Murray.

Kindleberger, C. P. and Aliber, R. (2015), *Manias, Panics, and Crashes: A History of Financial Crises*, 7th Edition, Palgrave Macmillan.

Lightner, O. (1922), *The History of Business Depressions*, The Northeastern Press.

Makasheva, N. (1998), Introduction to *The Works of Nikolai D Kondratiev, vol. 1: Economic Statistics, Dynamics and Conjuncture*, pp. xxvii–xxxiv, Pickering and Chatto.

Makewell, R. (2013), *The Science of Economics: The Economic Teaching of Leon Maclaren*, Shepheard Walwyn.

Martin, F. (2014), *Money: The Unauthorised Biography*, Vintage.

Mason, P. (2015), *Postcapitalism: A Guide to our Future*, Allen Lane.

Miller, G. (2000), *On Fairness and Efficiency: the privatisation of the public income over the past millennium*, The Policy Press.

Modelewska, M. (2016), *Financing public transport using value capture finance: an incremental assessment framework for investments in transport infrastructure ("I-FIT")*, PhD thesis, University College London.

Napier, R. (2016), *Anatomy of the Bear: Lessons from Wall Street's Four Great Bottoms*, Harriman House.

Napier, R. (2021), *The Asian Financial Crisis, 1995–98: Birth of the Age of Debt*, Harriman House.

Pepper, G. and Oliver, M. J. (2006), *The Liquidity Theory of Asset Prices*, Wiley Finance.

Perez, C. (2003), *Technological Revolutions and Financial Capital: The Dynamics of Bubbles and Golden Ages*, Edward Elgar.

Peris, D. (2018), *Getting Back to Business: why Modern Portfolio Theory files investors and how you can bring common sense to your portfolio*, McGraw-Hill.

Pilon, M. (2015), *The Monopolists: Obsession, Fury, and the Scandal Behind the World's Favorite Board Game*, Bloomsbury.

Pistor, K.(2019), *The Code of Capital: How the Law Creates Wealth and Inequality*, Princeton University Press.

Quinn, W. and Turner, J. D. (2020), *Boom and Bust: A Global History of Financial Bubbles*, Cambridge University Press.

Reinhart, C. M. and Rogoff, K. S. (2009), *This Time is Different: Eight Centuries of Financial Folly*, Princeton University Press.

Riley, D. (2001), *Taken for a Ride: Trains, Taxpayers and the Treasury*, Centre for Land Policy Studies.

Riley, D. (2001), *Taken for a Ride*, Centre for Land Policy Studies.

Rogers, M. T. and Payne, J. E. (2015), 'Was the Panic of 1907 a Global Crisis? Testing the Noyes Hypothesis', retrieved from www.atlantafed.org/-/media/Documents/news/conferences/2015/0511-workshop-on-monetary-and-financial-history/papers/rodgers-payne-noyes-hypothesis.pdf.

Ryan-Collins, J., Greenham, T., Werner, R. and Jackson, A. (2011), *Where Does Money Come From? A Guide to the UK Monetary and Banking System*, New Economics Foundation.

Ryan-Collins, J., Lloyd, T. and Macfarlane, L. (2017), *Rethinking the Economics of Land and Housing*, Zed Books.

Schumacher, E. F. (2011), *Small is Beautiful: A Study of Economics as if People Mattered*, Vintage.

Standing, G. (2019), *Plunder of the Commons: A Manifesto for Sharing Public Wealth*, Pelican.

Swarup, B. (2014), *Money Mania: Booms, Panics, and Busts from Ancient Rome to the Great Meltdown*, Bloomsbury Press.

Tippett, J. (2012), *A philosopher's take on economics*, Delphian Books.

Tooze, A. (2018), *Crashed: How a Decade of Financial Crises Changed the World*, Penguin.

Tooze, A. (2021), *Shutdown: How Covid Shook the World's Economy*, Allen Lane.

Vague, R. (2019), *A brief history of doom: two hundred years of financial crises*, University of Pennsylvania Press.

Werner, R. A. (2020), *Princes of the Yen: Japan's Central Bankers and the Transformation of the Economy* (2nd edition), Quantum Publishers.

Wessel, D. (2009), *In Fed We Trust: Ben Bernanke's War on The Great Panic; How the Federal Reserve Became the Fourth Branch of Government*, Three Rivers Press.

Wigglesworth, R. (2021), *Trillions: How a Band of Wall Street Renegades Invented the Index Fund and Changed Finance For Ever*, Penguin Random House.

Wood, C. (2006), *The Bubble Economy: Japan's Extraordinary Speculative Boom of the '80s and the Dramatic Bust of the '90s*, Equinox.

ENDNOTES

Introduction

1   Tooze (2018), p. 156, 160–163. Other sources: the UK tipped into recession in April 2008 and would not return to pre-crisis levels of output for five years. Unemployment peaked at 8.4% in July 2013. US unemployment peaked at 10%. The effect on emerging economies is highlighted in IPPR's 'Financial crisis and developing economies'. The contrast between the financial crisis and the 2020 pandemic can be found here: Gopinath, G. (14 April 2020), 'The Great Lockdown: Worst Economic Downturn Since the Great Depression', IMF Blog, retrieved from www.imf.org/en/Blogs/Articles/2020/04/14/blog-weo-the-great-lockdown-worst-economic-downturn-since-the-great-depression; Elliott, L. (13 October 2020), 'IMF estimates global Covid cost at $28tn in lost output', *The Guardian*, retrieved from www.theguardian.com/business/2020/oct/13/imf-covid-cost-world-economic-outlook.

2   Lemann, N. (2017), 'The Problem with Steve Bannon's Story About His Father', *The New Yorker*.

Prologue

1   Vague (2020) and Rogers and Payne (2015). The failures were linked to the sharp fall in copper prices which had become a key input in electricity, telecommunications and transport infrastructure. The fall was due to recessionary conditions that had in part been caused by a slowing housing market in the US and other countries, on which see Hoyt (1933).

2   Anderson (2008), p. 214.

3   Anderson (2008), Appendix 1, pp. 385–386 for quotes from papers of the time; in particular, this from the *New York Globe* and *Commercial Advertiser*: "I think if we should analyse the cause of most financial panics we should find that they were caused by the failure of American women to spend their money wisely and well."

4   Fridson (1998), p. 27.

5   Hoyt (1933) and Anderson (2008), p. 216.

6   In 1921 the Federal Reserve cut its lending rate from 7% and continued doing so until 1924 when it reached a low of 3%. The US Treasury Secretary, Andrew Mellon (the country's wealthiest industrialist), cut all manner of taxes.

7   Anderson (2008), p. 221.

8   Calverley (2009), p. 27.

9   Harrison (1983). Also Vague (2020), pp. 19–20: New York developers were given a ten-year exemption from real estate taxes.

10   Anderson (2008), on the use of technology to make banking more efficient. Vague (2020) has data on debt to GDP ratios during a lending boom.

11   Peris (2018), p. 5.

12   Fridson (1998), pp. 6, 39: such was the frenzy that even sober investors, such as Ben Graham, the father of 'value' investing, participated in the bull market. Graham's normal approach was to buy only stocks that were fairly valued, but even he could not resist buying during the good times.

13   Gaffney (2009), p. 31: the variable that demonstrates the investment frenzy in the land market most was the number of subdivisions taking place.

14   Vague (2019), pp. 43–44: in Japan there was a boom in housing that followed the railroads and electricity generation; and there was speculation in rice paddies. Urban land in Osaka appreciated 20–30% a year in the boom years. It crashed 74% in 1929.

15   Hoyt (1933), p. 398: the dullness is attributed to the fact that the drivers (or as he put it the 'factors') of the boom – population growth, rent increases and new construction – are preparing to reverse trend.

16   The stock market usually peaks just after the peak of the land market. But the 1920s was different. The stock market boom outlasted the land market by fully three years. According to Anderson (2008) the land cycle peaked in 1926. That was the year construction activity peaked. After 1926, while the commercial real estate boom continued apace, residential construction fell. Partly this was due to the halting of the Florida Land Boom (which was stopped in its track by major hurricanes in 1926 and 1928).

17   Anderson (2008), p. 243: as well as mismanagement and director fraud. Depositors had been taking money out of the latter over the prior eight weeks; the bank was insolvent.

18   Anderson (2008), pp. 249–251.

19   Hoyt (1933), pp. 3–4.

20   Hoyt (1933), pp. 39, 74, 119–120, 180, 218 and 268–270.

21   Harrison (1983), pp. 110–111.

22   Gaffney (2009), p. 23: citing the work of Ernest Fisher about a similar pattern observed in data on subdivisions.

23   Anderson (2008), esp. pp. vii and Chapters 1–4 for an account of the settling of the United States through its land sales and land speculation. See also Makewell (2013), p. 50: large tracts remained unused at the outskirts of cities, leading to newer settlers having to venture further, often hundreds of miles, into the frontier to acquire land. This led to the odd pattern of development whereby the far west was developed more quickly than the closer Midwest and in between the two coasts there are vast areas of empty land – a feature that remains today. In 1790 Thomas Jefferson had thought it would take a thousand years for the land as far west as the Mississippi to be settled. Land speculators ensured that the entire continent was settled in just 123 years with the closing of the frontier in 1923.

24   Harrison (1983), p. 81.

25   Harrison was not the only one who saw it coming. A number of other economists, influenced by Harrison and Hoyt, had publicly set out how the events of 2008 would unfold. See www.thesecretwealthadvantage.com for a list of relevant sources.

26   Appendix 1 compiles the historical dates for the cycle for the countries for which we have explicit evidence.

Chapter 1

1   The Chinese stimulus was distinctive: local authorities were given strict targets to meet; and much of this was done through land sales and a vast programme of city building and property development.

2   Lewis, P. (2009), 'Dubai's six-year building boom grinds to a halt as financial crisis takes hold', *The Guardian*, 13 February, retrieved from www.theguardian.com/world/2009/feb/13/dubai-boom-halt.

3   Macworld San Francisco 2007, Keynote Address. See www.thesecretwealthadvantage.com for further resources.

4   The worst collapses are often at the periphery of a country or a region. In the EU the southern rim (Greece, Italy, Spain and Portugal) and western flank (Ireland) were most affected. However, internal politics meant that bailing out those countries' banking systems was vetoed by the northern European countries, led by Germany.

5   Tooze (2018), pp. 167, 170–171, 184–185, 193. There was further coordination with other countries through the G20 forum. This was repeating history (see Anderson (2008), p. 302).

6   The US passed the *Wall Street Reform and Consumer Protection Act* (also known as the Dodd-Frank Act) in July 2010; the UK's *Banking Reform Act* was passed in 2013. The new international regulations (Basel III) were passed by the Basel Committee on Banking Supervision, convened by the Bank for International Settlements in Switzerland. In addition, banks were required to conduct periodic stress tests to prove that, in different economic scenarios, they would remain solvent. The committee that set them was established in 1974 (after the real estate crisis of the 1970s).

7   Tooze (2018), p. 367.

8   *Irish Independent* (2014), 'Record deal as US firm snaps up Anglo's UK loan book for €4.2bn'. The US fund paid 60 cents in the etc for the loan portfolio, 26 February.

9   CEPR (2013), 'The Reinhart-Rogoff Debt-to-GDP story: why it matters', 18 April. The reasons why this view of public spending is wrong is covered in Chapter 9.

10   Corporate Finance Institute, 'Bernie Madoff', retrieved from corporatefinanceinstitute.com/resources/wealth-management/bernie-madoff/#:~:text=Bernie%20Madoff%20is%20famous%20for,to%20150%20years%20in%20prison.

11   *New York Times* (22 August 2014); $150 billion in fines were levied in the US. The total included fines for other frauds such as market manipulation. JP Morgan was fined $13.3bn.

12   Furthermor 20,000 Indignados occupied the Puerta del Sol; 200,000–300,000 people protested in Syntagma Square in Athens.

13   *The Guardian* (2013), 'John Paulson is no longer the man with the Midas touch', 21 April.

14   There is an interesting, and relatively new, branch of economics focused on studying the ways in which human behaviour is not rational (as assumed by most economic models). Here, too, there is a greater focus on the great periods of speculative mania that grip people from time to time, rather than the Start of the cycle when investors are held back from investing.

15   The turn of the cycle always involves a low in land prices. The problem is that the one variable that would highlight the turn – land prices – is the one thing not properly measured by economists and statisticians in any meaningful way. We will see why in Chapter 5.

16   See note 6 (above). Other cycles included the first set of international regulations, Basel I (implemented in 1992); the Glass-Steagall Act (1933), the creation of the Federal Reserve system (1913).

17   The first actions tell you where the new cycle is going and where much of it will take place: for example, in China there was a massive expansion in transportation – air travel, railways, mining, shipping.

18   Within a few years of Obama coming to power, all major countries would see a new generation of leaders come to power: David Cameron (UK), Shinzo Abe (Japan), Xi Jinping (China), Narendra Modi (India), Emmanuel Macron (France). While none had the historicity of the Obama election, they all heralded the dawn of a new cycle.

19   Greater internal and external migration increases demand; lack of finance and sellers pushes people into the rental market. Suddenly, there is a major shortage of housing, despite the fact that there was a large oversupply in the run-up to the Summit of the prior cycle. The edges of cities and just beyond are blighted by unoccupied or half-finished housing projects that were conceived in the Land Boom of the prior cycle.

20 Hodgkinson (2008): rents/land prices are slow to reduce because investors may still be putting money into land, given lack of alternative investment assets (and also because of government efforts to prevent further falls in the price of property); hence it may take a while to come down to levels where business is relieved of excess burden and can revive. The land market retards the recovery, and so economic growth remains slow; which also explains why commercial real estate takes longer to recover.

21 The preparation for the new cycle should begin before the old one has completed (see *The Handbook of Wealth Secrets* Parts 12, 14 and 17).

22 The process of transition from one cycle to the next takes place over time. There is never any one day that can be defined as the start date of a new cycle. Therefore the actions in Part 1 of *The Handbook of Wealth Secrets* overlap with those in Part 17 (which covers the Rescue, the final stage of the cycle). While the emphasis of the latter stage is on preparation and the emphasis in this stage is on action, in practice there is a blurred line between the two stages and, depending on specific circumstances, may mean some suggested actions are taken sooner and some later.

23 See *The Handbook of Wealth Secrets* Parts 7 and 10.

24 This is the average percentage gain from the stock market low (at the Start of the cycle) to the high (at the mid-cycle Peak and Summit) for the stock markets of the seven largest/wealthiest economies (USA, UK, Japan, Germany, France, Canada and Australia) over three full cycles since 1955. Other average percentage change statistics quoted in this book work from the same data.

25 Fridson (1998). The years he analysed included those that occurred at the Start of the 18-year real estate cycle, that is 1908, 1933 (and 1935), 1975. He selected years based on performance in a calendar year; if we also include performance over a 12-month period (even if this straddles two calendar years) then we can add 2009–10 to this list, while 1990–91 narrowly misses out according to this definition as it 'only' appreciated 30% in 12 months from the cycle low. The finding is clear: the first year or two around the Start of the cycle are big years for the stock market.

26 Gann (1923), p. 93 provides examples of how to identify strong stocks.

27 Though developments are at a nascent stage in the metaverse, virtual real estate can be bought, sold and rented out in the market place. This will lead to 18-year cycles that involve this virtual component in the future.

28 Increasing the building footprint or adding floorspace unlocks additional land value; when infrastructure goes in, land values increase. This is the law of absorption, outlined in Chapter 2.

29 See *The Handbook of Wealth Secrets*, Part 2.

Chapter 2

1 Details drawn from data in the World Bank's Data microsite data.worldbank.org/country/PS; 'Business Report 2020', retrieved from www.doingbusiness.org/en/data/exploreeconomies/west-bank-and-gaza; UNCTAD (2020), 'Israeli occupation cost Gaza $16.7 billion in past decade – UNCTAD estimates', retrieved from unctad.org/news/israeli-occupation-cost-gaza-167-billion-past-decade-unctad-estimates.

2 Details from this story were taken from 'Unreported World: Gaza's Property Ladder' shown on the UK's Channel 4, Friday 25 November 2016. www.thejc.com/news/uk/it-s-boom-not-bombs-in-gaza-for-channel-4-documentary-1.44234.

3 Ricardo was analysing the yield on different agricultural sites; in this case, the differential yield arose from different fertility of soil. This is of course also related to location, as well as the natural productive powers of different soils and the like.

4 Harrison (2006), p. 47: "The fate of the nation – economically and sociologically – is sealed at the margin. In this place, people pit themselves against the toughest challenges. Here, they have to exercise ingenuity and determination to pare down their costs to remain economically viable. At the margin, the price of labour and of capital is determined in a way that shapes people's living standards throughout society. That is why it is in all our interests to make sure that life at the margin is good in all its senses."

5   Adams (2015), p. 7.

6   How high can land go? To whatever people are willing to pay. Land is supplied by nature for free and has no production cost, and as there is no more of it, especially in good locations, you have the ability to charge whatever you think people will pay. You don't have to worry about much competition. Because you don't get more of it, it is priced not in reference to how much it costs to produce (because no one is producing it and can increase production when prices go up like normal goods in an economy).

7   Riley (2001), p. 9.

8   Riley (2001), pp. 22–25. He did this by getting regular feedback from a local estate agents, conducting periodic appraisals of his own sites and observing selling prices around five of the new stations along the line (Waterloo, Southwark, Bermondsey, London Bridge and Canada Water). Through this detailed work he was able to calculate exactly what was going on in the local land market while the new line was being built. Most similar empirical studies look at percentage gains on property prices, rather than raw land, and do not attempt to calculate the absolute increase in the value of land.

9   Rising property prices is mostly due to an increase in the value of the underlying land. While the value of a building (as reflected in its replacement cost) does rise over time, broadly in line with general inflation levels, this increase is offset by wear and tear and building obsolescence. That property prices have risen so dramatically in the last few decades is therefore very significantly down to the increase in land prices.

10 Harrison (1983).

11 Modelewska (2016), Table 2.3, pp. 74–83. This provides a comprehensive review of the many empirical studies that have analysed the impact of a variety of transport improvements, particularly rail, on property prices. The review suggests that empirically the impact on commercial property prices is greater, especially close to the stations (while the effect on residential property, while seemingly lower, extends further out). Furthermore, the highest impact can be found in areas where banking and other advanced support service industries are located. Of the 55 studies reviewed, only one considered the impact on the value of land. The extent of development was highest in areas with high land values. Similarly, the biggest impacts on prices tended to be just before the construction phase; and the projects' greatest impacts accrued at the start of an upswing in the growth of the economy and population (p.89). Two of the studies cited considered the impact of the Jubilee Line extension on the selling price of property, finding a positive effect on commercial and residential property prices, one of which estimated the increase to be between 42% and 71%.

12 Savills News (2021), 'Value of global real estate rises 5% to $326.5 trillion', 21 September.

13 Riley (2001), pp. 79–81.

14 Riley (2001), p. 83.

15 For further references on this subject see www.thesecretwealthadvantage.com.

16 Harrison (1983), p. 129.

17 See *The Handbook of Wealth Secrets*, Part 10.2.

Chapter 3

1   The IMF suggested lending limits; restrictions on mortgage lending relative to house prices or household incomes; higher bank capital requirements for mortgage lending; and additional stamp duty for purchasers from overseas. Some of these measures were applied and cooled the market in places.

2   Gains in Germany's 'big seven' cities (Berlin, Cologne, Dusseldorf, Frankfurt, Hamburg, Munich and Stuttgart) were 123.7% in the decade to 2019, compared with 60% in London and 30% in Manhattan. The lowest percentage increase was 97% in Dusseldorf and 178% in Munich.

3   For example, the vacancy rate in Melbourne fluctuated between 4% and 6% of the total housing stock according to a series of detailed analyses by Prosper Australia.

4   *City AM* (7 July 2014): Each cycle involves innovations in the banking system – in the 1980s Britain opened its first telephone bank. In the 2000s, it was internet banking.

5   The ECB pushed interest rates into negative territory in 2014. It also extended €400bn in low-interest, fixed-rate loans to eurozone banks to provide credit to small businesses, a scheme modelled on the Bank of England's Funding for Lending programme. Japan's new prime minster, Shinzo Abe, instituted what was called 'Abenomics' – a set of policies to reflate the Japanese economy by boosting the money supply, increasing public spending, reforming the labour market (e.g., increased female employment), restructuring large corporate sectors (e.g., agriculture, pharmaceuticals, utilities) and supporting free trade initiatives.

6   This was also due to booming production in the United States, using an innovative technique called 'fracking' that enabled hard-to-access oil deposits to be extracted. Such was the boom that the US became the world's marginal producer. As costs of fracking came down, so did the price. OPEC failed to respond with production cuts, hoping that a lower price would cause US frackers to fail (they survived because they had access to plenty of low-cost loans). At the same time global oil demand reduced, especially in China.

7   Martin Fridson observed in the *Financial Times* on 5 August 2014 that investors were well aware they were not being compensated particularly well for the risk, but they did not have a good alternative to meet their return requirements.

8   *New York Post*, '*Wall Street Journal*, 22 August 2014', 26 April 2014. This was a repeat of history. During the previous cycle of the 1990s and 2000s, the flow of money came from Russia and ensured the real estate boom in Western countries was huge.

9   Partington, R. (2018), 'Home ownership among young adults has 'collapsed', study finds', retrieved from www.theguardian.com/money/2018/feb/16/homeownership-among-young-adults-collapsed-institute-fiscal-studies. See also Figure 8, p.50.

10   The struggle of young people to buy their first homes is one that is common to each cycle.

11   Gaffney (2009): as land prices increase, land use gets more intensive – i.e., building more on a site, which often means upwards. This is effectively substituting capital for land. (Similar processes occur when wages get high – businesses invest in capital equipment, substituting capital for labour.)

12   Wikipedia, '2015–2016 Chinese stock market turbulence', retrieved from en.wikipedia.org/wiki/2015–2016_Chinese_stock_market_turbulence#Stock_market_bubble; IndraStra Global (2017), 'Understanding the Causes of China's Stock Market Crash of 2015', 13 October, retrieved from www.indrastra.com/2017/10/Understanding-Causes-of-China-s-Stock-Market-Crash-2015-003-10-2017-0016.html.

13   Yahoo Finance (2016), 'Peter Thiel: The vast majority of the capital I give companies is just going to landlords', 16 March, retrieved from uk.finance.yahoo.com/news/peter-thiel-vast-majority-capital-give-companies-just-going-landlords-134709786.html.

14   Tooze (2021), p. 121.

15   Variously analysed as bull or bear flatteners depending on how short- and longer-term yields are moving. However, in relation to the 18-year economic cycle, at this stage, a few years into the cycle, the flattener is generally a good sign of robust growth over the next few years. years (see also Ch. 6, note 12).

16   In the cycles that began in 1911 and 1974, the US markets did not break out until the second half – the bull runs in the second half were far greater (in the 1920s and the 1980s respectively).

17   See Ch. 18: it remains to be seen how this will change in the future as China assumes greater economic importance and heft.

18   See www.thesecretwealthadvantage.com for further information.

19   See *The Handbook of Wealth Secrets*, Part 6.

Chapter 4

1   Saul, H. (2015), 'Courtney Love blasts Francois Hollande after her taxi is 'attacked' by anti-Uber protestors and driver 'held hostage' in Paris', *The Independent*, 25 June, retrieved from www.independent.co.uk/news/people/courtney-love-s-taxi-attacked-by-antiuber-protesters-and-driver-held-hostage-in-paris-10345040.html.

2   See Chapter 2.

3   Christophers (2020).

4   Moraff, C. (2008), 'The Medallion Financial Story', *monitordaily*, May/June, retrieved from https://www.monitordaily.com/article-posts/medallion-financial-stor.

5   Salam, E. (2021), '"They stole from us": the New York taxi drivers mired in debt over medallions', *The Guardian*, 2 October, retrieved from www.theguardian.com/us-news/2021/oct/02/new-york-city-taxi-medallion-drivers-debt.

6   Chumley, C. (2013), 'Mayor Bloomberg to cabbie: "I'll destroy your [expletive] industry"', *The Washington Times*, 22 May, retrieved from https://www.washingtontimes.com/news/2013/may/22/mayor-bloomberg-cabbie-ill-destroy-your-expletive-.

7   The role of banks, owners of banking licences, is considered in Chapter 8. The lack of competition also often results in lower service quality than would have been achieved in a properly competitive market. Pistor (2019) argues that over time the law has been co-opted to create rent-based assets out of almost anything (although she does not use the term 'rent', this is what she is getting at).

8   There are four (so far) categories of platforms for exchanging labour (e.g., Fiverr), capital (e.g., AirBnB), goods (e.g., Amazon) and attention (e.g., Google and Meta) – see Christophers (2020), pp. 186–188.

9   Standing (2019), p. 259; Christophers (2020), pp. 266–269. Network effects are equivalent to colonial powers benefiting from an influx of new settlers in the territory. Economies of scope are rather like such powers acquiring or taking by force new lands, especially ones which bring new advantages, such as access to navigable waterways.

10   Christophers (2020), pp. 206–207.

11   They also are very effective at lobbying governments, directing business away from their competitors, tax avoidance schemes (by booking profits in low-tax jurisdictions, exploiting tax loopholes) and exploiting gaps in labour law to generate a competitive advantage over non-digital retailers. They have, furthermore, turned much of their profit into new forms of rent (e.g., investment in financial services and space mining). All of this sustains their dominance.

12   Capturing this data and holding it privately also acts as a barrier to entry for newer competitors who will not be able to observe how users behave and therefore what products will best meet their needs.

13   Christophers (2020), p. 7: the thirty largest companies listed in the UK stock exchange exploit one or more forms of economic rent: six benefit from banking licences, seven from exploiting natural resources and 11 from intellectual property licences. They include two platforms companies, three public service contractors, three infrastructure providers and one land company.

Chapter 5

1   The details for the story regarding the origins of *Monopoly* are taken from Pilon (2015).

2   All of the details in this description of the rules of *Monopoly* are relevant to the subsequent discussion of our present economic system and why we can't identify the 18-year cycle.

3   Details of Henry George's life story are taken from Barker (1991).

4   Therefore, money would not get sucked into the land market for speculation. Profits and bank credit would be reinvested into businesses for increased production. Landowners would need to ensure that sites were used productively, rather than held out of use. This would generate opportunities for new business formation and job creation, leading to fiercer competition and increasing demand for workers.

5   This was another lesson of the game. The value of the house actually consists of two separate components: the ground rent, which reflects its locational value, and the housing rent, which reflects the quality of housing provided. The current game of *Monopoly* conflates the two – ignoring a crucial insight about real estate. This is ironic given that it is a game about real estate speculation.

6   To give it its full title: *Progress and Poverty: An Inquiry into the Cause of Industrial Depressions and of Increase of Want with Increase of Wealth: The Remedy.* The text can be read at www.henrygeorge.org/pcontents.htm.

7   At an event at Cambridge University, George met the prime minister's daughter and adviser, Mary, at a tea at Trinity College. She had read *Progress and Poverty* the previous summer and had spoken of it with her family. She found that despite its reputation as 'the most upsetting, revolutionary book of the age' she instead found herself upon reading it with 'feelings of deep admiration – felt desperately impressed', See Barker (1991), pp. 404–405.

8   It was this issue, along with the Liberal Party's championing of free trade, that caused Churchill to cross the chamber in 1904. Free trade was another issue about which George had written passionately and eloquently.

9   Hodgskin, T. (1832), 'The Natural and Artificial Right of Property Contrasted', retrieved from oll.libertyfund.org/title/hodgskin-the-natural-and-artificial-right-of-property-contrasted.

10   In fact, it was precisely his lack of attack on business owners (capitalists) and his support for markets and enterprise that alienated those offering competing alternatives in his day: socialists and Marxists.

11   As the Princeton historian Eric F. Goldman said (about the influence of *Progress and Poverty*): "For some years prior to 1952 I was working on a history of American reform and over and over again my research ran into this fact: an enormous number of men and women, strikingly different people, men and women who were to lead 20th century America in a dozen fields of humane activity, wrote or told someone that their whole thinking had been redirected by reading *Progress and Poverty* in their formative years. In this respect no other book came anywhere near comparable influence", retrieved from web.archive.org/web/20160513073711/http://www.earthrights.net/wg/q-about-george.html.

12   Wikipedia, 'A Great Iniquity', retrieved from en.wikisource.org/wiki/A_Great_Iniquity.

13   Miller (2000), pp. 377–379.

14   Gaffney (1994), pp. 50–53. Gaffney notes the irony that academics patronised George for not being an academic or understanding economics but then devoted such tremendous efforts to argue he was wrong. Clark was pretty open about his dislike of George's ideas. In the space of less than three decades he wrote no fewer than 24 articles or books targeted at George, a tremendous focus of intellectual attack. Patten was worried about George's successful use of Ricardo's insights: "Nothing pleases [an advocate of George] better than... to use the well-known economic theories... [therefore] economic doctrine must be recast", (Miller, 2000, p. 381). Here was the naked intention.

15   Other economists (e.g., Francis Walker, who became president of the American Economics Association and director of the United States Census) attempted to eliminate the distinction between land and labour, for example arguing that the fact that different quality locations earned different rents was matched by the fact that different quality employees could earn different wages – this was reward for different skill levels. As land and labour were also similar, they should not be treated differently. He even coined a term for it: employees that were particularly skilled earned a 'rent of ability' through greater management skills. This eventually justified the huge income disparities between different people, as if it were purely down to differential skill.

16   Harrison and Gaffney (1994), esp. pp. 45ff.

17   Harrison and Gaffney (1994), p. 7. See also Hudson et al. (1994), p. 7: "More people are graduating from universities than ever before, yet the social-science curriculum has narrowed to produce what Thorstein Veblen called an educated incapacity to recognise the flaws implanted in our economy, highlighted by the trained incompetence of professional economists."

18   In fact, the house itself will have depreciated in value over that period because of the natural wear and tear of materials.

19   Ryan-Collins et al. (2017), p. 50.

20   Environmentalists worry about pollution and climate change, without acknowledging that our use of land creates sprawl that massively exacerbates the problem. epidemiologists worry about the spread of disease without understanding the economic forces that lead to viral transmission through the unsustainable exploitation of land.

21   The best recent example of this was Thomas Piketty's *Capital in the Twenty-First Century*, which amassed impressive data sets to analyse wealth and income inequality in Europe and the United States since the 18th century. His main finding was that when the return on capital exceeded the rate of growth in the economy, there was an increasing concentration of wealth. It was an exceptional success for a modern economics book. It fell to an MIT graduate student, Matt Rognlie, to point out that this concentration was entirely down to housing (i.e., land). Piketty had stumbled upon George's insight but failed to articulate it properly.

22   There are notable exceptions in smaller countries or at local levels: this idea was implemented in parts of Australia, Canada, the USA, Denmark; and would later create economic miracles in Hong Kong, Singapore and Taiwan. But it could not be implemented at the heart of the British Empire. And so the revolutionary moments of the 20th century took a much darker turn, a descent into communist totalitarianism. The cost would be counted in the loss of life that numbered tens, if not hundreds, of millions of souls.

23   Donovan (2019), p. 95. To read the second set of rules, visit www.thesecretwealthadvantage.com.

24   Tideman, N. et al, 'An Open Letter to Mikhail Gorbachev', retrieved from www.wealthandwant.com/docs/Tideman_et_al_Gorbachev.htm. See also www.thesecretwealthadvantage.com.

25   See the Prologue. Harrison resurrected Hoyt's thesis of the 18-year land cycle and brought it up to date.

26   Belton (2020). After the Soviet Union fell and the scale of potential theft became apparent, the Yeltsin government made very little effort to identify where the stolen wealth had gone.

27   Gustafson (1999), p. 183; Harrison (2008), pp. 25–26.

28   Khodorkovsky had briefly been a deputy energy minister under Yeltsin. So he presumably knew exactly what the real worth of what he was buying was, and what it might potentially become.

29   In an infamous televised event, Khodorkovsky had humiliated Putin. Later, he was arrested. The grievance brought against Khodorkovsky was that he had stolen the resources of Russia through Yukos. There was some truth to this. Regardless of the fact that what he did was legally permissible, the moral right of the Russian people to their common wealth enabled such charges to be brought against him.

30   Belton (2020), p. 474. See also pp. 448ff for details of the links between Russian networks and the Trump Organization.

Chapter 6

1   The largest vessel on show, the *Tis*, is a 111-metre-long behemoth, and it drips with opulence. Its 18 guests can luxuriate in its Versailles-esque gold marble interior, go for a dip in its large swimming pool or visit its resort-inspired spa. Such yachts are a perfect reflection of the concentrated ownership of the economic rent; not least because a number of them are owned by Russian oligarchs.

2   Statista Research Department (2022), 'Corporate profits in the United States from 2000 to 2021', Oct 11, retrieved from www.statista.com/statistics/222130/annual-corporate-profits-in-the-us/#:~:text=The%20corporate%20profits%20are%20defined%20as%20the%20net,made%20profits%20of%20around%202.25%20trillion%20U.S.%20dollars.

3   Routley, N. (2020), 'Charting the Last 20 Years of Supertall Skyscrapers', Visual Capitalist, 13 June, retrieved from www.visualcapitalist.com/charting-the-last-20-years-of-supertall-skyscrapers.

4   Of G7 countries and Australia, only in Italy are house prices on average below where they were at the Summit of the prior cycle.

5   Credit Suisse, 'Global Wealth Report 2019', retrieved from www.credit-suisse.com/media/assets/corporate/docs/about-us/research/publications/csri-global-wealth-report-2016-en.pdf; 'Global Wealth Report 2016' retrieved from www.credit-suisse.com/media/assets/corporate/docs/about-us/research/publications/global-wealth-report-2019-en.pdf.

6   Global PMI was at the lowest level since a 2016 dip and at levels last seen at the Start. The levels for key bellwethers of the global economy – Chinese, Japanese and German manufacturing, for example – were dropping towards or below 50, indicating a contraction. The signs were clear, but many people questioned whether the yield curve could still be a reliable indicator at all given monetary policy in the last few years and the extent of quantitative easing.

7   This is in sharp contrast to 12 months earlier, when it had been the opposite (right before a strong year in the stock market).

8   Wang, L. and Hajric, V. (2020), 'Mom and Pop Are On Epic Stock Buying Spree With Free Trades', Bloomberg, 21 February, retrieved from www.bloomberg.com/news/articles/2020-02-21/free-stock-trades-are-stirring-an-epic-mom-and-pop-buying-frenzy?sref=xiYOZY7h. The volume of daily trades almost doubled in five months.

9   Across the seven largest/wealthiest economies since 1955, and three Start-to-Peak stages of the cycle, the stock market has only failed to achieve new highs (exceeding the prior peak) on four out of 21 occasions.

10   This is the average low-to-high percentage gain in the stock market for the seven largest/wealthiest economies across three cycles since 1955. See also Chapter 1, endnote 24.

11   Since 1970, only the Japanese property market after its post-1990 collapse failed to achieve new high average prices by the time of the mid-cycle Peak. The other advanced country property markets (the United States, United Kingdom, Germany, France, Canada and Australia) were at or above all-time highs by the Peak.

12   Normally, the yield on longer-term bonds is higher than on short ones. If the yields of shorter- and longer-term bonds are plotted on a graph, it normally appears with a gently upwards curve. This additional yield compensates investors for the longer payback period. Longer-term bonds are also riskier than short-term bonds because their prices are more sensitive to changes in interest rates. A factor determining the yield of a long bond is the expected average of short-term interest rates during the life of the bond. If interest rates are expected to rise and remain high, the average rises as the term of a bond lengthens, as do the yields of the bonds. This means that the upward slope of the yield curve is steeper than usual. If interest rates are expected to fall, the yield curve slope is shallower than usual. If interest rates are expected to fall substantially, the yield curve has a downward slope – that is, it is inverted. An inversion of a yield curve signals an economic slowdown is coming. See Pepper (2006), pp. 46–47.

13   The authors of the book, *Dow 36,000*, were James Glassman and Kevin Hassett.

Chapter 7

1   World Health Organisation (2020) 'Pneumonia of unknown cause – China', 5 January. Retrieved from www.who.int/emergencies/disease-outbreak-news/item/2020-DON229.

2   On 16 March the Dow Jones recorded the third largest drop in its history in percentage terms, larger even than the Black Monday crash of 1929. This took place just four days after a 10% drop on 12 March. The panic is compounded because traders are working from home using unreliable domestic internet connections.

3   Much of the selling pressure was coming from overseas – from Asia in particular. And so it provided liquidity swap lines to other central banks though which they could exchange their own currency for dollars – so that they could locally meet demand for dollars from entities in their own jurisdictions.

4   Tooze (2021), p. 131; see also Cassim, Z. et al, (2020) 'The $10 trillion rescue: How governments can deliver impact', McKinsey & Company, 5 June, retrieved from www.mckinsey.com/industries/public-and-social-sector/our-insights/the-10-trillion-dollar-rescue-how-governments-can-deliver-impact.

5   See Chapter 1, p.29.

6   See *The Handbook of Wealth Secrets*, Part 1, p.38.

7   NBER (2021), 'Business Cycle Dating Committee Announcement July 19, 2021', retrieved from www.nber.org/news/business-cycle-dating-committee-announcement-july-19-2021. Similarly the UK, having experienced the deepest recession on record, experienced one of the strongest growth years since the Second World War and was the fastest growing of the G7 advanced economies. Barnett, J. (2021), 'OECD: UK muscles out G7 to top economic growth rankings', cityam.com, 21 September, retrieved from www.cityam.com/oecd-uk-muscles-out-g7-to-top-economic-growth-rankings/#:~:text=The%20UK%20economy%20will%20grow%20the%20fastest%20among,the%20highest%20rate%20of%20growth%20among%20the%20G7.

8   Tooze (2021), p. 12: points out that real estate was solid, and if anything starting to appreciate. He noted that had banks been in as bad a position as in 2008 the crisis would have been catastrophic. But it was not, because they were in a much healthier position. (They were in a much healthier position because we are at the mid-cycle Recession and not the end-of-cycle Crash/Rescue stages).

9   Hanke, S. and Greenwood, J. (2021), 'Too Much Money Portends High Inflation', Cato Institute, 20 July, retrieved from www.cato.org/commentary/too-much-money-portends-high-inflation.

10 Gascon, C. and Haas, J. (2020) 'The Impact of COVID-19 on the Residential Real Estate Market', Federal Reserve Bank of St. Louis, 06 October, retrieved from www.stlouisfed.org/publications/regional-economist/fourth-quarter-2020/impact-covid-residential-real-estate-market.   Support measures cause the household savings rate to skyrocket, reaching 30% in the USA, the highest level ever recorded (it reaches similar levels in Europe).

11 The buyers are not always discerning. The share price of a small Chinese company at one point increases by 2500%, because buyers mistake its ticker symbol ZOOM for the Zoom technology company providing videoconferencing facilities (ticker symbol ZM). In another incident, coordinated buying (using social media platforms such as Reddit) causes a surge in the share price of a company, GameStop. It is a business that has been struggling commercially and its shares are some of the most heavily shorted on the New York Stock Exchange. But coordinated buying by an army of individual tech-savvy investors forces large hedge funds, with billions of dollars under management, to cover their positions for huge losses. Their opponents are motivated by a desire to bring them down. Finfeed.com (2020), 'How Robinhood and Coronavirus created a perfect storm for young new investors', 16 October, retrieved from finfeed.com/features/how-robinhood-and-coronavirus-created-perfect-storm-young-new-investors; Ferguson, N. (2021), 'GameStop, Robinhood, Reddit and the Wind Trade' Bloomberg, 7 February, retrieved from www.bloomberg.com/opinion/articles/2021-02-07/niall-ferguson-gamestop-robinhood-reddit-and-the-wind-trade?sref=x.

12   And tech companies, seeing permanently increased demand for their services, bought prime commercial space. Outside city centres, the demand for warehousing and logistics spaces boomed as the digital transformation accelerated.

13   Larter, D. (2020), 'The US Navy returns to an increasingly militarized Arctic', defensenews. com, 12 May, retrieved from www.defensenews.com/naval/2020/05/11/the-us-navy-returns-to-an-increasingly-militarized-arctic.

14   Miller (2000).

15   The heavy-handedness of the police is often the trigger for such protest and rioting when carried out in a recession at key points in the cycle: see also the killing of Mark Duggan that led to the London riots in 2011, or the beating of Rodney King that led to the LA riots in 1992. But these are not the true cause.

16   The UK managed to avoid the one the US fell into in late 2001, the mid-cycle Recession of the last cycle, for example.

17   Whether it be the measures to move the US out of post-war and pandemic recession in 1921 by Treasury Secretary Mellon; or Federal Reserve Chairman Paul Volcker tackling high inflation in 1981; or Alan Greenspan holding interest rates low and George Bush enacting tax cuts in the aftermath of 9/11, at the mid-cycle, the measures that governments use are seen to be effective at meeting the challenge of the day.

18   See *The Handbook of Wealth Secrets*, Part 1, p. 38.

19   The stock market rises in anticipation of higher corporate earnings as the recovery takes hold. This happened out of the mid-cycle lows of (for example) the post-Recession years 1921, 1962, 1982 and 2002.

20   Frick, W. (2019), 'How to Survive a Recession and Thrive Afterwards', *Harvard Business Review*, May–June, retrieved from hbr.org/2019/05/how-to-survive-a-recession-and-thrive-afterward.

Chapter 8

1   Details from this anecdote have been taken from Martin (2014).

2   Martin (2014): "The value of the coins depended principally on their size, but also on the fineness of the grain and the whiteness of the limestone."

3   Hodgkinson (2008), p. 142.

4   This is even true in a barter exchange because one person will hand over the good before receiving something in return; for that period, however fleeting it is, he or she will have a credit on the other party until the moment that the good being acquired is received.

5   This is an important function of money – to provide a unit of account. And it is done through quantity – often through weights or numbers of tokens; or more efficiently through a designation inscribed on a standardised token. Another important function is as a store of value, allowing one to defer desired exchange into the future (you can choose when to deploy the money to get something you want). To serve all these functions, money needs to be portable (you can carry it with you) credible (people will accept it) and durable (it is not easily destroyed).

6   George (2004), p. 229. See also Martin (2014): "currency is ephemeral and cosmetic. It is the underlying mechanism of credit accounts and clearing that is the essence of money."

7   But not all credit is money – money follows, in most cases, the granting of credit. See Tippet (2012), p. 87.

8   Martin (2014).

9   The National Banking Act 1863 effectively created a federal (as opposed to a state) banking system and ended the issue of bank notes by state or privately chartered banks. At the time the US had "7,000 genuine notes of 1,600 different state banks of issue…" (Hoyt, 1933, p. 76). A system of national banks could thenceforth issue notes; however, their notes were also retired after the 1930s.

10 Ryan-Collins et al (2011), pp. 12ff. The popular perception of the bank is as a channel between savers and borrowers or as a multiplier of savings, a notion which probably evolved from the practice of goldsmiths to issue deposit receipts against gold left with them for safekeeping. They soon worked out they could issue more receipts than the gold deposited with them (pp. 38–40).

11 Ibid., p. 4.

12 Bank of England Quarterly Bulletin (2014), 'Money in the modern economy: an introduction', 14 March.

13 In this sense, the repayment of all debts and loans is inherently deflationary, to the extent that it destroys money.

14 Ryan-Collins et al (2011), pp. 77–80 gives a detailed description of the arrangements. In reality central banks have very little control over how much money is created by the banking system.

15 This is because banks will want to maximise profits by extending as many loans as possible. Central banks are then, in this view of banking, expected to set the quantity of reserves banks have to hold back to ensure they don't over-extend themselves.

16 Ryan-Collins et al (2011), pp. 84–88.

17 See Chapter 1, note 6.

18 Werner (2020). Bank statisticians refer to broad money to encapsulate all of the money created by banks.

19 The amount of money should increase with the volume of production and trade, and this should go up to the limits of the productive capacity of the economy. As economies expand and all the factors of production are used up – the economy is running at full employment and businesses have reached full productive capacity – there should be no need for additional credit other than working capital needs (in general). Beyond this, bank money will push up inflation because the money created is chasing the same level of goods and services. This is when unsound money starts to be created.

20 From the perspective of a bank, lending against real estate makes a lot of sense. Banks have to appraise a loan, and this incurs a certain cost; from a profitability perspective it makes sense to incur that cost once against a long-term loan, especially if it is secured against a piece of real estate, earning interest over many years. Lending to businesses is seen to be higher risk and shorter term and requires much more in terms of upfront appraisal and monitoring during the life of the loan. Furthermore, lending against land is different to lending to acquire a piece of capital equipment for production. Capital is used up in production; land is permanent. A bank can lend against a piece of real estate; have the loan paid off and lend against the same piece of real estate again (usually at a higher value). This is an earnings carousel that is highly lucrative for the banking system.

21 The shaded areas represent the dates of the Summit of each cycle in US history (see Appendix 1). A similar pattern can be observed in the ratios for other countries, especially in the post-Second World War period (see www.thesecretwealthadvantage.com for further details). The rise in the ratio prior to each cycle Summit year is due to a surge in private debt; the further increase after the Summit's high point is due to the fall in GDP (and the overhang of debt).

22 Werner (2020), p. 112: when banks are keen to expand their loan books they are not much able to increase productive credit creation because they cannot force borrowers to borrow, and the amount of lending depends on the fundamentals of the economy. "But banks can increase unproductive credit creation almost at will. All they need to do is give borrowers the prospect of substantial capital gains. This can be done by focusing on collateralised loans – loans where an asset class, such as land or stocks, is used as a rationing and credit allocation device. By raising the ratio of the loan value to the valuation of the land, banks attract more borrowers who think they can make a profit. As the banks raise the appraisal value of collateral, its price is pushed up, providing capital gains to the borrowers and rendering their investment profitable. Both banks and borrowers feel encouraged to engage in further such activities, and as word gets around more and more individuals and companies want to join the game."

23   The essential service that banks provide is one of liquidity: production of different goods and services have different timescales, so the demand and return of money/credit varies. Banks enable a supply of money to be available at any point it is required. It is crucial to the functioning of the system that the demand for money is not coordinated. However, during the course of each property boom, the system gets notably less liquid because a greater proportion of the bank lending goes into relatively illiquid lending for real estate, which pays back over a long time. This increases the bank's reliance on the money market for short-term funding. In practice, if everyone were to demand their money at the same time the banks would not be able to honour their obligations. The problem is that such demand events arise at the end of each cycle, when depositors are fearful of the health of the banking system. In normal times banks can seek funding from each other at low cost; but if banks have reason to suspect each other's health then the market dries up overnight and rates on interbank loans spike.

24   Anderson (2008), pp. 228, 281–282, 317.

Chapter 9

1   *The Travels of Marco Polo*, Book II, Chapter 18.

2   Werner (2020), pp. 53–55.

3   *The Independent (2015)*, "'I am so sorry': Liam Byrne apologises for his infamous "no money' letter'", 10 May.

4   A quote from a speech given by Prime Minister Margaret Thatcher to the Conservative Party Conference, October 1983.

5   In modern public finance, expenditure generally consists of direct provision of services, transfer of payments to beneficiaries or procuring goods and services.

6   Administrative arrangements will vary from country to country but the essence is the same. Tax receipts are not the basis of public finance.

7   Ryan-Collins et al (2011), Appendix 2, p. 153. In relation to the flow of tax and public expenditure, it is important to distinguish between institutional arrangements that exist as a matter of custom and practice and those without which tax/spending could not happen. The UK's decision to draw tax into a consolidated fund which is drawn upon is an example of the former. It is not needed to finance public expenditure – that can be done as described in the chapter.

8   Tooze (2018), pp. 515–516.

9   Kelton (2020), pp. 32–35.

10   Graber (2014), pp. 49–50: this often started with governments needing to provision their armies with food and equipment.

11   Kelton (2020), p. 117.

12   Bill Mitchell: "Under current institutional arrangements, governments around the world voluntarily issue debt into the private bond markets to match dollar-for-dollar their net spending flows in each period…" the reality is that "A sovereign government within a fiat currency system does not have to issue any debt and could run continuous fiscal deficits (that is, forever) with a zero public debt." Retrieved from billmitchell.org/blog/?p=34945.

13   Godley had earned a reputation in the 1970s for gloomy, if correct, warnings. He forecast that the economic boom of the early 1970s would end in 1973 and that unemployment would hit three million in the early 1980s. These earned him the title the 'Cassandra of the Fens'. Like Cassandra of Troy before him, no one would believe him until after his dire prognostications had come about, by which time it was too late to act upon them.

14   Kelton (2020), pp. 104–105.

15   This is arguably a key consequence of the pandemic stimulus programmes, which boosted savings and then increased spending during and after them; but at the same time the economy endured a major supply shock from disruptions to supply chains and from millions of people choosing to leave the workforce. The effect was to increase the money supply more than needed and create inflation.

16   See Chapter 2.

17   See Chapter 5. This is the only way that rents of land, generated in the first place by public spending, cease to be capitalised into a market price. It will bring all land that is needed into the market so that it can be used productively. Furthermore, there would be far less need for government intervention in the economy, and therefore lower public expenditure (money creation). The only tax collected would be rents that had been generated by the government's prior investment, analogous to a bank's advance to a business to increase production.

18   See *The Handbook of Wealth Secrets*, Parts 1 and 7.

Chapter 10

1   History House, 'Who was the first British monarch to travel by rail?', retrieved from historyhouse.co.uk/articles/monarch_travel_by_rail.html.

2   Quinn and Turner (2020), p. 59.

3   Winton (2018), 'Railway Mania'. Retrieved from www.winton.com/longer-view/railway-mania.

4   Dimsdale and Hotson (2014), p. 60. This is an example of the stock market anticipating the recovery in corporate earnings.

5   Parliamentary approval was required because of the need to induce landowners along the route to sell their land.

6   Quinn and Turner (2020), pp. 60–63. The interconnectedness of the network increased the value – and therefore the share price – of all existing lines.

7   Quinn and Turner (2020), pp. 63–64. Some of these periodicals died in the subsequent bust, demonstrating that they were taking advantage of the boom conditions.

8   Dimsdale and Hotson (2014), p. 65.

9   Harrison (2010), pp. 104–105.

10   Vague (2019), p. 131; Anderson (2008), p. 159 provide examples. In the US boom that topped in the mid-1850s, it is reported that lots on the best street in Omaha (then a provincial town on the western frontier which owed its existence only to the railroad) were selling for $5,000, having appreciated ten times in just 12 months. Or in the following cycle, in the ten years to 1873, land values as a whole in Chicago increased five times, while on the city fringes gains of ten times were not uncommon.

11   *The Economist* (2008), 'The Beauty of Bubbles', 20 December.

12   Kindleberger and Aliber (2015), p. 69ff. "Displacement is an outside event or shock that changes horizons, expectations, anticipated profit opportunities, behaviour… the shock must be sufficiently large to have an impact on the economic outlook. Each day's events produced some changes in outlook, but few are significant enough to qualify as a shock."

13   Other examples include: political developments (Glorious Revolution, 1688), surprising success of a new security (the Baring loan of 1819, the first important foreign loan contracted by a British bank), deregulations of banks and financial institutions, derivatives, mutual funds, and hedge funds; the creation of Real Estate Investment Trusts (REITs).

14   See Chapter 2.

15 The market price for a finished building has to be at, or rise to, a level where, for a given level of build cost per square foot, a developer can secure sufficient return on capital invested. In the first half of the cycle property prices in many outer regions are too depressed to entice developers. It is different in the second half, which leads to a large boom in such areas, often of a far more speculative nature, on the back of optimistic forecasts of demand.

16 As pointed out by real estate economist Roy Wenzlick, the shortage of space in the office market only occurs after several years of business expansion, and even then the terms of leases delay the rise in commercial property values. By the time net income from commercial rents becomes high enough in relation to construction costs, the expansion is well underway. This explains why commercial real estate tends to perform more strongly in the second half of the cycle than in the first.

17 See also Chapter 12.

18 Dalio (2020): US debt to GDP increased by 12.6% per year in the boom of the 2000s. Vague (2019) provides other examples (see pp. 49, 68, 73, 165, 184–185). Into the top of the cycle in 2007, increases in private debt to GDP were 26% (USA), 34% (UK), 72% (Spain); into the top in 1990, they were 21% (USA), 41% (UK), 38% (Japan).

19 Wikipedia, 'United Kingdom parliamentary expenses scandal', retrieved from en.wikipedia.org/wiki/United_Kingdom_parliamentary_expenses_scandal. Many parliamentarians had been irregularly claiming expenses against second homes in London that had appreciated greatly in the property boom. They were able to pay off mortgages, add extra space, let them out to tenants and avoid capital gains tax. They also made efforts to exempt their expense claims from public disclosure under freedom of information rules. See Harrison (1983), p. 159, Wood (2006), pp. 54–55 for examples from the 1970s and 1980s booms in Japan; see Anderson (2008) for examples from other cycles in the United States, especially pp. 76–77, 116–118, 164, 434ff.

20 Though evidence is not so clear cut given that freely floating currencies are a relatively new phenomenon.

21 See *The Handbook of Wealth Secrets,* Part 1.1.c.

22 See Chapter 9: private sector earnings will be increasing from the positive trade balance and government spending, and are not offset by paying taxes or interest to foreign lenders.

23 See also *The Handbook of Wealth Secrets,* Part 11.

24 See *The Handbook of Wealth Secrets,* Part 2. It is not just apartments that can get overbuilt; that depends on planning regulations and other local factors. But when land prices are high, as in large cities, and regulations permissive, multifamily apartment blocks will be built in huge numbers during the Land Boom. In addition, because land prices are high it is likely that build quality will be low (because the developers need to find ways to make profits). The lower-quality build will lead to problems later.

25 See *The Handbook of Wealth Secrets*, Part 11 for further actions related to commodities.

Chapter 11

1 Makasheva, N. (1998), p. xxxii. The kulaks were a class of landowning peasant. Kondratiev was convicted as a 'kulak professor'. He favoured a market-led approach to industrialisation (an approach that Lenin had favoured) as opposed to Stalin's determination that the government should have total control of the economy. He was convicted in 1930 to eight years in prison, the final six of which were at Suzdal.

2 Mason (2015), pp. 33–34. As we will see, this coincided with the beginning of the next Long Cycle. In the 1980s, the study of the Long Cycle became prevalent in parts of the investment industry; and again after the 2008 global financial crisis.

3   A process of technological innovation, before the start of each Long Cycle, led to widespread adoption during its early stages. Perez (2003) refers to this explosion as "a powerful and highly visible cluster of new and dynamic technologies, products and industries, capable of bringing about an upheaval in the whole fabric of the economy and of propelling a long-term upsurge of development. It is a strongly interrelated constellation of technical innovations… [which] fosters a quantum jump in potential productivity for practically all economic activities…" (p. 8). Perez's study of technological cycles, and the 'irruptions' of technological progress was heavily influenced by Schumpeter and Kondratiev.

4   Chapter 10 covered the Railway Mania in the UK, which coincided with the beginning of the Long Cycle. The subsequent railway booms in other countries, including the United States, took place during the upswing of that Long Cycle. As we saw in Chapter 5, Henry George observed the effect of the boom on land values at the peak of the Long Cycle in the late 1860s.

5   See the quote by W. D. Gann that opens Chapter 1.

6   See Chapters 2 and 4.

7   See Chapter 2.

8   But the good times came to an end in the 1970s as many governments defaulted or were unable to service their debts in the ensuing agricultural depression of the 1980s and 1990s (the downside of the Long Cycle).

9   For example, MRI and CAT scanners, TV satellite dishes, smoke detectors, freeze-dried food, cordless tools and portable water filters.

10   The example of space is a demonstration how these conflicts get taken off the Earth. The Open Space Treaty of 1967 preserves space as the global commons and the common heritage of all mankind. It prohibits appropriation by countries and supposedly the capture of the economic rent. However, we are seeing increasingly private commercial interest in space resources to capture the rents of space for private benefit. Once established, such interests will need defending, including by military means.

Chapter 12

1   In this Japan was generously assisted by the Western allies. The yen was pegged to the almighty dollar at a low rate – ¥360 to the dollar – and Japanese companies could export their products easily to the huge American economy. It was further assisted by financial aid and technology transfers, through which it rebuilt its industrial base and then outcompeted economic rivals in industry after industry: first textiles, then steel and shipping, automobiles and then finally high-end electronics (see also Werner (2020), p. 90).

2   Note here how this links back to the themes of Chapter 9 – growth in the external sector was replaced by growth in the domestic one. Since the government was also to play less of a role, growth had to be maintained by boosting the private domestic sector through increasing access to bank lending.

3   Werner (2020), p. 95.

4   Vague (2020), p. 75

5   Werner (2020), p. 107.

6   Werner (2020), pp. 110–112: in Japan since the banking crisis of 1927, the majority of borrowers could only obtain loans if they could put up land as collateral (banks were then not interested in what the money would be used for). This was a limit was set by the Ministry of Finance to ensure there was always a safety margin. Bank officers would check the published land prices of each area, the *rosenka*, and then extend credit up to 70% of the value. Loan officers bypassed this problem by anticipating future growth in current valuations (see note 9 below).

7   Werner (2020), p. 107: the treasury divisions of companies were beefed up to enable speculation in land and the stock market.

8   While set up along Western capitalist lines, its economy was uniquely Japanese; built upon the dense social and hierarchical structures of 19th-century industrial Japan. Until the banking reforms were put in place, under a system of window guidance, the state directed credit in a way that would best help the economy to grow. And growth was the objective, not corporate profit. The state was interventionist to support their companies so they could be globally successful: they created regulatory barriers, offered subsidies and provided access to funds to nurture these large companies and their networks.

9   Loan officers got around the problem of loan-to-value restrictions by counting the anticipated growth in price for the following year (often projecting last year's increase to next year). In this way, it often became possible to extend 100% of the purchase price as a loan. As the bubble continued, they would sometimes anticipate two years' worth of price growth.

10 Other signs of excess: banks also lent to the *yakuza* (though sometimes risked their officers' health by asking for their money back); bank managers were given aggressive loan growth targets; fraudulent certificates of deposit meant that lending restrictions could be passed over.

11 The price-earnings (or P/E) ratio is a measure of how expensive the share price of a company is, as it expresses the price as a multiple of earnings per share of that company. So the higher the price, the greater the multiple.

12 Scheid, B. (2020), 'Key stock valuation ratio climbs above 1929 pre-crash level', S&P Global, 4 December, retrieved from www.spglobal.com/marketintelligence/en/news-insights/latest-news-headlines/key-stock-valuation-ratio-climbs-above-1929-pre-crash-level-61586487.

13 Iwamoto, Y. (2006), *Japan on the Upswing*, Algora.

14 Werner (2020), p. 106.

15 Wood (2006), p. 129

16 Vague (2019), p. 72; Werner (2020): land prices increased 245% between 1985 and 1989.

17 And the land beneath just the Imperial Palace in the city was estimated to be worth more than the land of the entire state of California.

18 The Pack Database, 'The Japanese Theme Park Bubble', retrieved from www.theparkdb.com/blog/japanesethemeparkbubble.

19 Werner (2020), p. 99.

20 High-profile acquisitions in the United States included the $831m purchase of Pebble Beach golf course, the $1.4bn purchase of the Rockefeller Center by Mitsubishi, and the $3.4bn purchase of Columbia Pictures by Sony.

21 Other films expressing this disquiet included *Bladerunner* and *Rising Sun*.

22 Alt (2020), pp. 159–160.

23 Yates, R. (1990), 'In Japan, golf is a pastime only for those with plenty of green', *Chicago Tribune*, 31 May, retrieved from www.chicagotribune.com/news/ct-xpm-1990-05-31-9002140319-story.html.

24 The painting by van Gogh was the *Portrait du Dr Gachet*. This would be a record price paid for a piece of art that endured until 2004. The painting by Renoir was the *Bal du Moulin de la Galette*.

25 da Costa, C. (2022), 'The Seagaia Ocean Dome Was The World's Largest Indoor Beach', *Gadget Review*, 27 June, retrieved from www.gadgetreview.com/the-seagaia-ocean-dome-was-the-worlds-largest-indoor-beach.

26 Harrison (2010), p. 89.

27 See Chapter 8. Also visit www.thesecretwealthadvantage.com for further resources on this point.

28 So even if banks stay within regulations, their lending would get more risky given where the projects they are lending to are.

29 Gaffney (2009), p. 32: "A bank that is all loaned out, no matter how sound its balance sheet, cannot make new loans much faster than its debtors pay back the old ones."

30   In the formulation of Hyman Minsky on speculative bubbles this is the point at which finance becomes speculative, as opposed to hedge finance. Speculative finance can only be paid back from sale of the asset (at the same or higher price) at a future date – because the earnings from it cover at most the interest and not a portion of the principal.

31   Hoyt (1933), p. 383: there is a rapid increase in construction. The volume of activity is five times higher in the busiest years compared to the quietest.

32   Hoyt (1933), pp. 385–386.

33   Gaffney (2009), pp. 34–37 documents the full sequence. Land becomes overpriced (it is not produced and has no cost of production to check its overvaluation); this brings marginal land into the market and induces sprawl as developers move outwards. Construction ties up scarce capital; sprawl also reduces the efficiency of the economy because it scatters activity over a broader space. Marginal investments reduce the rate of return across the economy. A less efficient economy where the rate of return on capital is decreasing is more vulnerable to a crisis.

34   See Gaffney (2009), p. 31. There is an overhang of ripening land.

35   Gaffney (2009), p. 32: there is no equilibrium in a market such as this; if prices are not continuing to rise they have to fall. Ironically it is near the top of the cycle that authoritative commentators come out and talk about how the world has reached a new plateau of permanently high prices.

36   Werner (2020), p. 106: "Companies who owned land were valued higher as land prices rose." The same happened in 2006 when shareholders of large US companies with huge real estate portfolios (such as McDonald's) forced management to engage in sale and leaseback activities to realise the value of their holdings during the boom times.

37   During the 1920s the proportion of American households investing in the stock market increased tenfold; in the 1960s this was seen by the large increase in mutual funds; in the 1980s by derivatives traders; in the 2000s in ETFs.

38   Economists call this the 'wealth channel effect' and it is one of the reasons why policy makers and central bankers pay attention to how the stock market is doing. If it goes up people are likely to spend more money and so boost economic growth.

39   The skyscraper is the simplest and most reliable indicator of a financial crisis and severe recession. The economics of such buildings require three things: high land prices, lots of (cheap) credit and grand plans supported by rosy forecasts of growth. The tops of prior cycles have been marked by buildings such as the Burj Khalifa in Dubai (2010), One Canada Square in London (1991), the Sears Tower in Chicago (1974), or, perhaps most famously, the Empire State Building in New York in 1931. Given construction timescales, such buildings invariably open during the subsequent economic depression and their owners struggle to find tenants and so remain partially vacant for several years.

40   More broadly, the era is characterised by wildly speculative schemes. In an echo of the Seagaia resort, at the time the Burj was under construction, there was a plan in Dubai to build a series of artificial islands, each one with its own microclimate. It was a little too late and, years later, the reclaimed land remained undeveloped and was sinking back into the sea.

41   Vague (2020), Figure 1.3; data available from www.bankingcrisis.org.

42   The cause of this inflation is different to those relating to, for example, supply chain disruptions brought about by the pandemic or high commodity prices due to the conflict in Ukraine that began in February 2022.

43   On the inverted yield curve see Chapter 6, note 12.

44   For example, in the 2000s the exploits of Paris Hilton and friends took up a huge amount of attention.

45   Swarup (2014), pp. 113–115 summarises a number of behavioural biases, several of which apply to the late stages of a bull market. These include cognitive dissonance, confirmation bias, hedonic biases, illusion of control, overconfidence.

46   See Chapter 14.

47   See also *The Handbook of Wealth Secrets*, Part 10 and Part 14.

Chapter 13

1   "One of the most striking features of the economic landscape over the past twenty years or so has been a substantial decline in macroeconomic volatility." Bernanke, B. (2004), in 'Remarks by Governor Ben S. Bernanke', The Federal Reserve Board, 20 February, retrieved from www.federalreserve.gov/boarddocs/speeches/2004/20040220.

2   With an exquisite sense of timing, he handed over the job to his successor, Ben Bernanke, on 1 February 2006, right at the apex of the land market in the US. It was quite the legacy. Immediately he was appointed by Gordon Brown, then head of the UK finance ministry, to be an 'honorary adviser'. It was quite the compliment. Greenspan returned the favour, saying that Brown was "without peer among the world's economic policymakers". This was the Gordon Brown who had confidently claimed he too had tamed the economic cycle.

3   Peris (2018), pp. 63–87. These were Graham and Dodd's *Security Analysis* (1934); John Maynard Keynes's *General Theory of Employment, Interest and Money* (1936) containing a chapter on capital markets; and John Burr Williams's *The Theory of Investment Value* (1938). Irving Fisher's *Theory of Interest* (1930) was also a key contribution.

4   It was at this time that systems were developed to measure national income. This work was led by Simon Kuznets and led to such measures as Gross Domestic (or then National) Product that are widely used today.

5   Markowitz expressed some scepticism that volatility might be the only measure of risk and suggested other ones; however, these were not taken up more widely.

6   Beta is the measure of covariance of a stock against the market benchmark, its sensitivity to the overall market. Beta is the critical datapoint about any stock. A low-beta stock tends to be less volatile, or risky, than the market; a higher-beta stock is more risky.

7   To do so would mean, in mathematical terms, your portfolio was not exposed to the specific risks attached to any one stock – it only had the same risk as the overall market.

8   The only hard data required for CAPM are the stock's beta value and the market risk premium (the amount of risk in the market above the rate on a risk free asset, i.e., the yield on a US government bond). If an investor wanted more return, they would go for a stock with higher sensitivity to market movements (higher beta). The greater the sensitivity, the higher the expected return to compensate investors for their higher risk.

9   Peris (2018), pp. 67–69.

10   Samuelson, P. (1965), 'Proof that Properly Anticipated Prices Fluctuate Randomly', *Industrial Management Review*, Vol. VI, Spring, pp. 41–50.

11   Wigglesworth (2021).

12   Indeed a new strand of economics and finance has recently questioned this assumption strongly – and in fact argues that humans are systematically irrational, so much so that their irrationality is in fact rather predictable. Over time the models have become more sophisticated and incorporate a broader range of factors, human biases and market frictions.

13   This is also known as the Grossman-Stiglitz paradox. Other problems include the assumption about how to measure a company's risk. Is there only one way to measure it, and is the daily movement or volatility of the price of a stock the best way to do it? If you are an investor you are not going to be buying and selling every day. So the daily movement of prices is not really relevant to you.

14   Sharpe, W. (1964), 'Capital Asset Prices: A Theory of Market Equilibrium under Conditions of Risk', *The Journal of Finance*, Vol. 19, Issue 3, pp. 425–442.

15 There is a vigorous debate in academia about whether their performance as an industry is better than the market over a significant period of time (and if it is, whether this is simply down to investing in higher beta companies). Fama himself, while a proponent of market price efficiency, argued strongly that CAPM was wrong – that investors needed to focus on things other than beta, such as investment styles, quality of earnings and size of company.

16 Markowitz, H. (2005), 'Market Efficiency: A Theoretical Distinction and So What?', *Financial Analysts Journal*, Vol. 61, No. 5, pp. 17–30.

17 CAPM assumptions were built into their design: a diversified property portfolio was contained in each tranche so that if one borrower defaulted the others would not, thus maintaining a flow of rents; the tranche was insured against losses, again on the assumption that the insurer would not face defaulting tranches all at once; the pricing of such securities was assumed to correctly reflect their underlying risks and so on.

18 "In our view, however, derivatives are financial weapons of mass destruction, carrying dangers that, while now latent, are potentially lethal." Buffett, W. (2002), in 'Berkshire Hathaway Inc. 2002 Annual Report', retrieved from www.berkshirehathaway.com/2002ar/2002ar.pdf.

19 Credit built up in the land market as it has done throughout history. In fact, despite his faith in markets, he held interest rates too low for too long, boosting the price of land and drawing further credit and capital into the land market. And he cultivated a sense, based on his interventions in financial markets, that should there be a sharp fall in asset prices the Federal Reserve would be on hand to lower interest rates and flood the system with liquidity. This increased the price of land even more.

20 See Introduction.

21 For markets to be self-regulating they must smoothly and continuously adjust to new information such that excesses in one area are corrected through the pricing mechanism. But if excesses cannot be seen, the adjustment is not smooth and prices enter into very quickly reinforcing feedback loops that create large losses.

22 Recent academic research can show that when market volatility is below average over a long period, it will bring about a crisis a few years later, the presumption being that investors grow in confidence during periods of low volatility and build up riskier and more leveraged positions which unravel once the quiet periods end. The questions are why do they do so and when will it unravel? For this, knowledge of the 18-year cycle and its link to the land and credit markets is key.

23 See www.thesecretwealthadvantage.com for regular updates on the progress of the cycle.

24 See *The Handbook of Wealth Secrets*, Part 1 for a definition of a 'very good year'.

25 See *The Handbook of Wealth Secrets*, Parts 1, 3, 10 and 17.

Chapter 14

1 Examples from prior cycles include: Christina Romer, chair of the US Council of Economic Advisers: "Better policy, particularly on the part of the Federal Reserve, is directly responsible for the low inflation and the virtual disappearance of the business cycle in the last 25 years." (September 2007); Nigel Lawson, UK chancellor of the exchequer: "In short, after two years of unexpectedly rapid expansion, growth next year is forecast to return to a sustainable level." (November 1988); Myron Forbes, president of the Pierce-Arrow Motor Car Company: "There will be no interruption of our permanent prosperity." (January 1928); even as far back as 1825, British Prime Minister Benjamin Disraeli claimed that the boom would not turn to bust because of superior knowledge (Anderson (2008), p. 228).

2 Gaffney (2009), pp. 32–35.

3 Anderson (2008), p. 355.

4 Werner (2020), p. 114: "Asset prices only rise as long as new money enters the market. All it takes to burst a credit-driven asset bubble is for loan growth to slow. Then the whole credit pyramid must collapse like a house of cards."

5 Gaffney (2009): there are effectively two real estate peaks in each cycle. Residential construction slows down but this is hidden by a surge in non-residential construction spending that keeps economic variables appearing solid (p.8). Land prices peak 12–36 months before the recession (Anderson (2008), p. 355).

6 As they do not see the land cycle, or focus on the land market, they do not see what the effects of their actions are likely to be and where the key risks in the system are. As we saw from the quotes by Trichet and Greenspan in the Introduction and Chapter 13, central bankers did not have the tools or the knowledge to manage the economy at the key stages of the cycle. See also quotes in Anderson (2008), pp. 203, 269.

7 Examples of such events: September 1857 – a steamer bound for New York sank, killing 400 passengers and leading to the loss of $1.6m in uninsured gold; 1925 – a rail strike halted supplies of building materials for the booming Florida real estate market and in early 1926 a ship capsized in Miami harbour, taking with it building supplies and delaying shipments of replacements; September 1926 saw a major hurricane in Miami. See Anderson (2008) and the key observation: "Here is demonstrated the psychology of the crowd. If the trend in markets is up, bad news tends to be shrugged off; in a downturn it is seized upon by the public mind and any glimmer of light is overlooked. In a situation where speculation, especially in land value, is out of control, a disaster takes on vivid significance (p. 122).

8 See The Handbook of Wealth Secrets, Part 12. Real estate-related stocks need to be sold prior to the Summit because they start trending down even though the broader market is going into new highs (indeed this is one of the signs that we are approaching the Summit). Focus on the situation in the American stock markets in particular, because the US leads the cycle.

9 Commercial property peaks after residential property, so you may have a bit more time in this part of the market. If a buyer can be found, prioritise a quick sale to a well-resourced buyer over maximising the price from a borrower who has to raise finance.

10 See The Handbook of Wealth Secrets, Part 6.4, Part 7.3; and Part 12.5.

Chapter 15

1 Tacitus, Annals, Book VI, 17. As we saw from Chapter 8, the banking system's function is to provide liquidity, but property loans are long term. And so there is a reliance on the money markets for liquidity to meet demands of depositors and short-term financing needs.

2 Banking regulations then, as now, tend to be bypassed during bouts of speculative mania. Governments are part of the system that they have created, not above it; their efforts to 'manage' it inevitably make things worse. At the Summit of the cycle, this often involves belatedly reimposing regulations that should have been enforced all along. This usually leads to a contraction in the money supply, which at this point in the cycle will precipitate the downturn and Crash.

3 Anderson (2008), p. 316: examples from 1792 and 1819 – the authorities attempted to contract the credit supply; in 1986, US government reversed a 1981 law that had promoted overbuilding of real estate (p. 286); Kindleberger (2015), p. 126: in 1990, the Bank of Japan attempted to slow the growth of real estate loans.

4 Even those who know about problems within the property market are probably not able to fathom how widespread the impact will be. But the reality is that banks and many borrowers are over-extended.

5 Lightner (1922), p. 20: "The important firm of Seuthes & Son, of Alexandria, was facing difficulties because of the loss of three richly laden spice ships in a Red Sea storm." He cites other troubles: "The great house of Malchus & Co, of Tyre, with branches at Antioch and Ephesus, suddenly became bankrupt as a result of a strike among Phoenician workmen and the embezzlements of a freedman manager." Kindleberger (2015), p. 124 provides other examples. Often these might be weather-related: see Chapter 14, note 7.

6 Vague (2020). See also Anderson (2008), p. 317: "Lending institutions don't actually care how high the land price is; they just make the loan and then securitise it into the market. Rising interest rates will at some point just find the weak link in this chain, which may or may not be obvious as land price turns down with the inevitable… higher interest rates. The insiders will know, though, so reference to the appropriate charts, if any are available, will be instructive. The relevant stock market indices are a starting point, then the charts of individual banks, finance companies and mortgage brokers."

7 Calverley (2009), pp. 136–137: behavioural economists borrow an idea from physics: critical state theory. At the Summit of the cycle, when everything is overextended, markets have reached a 'critical state', and it does not take a huge trigger event to initiate the Crash. It is hard to know in advance what possibly small event will cause a bubble to burst, and it will typically be fairly small and seemingly unrelated to where the risks are in the system. The advantage of understanding real estate cycles is that you know the greatest risks will ultimately be in the land market and that these trigger events tend to take place around two decades after the prior Summit and Crash.

8 Anderson (2008), p. 355. Kindleberger (2015), p. 124 talks about the *causa proxima* – the immediate cause – of people selling (as opposed to the *causa remota*, the more fundamental but less immediate cause). The *causa remota* causes people to reverse expectations of future growth; large investors sell and prices begin to slide. The most important *causa remota* is speculation in the land market.

9 Lightner (1922), pp. 21–22: the banking houses of Maximus & Vibo and Pittius & Pittius; the trading problems originated with the fall in value of luxury items (ivory and ostrich feathers) and the loss of three ships carrying expensive cargo. The Via Sacra, or "Sacred Street" was at the centre of Rome and was the Empire's financial centre.

10 Wessel (2009), pp. 100–101. On 9 August French bank BNP Paribas suspended withdrawals from three funds that had invested in US sub-prime mortgages. "The bank said it couldn't put a value on the funds assets because of the 'complete evaporation of liquidity in certain market segments of the US securitisation market'. This news was as unsettling to investors in 2007 as it had been to depositors in 1907 when a bank shut its doors and said the cash vault was empty. Rumors circulating that the other banks were similarly exposed. Those with cash husbanded it, reluctant to lend even to other banks because they were no longer sure they would get paid back."

11 Calverley (2009): the investment bank had to take two months to value the funds largely because the market for CDOs had dried up and there was no price; when they reported the values in July 2007, revealing losses of more than 90%, the market was shocked and all such assets started to be revalued.

12 The young, media-friendly guru, who had told everyone at the Summit that things would never go down, now panics. And his gullible followers copy him. In the present cycle, social media might propagate the panic greatly.

13 Werner (2020), p. 114: "Then the whole credit pyramid must collapse… Asset prices would fall. That would leave many speculators heavily exposed, for they need asset price rises to service their loans, let alone repay them. Thus they are forced to sell the asset. As more speculators sell, asset prices fall. More speculative borrowing schemes unravel. Many speculators are driven into bankruptcy. That creates large bad debts for the banks. In aggregate, it is easy to estimate the ultimate scale of the problem: when the bubble bursts, all the speculative lending must turn into bad debts."

14   Hodgkinson (2008), p. 317: "Hence a recession cuts a swathe through firms rendered marginal by falling business. At the intensive and extensive margins firms can no longer pay the prevailing wage rates. Unemployment rises, even while workers retained in employment may not be a great deal worse off. Thus the business cycle does not merely involve all alike in minor adjustments of output and income, but causes major adjustments of entrepreneurship and employment." See also p. 319: rising land prices draw in speculative funds, increasing prices further; investors may sell shares and bonds and re-direct funds into the land market; firms may borrow temporarily to meet cashflow needs, but this process cannot last long. "Sooner or later profits collapse for some firms. Then credit contraction sets in. Banks call in advances; firms offer less trade credit. Closures of firms rapidly lead to a fall in demand for intermediate goods and for labour. The process of the downturn is familiar enough. The largely hidden movement of land prices that intensifies it is not so familiar."

15   Reinhart and Rogoff (2009), Figure 14.4, p. 230.

16   Reinhart and Rogoff (2009) in their analysis of systemic banking crises, find that on average a crisis leads to a stock market decline of over 55% in real terms, lasting 3.4 years.

17   Reinhardt and Rogoff (2009), Figure 14.2, pp. 226–227. The data is drawn from major systemic banking crises, 21 in total. While they do not include data from all real estate downturns, all of the examples cited correspond with real estate cycle downturns. On pp. 160–161 (on the basis of a slightly larger data set) they note that the extent of the decline is not appreciably different in emerging and advanced economies.

18   See *The Handbook of Wealth Secrets,* Parts 12 and 14 for the key things you need to do to prepare.

19   See also *The Handbook of Wealth Secrets*, Parts 1 and 17. This phenomenon takes place across the end of the Crash, and Rescue and Start stages of the cycle.

Chapter 16

1   See Fisher (2009), Kindleberger and Aliber (2015), Chapter 7, p. 143ff, Anderson (2009), especially pp. 387–440.

2   While not every case will involve all rules being violated, the vast majority of them will involve the decision-maker custodian rule being broken. So get that right and, while your investments may not do well, you should at least have the chance of getting some of your money back if things go wrong.

3   Some of these frauds are 'honest' in the sense that the perpetrator might have genuinely believed, at least initially, that they could have achieved the stellar returns they promised. They just lacked the skills or the ability to manage risks. To save face or keep the scheme going they resorted to false statements, using new capital to return money to old. Every Land Boom and Mania stage of the cycle will also involve those who are going to use deceit to part you from your money. It is inevitable that someone will try this on you.

4   Data on long-term returns on stocks, bonds and real estate can be found here: pages.stern.nyu.edu/~adamodar/New_Home_Page/datafile/histretSP.html.

5   There is a reason why, for example, the interior of Trump's buildings drip with gold and chandeliers, gaudy paraphernalia, reeking of extravagance and excess; and why Warren Buffet, even now, occupies a modest office, drives a modest car and lives in a modestly proportioned house. One of them has been a highly successful investor for decades. The other gets burned by each real estate cycle crash.

6   Galbraith (2009), pp. 132–133: "Alone among the various forms of larceny embezzlement has a time parameter. Weeks, months or years may elapse between the commission of the crime and its discovery. (This is a period, incidentally, when the embezzler and the man who has been embezzled, oddly enough, feels no loss. There is a net increase in psychic wealth)."

7   A common way to do this is to ask for an advance fee that unlocks a much greater reward; for example by showing a paper profit but then requiring a commission (or a tax) to be paid as a percentage of the larger amount, which somehow cannot be paid for out of profits. That is rarely made clear before you have made your initial investment.

Chapter 17

1   Bank lending was hard to come by in the late 1960s, which is one of the reasons why REITs became so popular initially as a means of funding property deals. However, credit restrictions eased in the early 1970s, and commercial banks lent freely for real estate. This also illustrates that even if restrictions are placed on banks, investors find ways around them to push money into the real estate market.

2   Harrison (1983); Werner (2020), p. 92. After the 'Nixon shock' of 1971, when he removed the dollar's gold convertibility, the Bank of Japan resorted to stimulus measures. They were not needed; the economy was at full capacity. As usual, government policy ignited the Mania phase of the cycle. The credit being pushed out of the banking system went straight into land, assisted by policy: the government had launched a 'Plan for Rebuilding the Archipelago'.

3   Harrison (1983), pp. 97, 131.

4   See *The Handbook of Wealth Secrets*, Part 1.1. As we now know, this is a common occurrence out of lows of the cycle once the system has confidence that the problems in the property market have been contained. Fridson (1998), pp. 174-187.

5   Harrison (1983), p. 246.

6   See Chapter 1.

7   Kindleberger and Aliber (2015), p. 239 – "The list of regulations would fill a small phone book and includes capital requirements, reserve requirements, liquidity requirements, portfolio diversification regulations, limits on the maximum size of a loan to any one borrower, limits on the loan to insiders, and limits on trading risky securities. Limits or ceilings have been placed on interest rates that banks can pay on deposits. At one stage, banks were limited in their ability to expand beyond their local market area, although most of these limits no longer exist. Moreover, U.S. banks and those in many other countries are examined to ensure that their assets and liabilities correspond with the values that they report. The pattern is that each crisis leads to a new set of regulations."

8   Ibid. pp. 236–237. Russell Napier points out that investors do believe that government will ride to the rescue; the decision is ultimately political because these crises have such wide-reaching effects that the government must intervene lest it be overwhelmed by the backlash from citizens facing economic hardship.

9   One example during the 19th century was to redeem deposits using low denominations (e.g., sixpence pieces) which would take a long time to count out. Or they might create a charade to show that people are buying and thus alleviate the sense of panic among others waiting in line to withdraw money.

10   Japan of the 1990s and the eurozone of the 2010s are standout examples for the inefficiency of resolving problem loans in the banking system – which is why the recoveries in those locations took so much longer than in others.

11   But the passing of dividends at this point in the cycle marks the passing of the stock market lows (Anderson, 2008, p. 300).

12   See *The Handbook of Wealth Secrets*, Parts 12 and 14.

13   See Campbell (2010), p. 48 for the key real estate timing signals.

Chapter 18

1   In English this famous phrase translates to 'the more it changes, the more it is the same thing'.

2   Witness the troubles that highly indebted property developers had in servicing their overseas loans (or rolling them over) during 2021 and 2022.

3   Vague (2020), pp. 190–191.

4 This view has been reinforced by the recent sanctions imposed by the US on Russian dollar reserves. Why would central banks hold dollar reserves if the American government could take them away?

5 The Atlantic, 'A Mapped History of Taking a Train Across the United States', 21 February 2013.

6 See Figure 7, p. 50.

7 IMF Working Paper (WP/18/250), 'House Price Synchronicity, Banking Integration and Global Financial Conditions': the empirical study found that "the abundance of liquidity owing to accommodative financial conditions is positively associated with house price synchronicity at country and city levels... [this also suggests] a stronger transmission of external shocks into the domestic economy... [and that this] positive association... was stronger preceding the global financial crisis" (p. 26). Overlay the knowledge of the real estate cycle and you see that during the Land Boom house prices go up together in most countries.

8 See Chapters 2, 4 and 11.

9 See Chapter 5 on the corruption of economics and Chapter 13 on why your financial adviser is unlikely to be able to advise you properly either.

10 On money creation by private banks, see Chapter 8; by government, see Chapter 9; and on the cost of rescuing the system see Chapters 1 and 17.

INDEX

ABOUT THE AUTHOR

Akhil Patel is the Director of Property Sharemarket Economics, an investment research service that teaches subscribers how to 'remember the future' based on leading knowledge of economic and financial cycles.

Akhil became interested in such cycles after his family's business went through difficult periods during the major recessions in the early 1990s and 2008. He refused to accept the conventional wisdom that these events could not be forecast in advance. After much study, he decided to develop a body of work that would help people – whether they were investors, business owners or those just interested in doing something with their savings.

With professional experience in the UK civil service and international development, Akhil has worked on a range of issues from reviewing large infrastructure deals to helping establish the UK's £3bn International Climate Fund. He has two masters degrees (in finance and public policy) and a first degree in classics from Oxford.